European Family Therapy Association Series

More information about this series at http://www.springer.com/series/13797

Roberto Pereira • Juan Luis Linares
Editors

Clinical Interventions in Systemic Couple and Family Therapy

Springer

EFTA

Editors
Roberto Pereira
Vasco-Navarra School of Family Therapy
Bilbao, Spain

Juan Luis Linares
Department of Psychiatry
Autonomous University of Barcelona
Barcelona, Spain

European Family Therapy Association Series
ISBN 978-3-030-08720-3 ISBN 978-3-319-78521-9 (eBook)
https://doi.org/10.1007/978-3-319-78521-9

Printed on acid-free paper

This Springer imprint is published by the registered company Springer International Publishing AG part of Springer Nature.
The registered company address is: Gewerbestrasse 11, 6330 Cham, Switzerland

Foreword

This book is a superb resource for practitioners. Throughout its 15 chapters, divided into three parts, it offers thorough accounts of the practice of each author in turn, in every case showing the systemic rationale and the contexts of application in which the approach was created and refined. Our field of systemic family and couple therapy has always placed a high value on sophisticated theorizing and, more recently, on using research to identify what works best. Each of these thrusts is essential, but practitioners also need to know what the most advanced practitioners actually do when they are seeing clients. The great strength of this book is that, while each chapter provides a full rationale to help us understand how the approach was derived, they all progress to detailed descriptions of the practice of the authors. The result is a compendium of ways that therapists have successfully worked with the most serious and difficult of cases.

When Maria Borcsa and Peter Stratton launched the EFTA book series, we intended that it would use the strengths of EFTA to make available a full range of the high standards of systemic work that is going on in Europe. In terms of a difference that makes a difference, this book makes a perfect third volume in the series. Where Volume 1 *Origins and Originality* provided a survey of the current thinking of senior practitioners, who had all made major contributions to EFTA, and Volume 2 *Routine Outcome Monitoring in Couple and Family Therapy* focused on current research-informed advances, the current volume provides an extensive overview of actual practice and the thinking behind these choices of ways to practice. Also, Volume 1 covered the full geographical range of EFTA by virtue of the systemic practitioners who had made pivotal contributions to the development of EFTA from South to North and East to West. Volume 2 took a Northern and especially Norwegian perspective. Volume 3 has a Southern European orientation, being rooted in systemic therapies of Spain, Italy, and Portugal.

What is special about the book is that it reports use of the full range of systemic thinking and practice, including building on origins, to tackle serious psychological conditions and multi-problem families. The book in its entirety constitutes a major claim: that when the therapeutic approach is rooted in sound systemic principles and practices, then the therapist can take on the most complex and demanding cases.

As an indication of this confidence, the book opens with a chapter by one of the editors, Juan Luis Linares, describing his relational treatment for people with schizophrenia. The subsequent chapters in the Part also focus on therapy with people suffering from severe conditions with two chapters on borderline personality disorders, couple therapy for depressive disorders, and eating disorders.

With the most challenging territory marked out, we need the additional reassurance of innovative therapeutic resources that have not yet been fully exploited. Rodolfo de Bernart, current President of EFTA, chooses to elaborate the resource that siblings can offer the systemic therapist. Modern life provides an unprecedented array of ways in which it is possible to be unfaithful to a partner, therefore requiring highly adaptable techniques for reconstructing the relationship. Another cultural change that demands an extension of our capabilities has been the increasing population of healthy older people who are, at least potentially, active romantically and sexually. The final inescapable challenge of our times is the growing role of Internet resources. We need to be aware of the possibilities they offer the therapist and client while being guided by experienced therapists about the potential risks and how to handle them.

As we enter the third Part of the book, we do not leave the salient challenges of current times behind. We start with drug taking and addictions, at once an increasing problem for society and an area in which we have some of the best evidence for systemic approaches. Another classic for our field has been the multi-problem family which requires a systems approach to both the family and all the professional agencies. The multifamily group has an interesting pre-history but is now an established approach whose practice can be described. It is encouraging to find that there are ways of creating alliances with families that are not attending voluntarily, in ways that have proven effectiveness. We have limited background in working with disability and the effects on all family members so it is good to have such an authoritative account of how to do this work. And finally Roberto Pereira, first editor of this fascinating collection, analyses the impact of loss of a significant member on the family system, the roles people may adopt in the aftermath. He then provides a series of family interventions that have been developed during his extensive work with "the mourning family".

This fearless survey of the most difficult problems that present-day therapists will encounter, and encouraging indications of how to work with them, has only been possible because of the ethos in these countries in which psychopathologies and psychological problems can be named as such without equivocation or minimization of the difficulties. It has required a consistent systemic frame of thinking that is widely shared in the region and beyond which maintains contact with the strong and highly creative roots of the mothers and fathers of our field.

This book will make a major contribution to training systemic therapists. Although drawing primarily on the work being done in specific countries of Southern Europe, it will have immense value throughout the world. Its major contribution is to widen horizons about the whole range of levels of distress in which we can confidently intervene. It will also have great value in putting established practitioners and training courses (back) in touch with the origins of systemic psychotherapies and how they have been developed by contemporary leaders in the field.

Peter Stratton
Leeds Family Therapy and Research Centre
Institute of Health Sciences
University of Leeds
Leeds, UK

Introduction

In terms of a psychotherapeutic model, family therapy has a rich clinical tradition that was initially articulated around psychosis. In fact, schizophrenia and its fascinating communicational characteristics were the source of inspiration for the double bind theory, the real emblematic construction behind the origins of family therapy. Nor should we forget that multi-problem families (the heirs to the psychopathy and sociopathy of days gone by and, as such, related to younger entities such as borderline personality disorders) were also given considerable attention by family therapy in its early stages, when psychotherapy as it was at that time did not venture into such difficult and complex terrain.

All this points to a glorious history, in which family therapy forged its path as a psychotherapeutic model in "major clinical practice". Unfortunately, this privileged relationship has weakened with the passing of time, resulting in post-modern family therapy having distanced itself from clinical practice. We have already witnessed the negative consequences of this in such situations as that of German family therapists who had to laboriously demonstrate that their professional practice was indeed useful and capable of obtaining outstanding clinical results.

This book continues in the vein that was initiated in recent times by German family therapy, but which has not yet been reflected in sufficient relevant publications. Its goal is to demonstrate that systemic clinical contributions are not limited to those that took the scientific world by storm and made such an impact 50 year ago, rather that they have continued to ensue in such fields as eating disorders, drug addiction, depression and, always, psychosis, multi-problem families, and personality disorders. In addition to these, we must add problems of unquestionable clinical significance, such as grief and infidelity between couples, and therapeutic strategies especially appropriate to systemic sensitivity, such as working with siblings, multi-family groups, and working with new technologies.

Simultaneously, the book presents the developments in family therapy in southern Europe, which, unlike other regions, has never lost the perspective of the clinical use of family therapy in psychiatry and clinical psychology and has continued to make progress in that way.

The book is divided into three parts. The first part "Family Therapy and Clinical Psychopathology" makes a significant contribution to the recovery of family therapy in the treatment of severe psychopathologies, without fearing to venture into clinical diagnosis.

This part begins with a chapter devoted to the therapy of psychosis. In the same way that the clinical application of family therapy begins with schizophrenia, so is this book and this part symbolically and specifically devoted to that clinical practice: it really could not begin any other way. The chapter reviews the relational basis of psychotic disorders, compiling and updating the proposals of the pioneers of family therapy on the communication bases of schizophrenia. It goes on to propose a psychotherapeutic treatment based on a process of "reconfirmation" that includes the entire family of the designated patient.

Its author, **Juan Luis Linares**, a Psychiatrist, Psychologist, and Systemic Family Therapist, is Professor of Psychiatry at the Autonomous University of Barcelona and Director of the Psychotherapy Unit and the Family Therapy School at the Hospital of St. Pau in Barcelona. A Past President of EFTA and Honorary President of RELATES, he has devoted much of his professional life to working with severe psychotic pathologies, developing his own model of intervention based on disconfirmation as the primary relational dysfunction in such disorders.

The second chapter studies the borderline personality disorder storyboard, from childhood to adult life, from the systemic family therapist's perspective. With the support of several clinical cases, the authors describe interventions in children, adolescents, and adults afflicted by borderline personality disorders.

Luigi Cancrini, a Psychiatrist and Psychotherapist, is Chairman of the Centro Studi di Terapia Relazionale and Director of the Centro di Aiuto al Bambino Maltrattato e alla Famiglia in Rome. He has dedicated a considerable part of his research work in recent years, illustrated with numerous publications, to the study of borderline personality disorder. Dr. Cancrini shares the authorship of the chapter with **Francesca Romana De Gregorio**, a psychologist and psychotherapist at the Associazione Bambini nel Tempo Onlus in Rome, Italy.

The following chapter focuses on one of the main psychopathological diagnoses, that of depressive disorders. The author proposes couple therapy as the preferred treatment, especially for handling resistant depressive disorders that present a specific diagnostic and intervention procedure in couple therapy, the aim of which is to clarify unresolved conflicts that are masked by the symptoms, to give meaning to pathological behaviour and to enable the design of relevant strategies to promote change. Another priority objective is to encourage the construction of a therapeutic alliance, an essential component if one is to obtain the collaboration of the patient and their spouse as the therapeutic process progresses.

Carmen Campo, a Psychologist and Systemic Family Therapist, Senior Consultant at the Sant Pau Hospital Psychiatric Service, and Assistant Director of its family therapy school, is highly experienced in both the treatment of depressive disorders and in couple therapy. In this instance, she combines the two.

The fourth chapter addresses one of the most serious pathologies in which systemic family therapy has been traditionally used for a considerable length of time: eating disorders, in particular anorexia nervosa. Each of the two authors have more than 20 years' experience in the treatment of severe cases of anorexia nervosa, in the context of two confinement units, one of which is specifically for eating disorders, in Barcelona (José Soriano), and another non-specific centre which receives all manner of patients with serious mental disorders, in Las Palmas de Gran Canaria (Jorge Vega). Between them they have treated almost 900 patients who will normally have been admitted due to their having a BMI (body mass index) below 15 and to serious risk to their life having been recognized. During admission they attend both the patient and their family, and they provide ongoing care, once the patient has been discharged, for several months and even, in certain cases, for years.

Jorge Vega is a Clinical Psychologist, Family Therapist, and Director of the Rayuela Family Therapy School, in Las Palmas de Gran Canaria, and Associate Professor at the University of Las Palmas, Spain. **José Soriano** is a Psychiatrist, Family Therapist, and Associate Professor at the Autonomous University of Barcelona and Deputy Director of the Family Therapist School of the Hospital de Sant Pau in Barcelona, Spain.

Matteo Selvini, a Psychologist, Family Therapist, and Co-director of the MARA SELVINI PALAZZOLI Therapy School in Milan, Brescia, and Turin (Italy) and in Mendrisio (Switzerland), then delves into a complex issue: the diagnosis of borderline personalities, connecting personality traits to the patient's development within their family, through the investigation of post-traumatic personality disorders.

According to Selvini, systemic therapy theories should highlight the development patterns that lead to personality disorders. It is often a mistake to connect a symptom to the way in which the family acts in the here and now. Research into family deficiency, traumatic development, attachment disorganization, and the five types of reorganizations that he proposes are the fundamentals for family and individual treatment of personality disorders. "Borderline" and other stigmatizing diagnostic labels should be replaced by words that emphasize trauma and family deficiency.

The second part "New Resources in Systemic Therapy" includes four chapters that present innovative therapeutic resources, or resources whose potential has not been fully explored, or that address problems or people not sufficiently taken into account until now.

In chapter 6 "The Importance of Being Siblings", **Rodolfo de Bernart**, M.D. Psych., Psychotherapist, Director of the Istituto di Terapia Familiare di Firenze, President of EFTA (European Association of Family Therapy), and IASA Co-chair (the International Association for the Study of Attachment), introduces us to one of those insufficiently used family resources whose potential he explains with clarity: siblings. As De Bernart explains, "Traditionally in Family Therapy we work with the complete family or with the subsystem of the parents. Sometimes this subsystem doesn't collaborate or doesn't exist, so we need different resources other than the "vertical roots" (Parents and Grandparents). Siblings represent the "horizontal roots" and are the members of the family which usually live together or near to one another for the longest period of the family life cycle (Parents go before, partners, spouses and children arrive later). The building of the "mind of the Siblings" creates a tool through which we can obtain new points of view on the whole family and on the parents and siblings subsystems, and which we can use in therapy".

In chapter 7 "What If There Is Another Person in His/Her Life? Infidelity in Couple Therapy", we find a classic theme in couple therapy, infidelity, updated to an age such as ours in which "new technologies enable both multiple forms of contact and control in dual relationships". There can be no doubt that the therapist who works with couples must know the ins and outs of marital infidelity and how to address it. In the words of Annette Kreuz, the author of the chapter, "balancing freedom, mystery, togetherness, differentiation, responsibility, transparency and privacy is extremely complex and complicated". To consider a love triangle, she adds, assigning the dynamics of a lover, husband, and wife to the roles of victim, guilty perpetrator, and a third person clearly oversimplifies the issue. However, the experience of a person cheating on their partner is nevertheless highly traumatic in the majority of cases.

Working with competence and sensitivity may help regain confidence and reconstruct a couple's relationship. This chapter offers diagnostic key concepts and specific techniques based on the bio-psycho-social model of mutual confirmation required in couple relationships.

Annette Kreuz is a Clinical Psychologist and Director of the "Phase 2 Centre" for Family and Couples Therapy (Training and Assistance) in Valencia, Spain, and an expert Couple and Family Therapist with a lengthy experience in private practice.

The next chapter deals with a theme which, without being taboo, is often socially hidden, ignored, or treated with certain condescension: love, sexuality, and ageing. Nevertheless, in the twenty-first century, it is no longer possible to ignore the fact that sexuality is extending to a part of life that is becoming more and more prolonged in time, and which can no longer be considered "senescence": the improvement in the health of the population is making the stage of "adulthood" extend much farther in time, so much so that it now includes what used to be considered "senescence".

Of course, this prolongation of love relationships to ages that used to be considered periods of "decline" implies that relational problems in couples do so also. As a result, in our consultations we are finding ever more senior and elderly couples. We need then to get ourselves up to date and see whether the problems faced at these ages are the same as those faced by younger couples, or whether they have characteristics that distinguish them. This is what the chapter written by Ana Gomes deals with: "To reflect on the concepts of love and sexuality, further contributing to update the representations and myths about the final phase of the life cycle", based on three cases of couple therapy from her consultancy.

Ana Gomes is a Clinical Psychologist, Couple and Family Therapist, President of the Portuguese Society of Family Therapy, Trainer and Supervisor in Family Therapy, as well as Director of the Social Affairs Department in the Ministry of Work, Solidarity and Social Security. As a result, she brings to the table a wealth of experience in both fields: couple Therapy and care for the elderly.

And in the last chapter of this part, Manfrida, Eisenberg, and Albertini set before us a reality that we cannot ignore: the use of new technologies in psychotherapeutic practice. The use of telephone messages, emails, or video chats is a growing practice in psychotherapy. However, the authors warn us that the use of these new resources has an impact on the therapeutic relationship that we should be aware of. Resources can help a great deal, but they should be used with caution and being aware of the risks inherent in their use, which they detail thoroughly and with great rigour.

Gianmarco Manfrida is a Psychiatrist, Psychologist, Psychotherapist, Director of the Centro Studi e Applicazione della Psicologia Relazionale di Prato, in Italy (CSAPR), and Past President of the Società Italiana Psicologia Relazionale e Psicoterapia Relazionale (SIPPR). Working in the same centre are his collaborators **Erica Eisenberg**, a Psychologist, Psychotherapist, and Executive Board Member of the CSAPR, and **Valentina Albertini**, a Psychologist, Psychotherapist, and Chief Researcher of the CSAPR.

Comprising six chapters, the third and last part "Systemic Interventions in Different Contexts" is the most comprehensive. It describes systemic interventions in specific problems, both from the point of view of the characteristics of the problem and from that of the techniques used, or the characteristics of the context in which they occur.

The tenth chapter, and the first of this part, is dedicated to systemic intervention and family therapy in addictions. The field of addictions is one of the fields that have received most attention from the systemic model, given the good results obtained by the implementation of family therapy. As pointed out by the author, "drug-taking should be seen as a message from the individual that transmits aspects of him or herself and of their context. The existing tensions between the needs of the patient, their frames of reference such as the family, the educational environment, the peer group etc., along with their physical and mental health complications create a therapeutic workspace in which it is possible to develop intervention strategies on a per case basis".

Juan Antonio Abeijón, a Psychiatrist, Family Psychotherapist, and Supervisor in the Vasco-Navarra School of FT, is Head of the Julian Ajuriaguerra Mental Health Centre of the Basque Health Service and the current President of the Spanish Federation of Family Therapy Associations (FEATF). He has wide experience in working with drug addictions, to which he has devoted his entire professional career both in Spain and in various European organizations dedicated to their study.

Chapter eleven delves into one of the problem areas at the core of family therapy: the multi-problem family. In effect, ever since the early work of the structuralists, destructured families that receive simultaneous attention from multiple professional agencies of the socio-health field have been the subject of intense study by systemic professionals, particularly in Italy, where a model of intervention has been developed that has become a benchmark for numerous countries. Interventions involving multi-problem families is a challenge for the therapist, who must add to the difficulty presented by the families themselves the coordination of all those who are simultaneously involved in these cases. In his chapter, as a leading expert on the subject, the author presents a thorough review of the existing literature, proposing an intervention and analysing the potential results of that intervention.

Maurizio Coletti is a Psychologist, Family Therapist and Researcher, and Director of the European Institute for Systemic Training and Counselling (I.E.F.Co.S.) in Rome. He is a former President of ITACA, the European Association of Professionals Working in the Field of Drug Abuse.

The next chapter is dedicated to an intervention resource which, while by no means new, is currently the subject of renewed interest especially to professionals working with serious pathologies: the multifamily group. In the chapter, the author presents a brief overview of the history of multifamily groups, placing the emphasis on how they function as a therapeutic instrument, particularly to restore the social ties that break during a severe psychiatric pathology. This rebounding, particularly important to meet emotional needs, finds a suitable vehicle in group meetings between patients and families.

Norberto Barbagelata, a Psychiatrist, Family Therapist, and Director of the Zurbano Group of Family Therapy in Madrid, is the Teaching Supervisor at the Spanish Federation for Family Therapy. He has been working in Madrid with this reborn technique for years, with highly satisfactory results.

Chapter thirteen endeavours to answer a question that many therapists ask themselves when they have to work with a family that does not attend therapy on a voluntary basis, either because they are legally obliged to attend or they must do so because of some other circumstance. What can we do in these cases? How can we establish a suitable alliance that will enable us to reach our therapeutic goals? The authors, with many years of experience working with such families, respond to these issues in a comprehensive, reasoned, and convincing manner. If one creates a therapeutic alliance properly, they argue, there is no difference in the result obtained with families obliged to attend than with those who attend on a voluntary basis.

Ana Paula Relvas is a Psychologist, Family Therapist, PhD in Clinical Psychology, Full Professor of the Faculty of Psychology and Education Sciences, and Researcher of the Social Studies Centre (SSC/Research Unit), both of the University of Coimbra, Portugal. **Luciana Sotero** is also a Psychologist, Family Therapist, PhD in Clinical Psychology, and Invited Professor of the Faculty of Psychology and Education Sciences of the University of Coimbra, Portugal.

Chapter fourteen focuses on a field that has not received much attention from psychotherapy in general and from the systemic model in particular: intervention on disabilities. In Western culture, the socio-cultural perspective on disabilities has been changing in recent decades: from their having originally been the subject of care that focused on the deficit and was dispensed from "charity" to the current proposals that seek to achieve the social inclusion of all those who suffer from some type of handicap. "Disability, a concept that includes multiple pathologies, has mainly been aimed from the systemic view towards the caring for people with an intellectual retardation. The arrival of children with a handicap, together with their evolution throughout the life cycle, transforms family dynamics, changing the roles and giving rise to risk factors for the family and its members".

This proposal for systemic intervention in disabilities is presented by **Javier Bou**, a Clinical Psychologist, Family Therapist, Director of Dictia Valencia (Systemic Training Institute), the Spanish Representative in EFTA, and Scientific Advisor to the Official Association of Psychologists in Valencia.

Finally, the last chapter of the book is devoted, in a symbolic way, to grief, more specifically to the mourning family. Grief, that is to say, the emotional reaction after a loss, has been studied from the individual point of view, albeit not so much from that of the family, despite the fact that the presence and support of a social-family network is a very important factor in its evolution. This has been changing in recent years, and there is a developing systemic literature that studies grief reactions in functional and dysfunctional families. The chapter looks at both types of evolution, placing the emphasis on the stages of family mourning and on the frequent appearance of the role of the "mourner", which sometimes adds another element of difficulty to the already often difficult process of family mourning. At least one assessment of family functioning would always be necessary in a process of mourning that presents a risk factor that may lead to complicated mourning, and were this to appear, the chapter proposes a number of useful family interventions for its resolution.

Roberto Pereira, a Psychiatrist and Senior Consultant at the Basque Health Service, Family Therapist, Director of the Vasco-Navarra, School of Family Therapy in Bilbao, Spain, is President of the European and Latin American Network of Systemic Schools (RELATES) and former President of the Spanish Federation of Family Therapy Associations (FEATF). His in-depth study into family mourning processes has contributed to the knowledge of such processes, and he has an extensive bibliography on the subject.

In short, the volume provides an up-to-date approach to the clinical practice of family therapy and systemic intervention, adapted to the new resources offered by the world we live in today, without ignoring the contributions of the pioneers of family therapy, who turned the attention they dedicated to psychiatric clinical practice into the rationale for the development of a new paradigm. The different chapters reflect both major psychopathology and the principal vital conflicts and crises that cause the majority of consultations in our field.

Roberto Pereira
Vasco-Navarra School of Family Therapy
Bilbao, Spain

Juan Luis Linares
Autonomous University of Barcelona
Barcelona, Spain

Contents

Contributors

Juan Antonio Abeijón Vasco-Navarra School of Family Therapy, Bilbao, Spain

Valentina Albertini Centro Studi e Applicazione della Psicologia Relazionale (CSAPR), Prato, Italy

Norberto Barbagelata Zurbano Group of Family Therapy, Madrid, Spain

Javier Bou Dictia Valencia (Systemic Training Institute), Valencia, Spain

Carmen Campo Escuela de Terapia Familiar del Hospital de Sant Pau, Barcelona, Spain

Luigi Cancrini Centro Studi di Terapia Relazionale, Rome, Italy

Maurizio Coletti European Institute for Systemic Training and Counselling (I.E.F.Co.S.), Rome, Italy

Rodolfo de Bernart Instituto di Terapia Familiare di Firenze, Florence, Italy

Francesca Romana De Gregorio Associazione Bambini nel Tempo Onlus, Rome, Italy

Jorge De Vega Rayuela Family Therapy School, Las Palmas de Gran Canaria, Spain

Erica Eisenberg Centro Studi e Applicazione della Psicologia Relazionale (CSAPR), Prato, Italy

Ana Maria Gomes Sociedad Portuguesa de Terapia Familiar, Lisbon, Portugal

Juan Luis Linares Universidad Autónoma of Barcelona, Barcelona, Spain

Gianmarco Manfrida Centro Studi e Applicazione della Psicologia Relazionale (CSAPR), Prato, Italy

Roberto Pereira Vasco-Navarra School of Family Therapy, Bilbao, Spain

Ana Paula Relvas Faculty of Psychology and Education Sciences of the University of the Coimbra, Researcher at Center for Social Studies, University of Coimbra, Coimbra, Portugal

Matteo Selvini Selvini Palazzoli Psychotherapy School, Milan, Italy

Annette Kreuz "Centro Fase 2" for Family and Couples Therapy, Training and Clinical Practice, Valencia, Spain

José Soriano Universidad Autónoma de Barcelona, Barcelona, Spain

Luciana Sotero Faculty of Psychology and Education Sciences of the University of the Coimbra, Researcher at Center for Social Studies, University of Coimbra, Coimbra, Portugal

---

The original version of this book was revised. A correction to this book can be found at https://doi.org/10.1007/978-3-319-78521-9_16

Part I
Family Therapy and Clinical Psychopathology

The Family Therapy of Psychosis: A Reconfirmation Process

Juan Luis Linares

Introduction

Although psychoses are still the primary challenge of psychiatry, not to mention psychotherapy, they long ago ceased to occupy the emblematic position they had once held in the mental health field, ever since the modern psychiatric era was in its infancy. Nowhere is this so noticeable as in systemic family therapy which once considered them its primary source of inspiration. Among the myriad causes that have contributed to this situation, let us not underestimate the importance of what we might refer to as the comfortable self-complacency of the systemic professionals, which have discovered in less compromising and complex problems more comfortable and cost-effective areas on which to project themselves.

And yet, the mystery of psychoses, as current today as ever before, and the fascination generated by their communicational idiosyncrasies, not to mention the suffering endured by patients and their relatives, requires that we persevere in the investigation of their relational bases. Such is the fundamental objective of our clinical practice, the principal characteristics of which we shall endeavour to communicate in the lines that follow.

Disconfirming Triangulation

Our development of a relational theory of psychoses stems from two time-honoured concepts in the field of systemics, namely, triangulation and disconfirmation. Both have their roots in the most prestigious enclaves of the systemic map; triangulation

---

J. L. Linares (✉)
Universidad Autónoma of Barcelona, Barcelona, Spain

R. Pereira, J. L. Linares (eds.), *Clinical Interventions in Systemic Couple and Family Therapy*, European Family Therapy Association Series,
https://doi.org/10.1007/978-3-319-78521-9_1

is a major benchmark of structural therapy, while disconfirmation carries the unmistakable stamp of Palo Alto communicationalism.

For some authors, whether systemic or non-systemic, (Bowen, 1960; Freud, 1915–17; Goldbeter, 2003; Guerin, 1976; Guerin, Fogarty, Fay, & Kautto, 2010), triangulation amounts to a fatality or a structural constant in the organization of families. Our proposal, on the other hand, considers it to be the result of the inclusion of children in their parents' dysfunctional relational games (Linares, 2012). It is therefore, a negative situation, an antechamber to numerous pathologies, that allows multiple variants and should under no circumstances be considered normal or physiological.

We agree, therefore, with the first proposal on *triangulation* from the field of family therapy, coined by Haley (1967), who uses the term *perverse triangle* to refer to a relational triangle in which the generational barriers are broken—even though this fact may be denied by those involved. Its key features are the following: at least two of the people involved belong to different generations, and the coalition between a member of each generation against the third party is hidden or denied.

The most frequent form of triangulation in a family is the coalition of one of the parents with a child in opposition to the other parent. There are, however, other variants that can be very significant. In one of them, the parents line up side by side in a clear and close-knit relationship with one of the children, while another child remains outside that game. Another modality is a coalition of members of the first and third generations against a member of the second generation (for instance, the frequent coalition of a grandmother and granddaughter against the mother).

Disconfirmation is, as we have said, a concept that has a communicationalist origin, as brilliantly proposed by Watzlawick, Bavelas, and Jackson (1967). However, the authors from Palo Alto do not clearly define its meaning vis-à-vis that of *disqualification* which gives rise to subsequent confusion.

Recognition is a psychological movement of a primarily cognitive nature which consists in accepting the relational existence of another person. This may seem banal, but that is far from being the case as accepting the existence of another person implies that in some way or another one is limiting one's own existence. Lack of recognition, therefore, when it becomes stabilized in permanent relational behaviour, generates *disconfirmation*, which is the perception of one's own non-existence in relational terms. Recognition implies a perception of the needs of the other, as opposed to what we find in disconfirmation, in which they are subordinated to the needs of the interlocutor. What is more, the entire process is implicit, which further hinders the understanding of the phenomenon. If someone says to another person, "as far as I am concerned, you don't exist", they are expressing rejection, but they are certainly not disconfirming that person, on the contrary, they are recognizing him or her as an antagonist.

Two important questions define the unique complexity of disconfirmation. The first is *how can I feel that I do not exist, given the sensory evidence of my existence?* And, indeed, although many delusions and hallucinatory dynamics, especially cenesthopathic ones, lead us to the very gates of the experience of physical decay, the non-existence to which we refer is a metaphorical, psychological and relational phenomenon which has nothing to do with physics. I feel that I do not exist because I am not important to those on whom I depend even though they are everything to me. And this experience of not being important contains *double binding* qualities, registered within a logic of "*yes but no*". In short, "*I exist but I do not exist*", "*it seems that they include me, but then they forget about me...*".

The second question is *how can I ignore the person I have carried inside me for 9 months, whom I have borne with pain, breastfed and cared for day and night when they were a baby; or the person I took to the civil registry office to be registered with my name, endowing them with social existence?* And here again it is necessary to remember the metaphorical and complex nature of disconfirmation processes. Even though there are parents who do in fact ignore one or other of their children in quite dramatic circumstances (e.g. a child who is left forgotten for a time among the smoky or crumbling walls of the family home after an earthquake or fire), more often than not such real oversights do not occur, rather other symbolic or metaphorical ones, within the same double binding atmosphere described above. For example, systematically confusing a child's name with that of another child.

And so we come to the key concept of our proposal on the relational bases of psychotic disorders, which is *disconfirming triangulation*. This elusive and difficult-to-grasp phenomenon of disconfirmation, takes shape and becomes more understandable when it is associated with triangulation, which serves as its preferred vehicle. We have already said that this involves the inclusion of a child in their parents' dysfunctional relational games or in those of the fundamental figures in their system of belonging. But in what way?

Imagine a room in which two subjects, A and B, are interacting in isolation from everyone else. They may love, hate or bore one another or they may share many other experiences, but it is unlikely that either one will be able to ignore or forget the presence of the other. However, what happens if the door opens and a third person, C, comes in? The situation will change qualitatively. It may happen that A becomes enthralled by his relationship with C, his or her new interlocutor, bonding with him or her in such an intense way that B disappears from their perceptual field; in other words, the person who up to that moment had polarized the attention of A becomes blurred and is to all intents and purposes relegated to oblivion. Probably B will experience disconfirming triangulation, or, more accurately, he or she will experience disconfirmation, conveyed by the triangulation in which they are participating. The hypothesis is that B will experience relational conditions that lead to the development of a psychosis.

Personality and the Symptoms of a Psychotic

From a systemic perspective, personality in general (and that of a psychotic cannot be an exception) must be defined by referring to his or her relational systems of belonging, and very particularly, to their family of origin. In this way, it is possible to proceed to a definition involving three steps.

1. Elsewhere (Linares, 2012 op. cit., p. 95) we have defined personality as "*the individual dimension of accumulated relational experience in a dialogue between past and present, doubly contextualized by a biological substrate and a cultural context*". The dialogue between past and present makes reference to the fact that, even though we are historical beings, humans avoid being slaves of the past thanks to our ability to reformulate it from the present. The construction of one's personality is a process that lasts practically all one's life, in which this recursion between the past one has lived and the reformulated present occurs continually. Thanks to this capacity, psycho-relational changes, including therapeutic changes, are possible without the need to actually relive what we have already experienced in the past: it is enough to find new meanings. This also applies to the psychotic, albeit with the peculiarity that, as a relational experience dominated by disconfirmation is so intensely destructive, its subsequent reformulation is particularly laborious and difficult.

   The relational experience that a future psychotic accumulates in their family of origin is governed by disconfirming triangulation. Disconfirmation impacts on and disintegrates identity, generating a negative psychological dynamic that translates into a kind of experience of non-existence: "*If I do not exist or I am not important to the people who are everything to me, I am nobody*". These experiences will give rise in time to the so-called negative symptoms of schizophrenia: poverty of thought, social withdrawal with disorganized language and behaviour, inappropriate affectivity, etc. The living image of this terrible situation is that of the schizophrenic patient staring at himself in the mirror and laughing. "*Unmotivated laughter*", is what the researcher on duty will note down in their case history. However, if you make the effort to try to understand him, you will realize that his laughter is sardonic, very painful and full of contempt for himself in the face of the sorry spectacle of his own destruction.

   And as it is not possible to live "*not being anyone*", if the destruction of the identity does not reach the point of annihilation, from the rubble of its ruins the subject will try to obtain material with which to initiate a process of reconstruction. This is a positive process involving the search for an alternative identity, which, however, must comply with the requisite of being immune to disconfirmation. "*As I cannot bear not existing, I shall be someone quite unique, someone who cannot be ignored ever again. I shall be...Napoleon!*" This process shall give rise to the positive, delusional and hallucinatory symptoms that are so characteristic of paranoid schizophrenia.

   Not in vain, for nearly two centuries the figure of Napoleon has inspired jokes about crazy people in the western world. A small corporal from the confines of France, conquers the world and proclaims himself its emperor. There can be no more appropriate metaphor for the longing of the psychotic, which is none other than that of ensuring his or her recognition to the end of time. And if we aren't keen on Napoleon, then there is no shortage of figures who provide an unquestionable identity: Jesus Christ, the Virgin Mary, etc. It is not even necessary to embody a specific character. It is enough to live a unique situation, one "*that can only happen to me, like Martians kidnapping me or the neighbours tapping my conversations, or my thoughts appearing on TV*". The logic of delirium is always exclusive: "*The Martians don't abduct the people in my town, just me and nobody else than me*". It is, let us not forget, a question of protecting and shielding an identity against disconfirmation, although the cruel irony of the psychotic is that the more he is recognized as Napoleon (or she as the Virgin Mary), the less possibility there is that they will be recognized as the common or garden people they could once have become. Thus is sealed the social marginalization of the madman, among impossible dreams of a fully recognized unique identity.

2. In the light of the above, a psychosis may be understood as the identity disorder par excellence, since that identity is seriously affected in a twofold way, in its destruction by disconfirmation and in its delirious reconstruction, both of which pose a problem. But what do we mean when we talk about identity?

   To understand the concept of identity, we ought first to define *narrative*, which is the process of attributing meaning to relational activity. Ever since it exists, that is to say, virtually from the beginning of an individual's life, that subject builds stories, always of increasing complexity, giving a meaning to what takes place and also therefore attributing a meaning to his or her existence in this relational context. From this perspective, the narrative is the basis of the psychic activity, akin to the fundamental magma with which personality is built.

   Simultaneously with the construction of the narrative, and also closely linked to the relational activity, a second process takes place during which we select narrative material with which to build an *identity*. This is the part of the narrative in which the subject decides to define himself or herself: "*Of all these stories I have built, I identify myself with this one, that one and this other one. This is me, and therefore I do not accept any transactions or negotiations as far as these stories are concerned*". The word identity comes from the Latin "*Idem*", which means "*the same*", that is to say, that which does not change. And this relative immutability gives rise to certain consequences. On the one hand, it is clear that identity (also referred to as "*identitary narrative*") may not occupy too large a space in the narrative, rather just enough to serve as an anchor to the "*non-identitary narrative*", which must be extensive, rich and varied if it is to ensure a healthy and balanced personality.

   The narrative and the identity are generated in the individual, in close liaison with their systems of belonging and, especially, with the family of origin. And in these, as a relational system, there are two fundamental instances: organization and mythology.

   The *organization* of a relational system is equivalent to the longitudinal dimension of its structure, the projection of this dimension throughout the life cycle. If the structure is displayed in a synchronous section or a cross section, the organization is perceived as a diachronic or longitudinal cut. The structure changes during the various stages of the life cycle, becoming, for example, more cohesive in some of them (e.g. the courtship of the couple or the birth of their children) and less so in others (e.g. their children's adolescence). In principle however, the organization will remain unchanged during these stages. Unless certain changes take place, for example, in those who play important roles: deaths, separations, divorces and new partners. These are organizational changes, and after they have taken place, we may say that we are facing a new system.

As far as *mythology* is concerned, this is the space within the system in which the individual narratives of its members converge. Or, viewed from another perspective, the space from which these narratives emerge. Mythologies are, therefore, spaces of narrative consensus, shared to a greater or lesser extent, sometimes despite themselves, by the different members of the system: "*Mary is intelligent and hardworking but she does her own thing, while John is friendly, lazy and very generous*". Here we have a mythology in which, whether they like it or not, Mary and John are involved and which, inevitably, will influence the development of their personalities.

In a psychotic, these four functions have specific characteristics, as shown in Table 1:

Identity, consistent with the positive logic that we might call "*Napoleonic*", is hypertrophied, invading all corners of the narrative. If one is Napoleon, one is Napoleon to all intents and purposes, at any and every time and place. Non-identitary narrative is reduced to an insignificant minimum. It is impossible to speak with a psychotic in full delusion without his or her delusional identity making an appearance. In a delusional context, weather, for example, normally a non-identitary construction allowing banal and relaxed conversations, can easily become identitary:

> "*Aha! So you say it's a beautiful morning, do you? Surely it's just the weather you were waiting for to be able to set sail to take me to Santa Elena...*"

We will see what consequences this has for therapeutic intervention. Otherwise, triangulated organization and disconfirming mythology define the most important systems of belonging and, especially, the family of origin. For this reason, the personality of the psychotic will be marked by a bias of triangulation and disconfirmation.

3. The third step in defining a psychotic personality shows the two major dimensions that preside over the relational atmosphere in the family of origin: conjugality and parentality. In the psychotic's family of origin, exercising a decisive influence on the construction of his or her personality, a disharmonious conjugality is often to the fore (the infamous covert symmetry, symmetrical hubris, relationship stalemates, etc.) and a primarily preserved parentality, which deteriorates secondarily when faced with the impact of conjugality. This is the common denominator of triangulations: parents who are initially interested in their chil-

Table 1 Identity and narratives: developments of psychotic personality

Identity or identitary narrative (hypertrophic)	Organization (triangulated)
Non-identitary narrative (small)	Mythology (disconfirming)

dren and do everything possible to treat them well, but whose good intentions wane in the heat of marital conflict. On the other hand, in the psychotic's family of origin, the presence of pseudo-conjugal and pseudo-parental figures is frequent, people who exercise in a dysfunctional way the respective parentality and conjugality and who participate in several triangulations: prestigious siblings or members of the extended family.

This third defining level of personality, the relational atmosphere experienced in the family of origin, defined by conjugality and parentality, is linked to the first level, always under the sign of disconfirming triangulation in the case of a psychotic.

Therapeutic Intervention

The approach to psychoses is the greatest challenge that any psychotherapeutic model can face, but of all of them, family therapy is best equipped to survive the test reasonably well.

We have already seen how a delusional identity hypertrophies, reducing non-identitary narrative to an irrelevant minimum (Table 1). For a psychotic in full symptomatic activity, everything is delusion: *If I am Napoleon, I am Napoleon 24 h a day, and I can't waste time on banalities unless they have to do with my imperial condition.*

This explains how difficult it is to therapeutically address a psychosis from the individual who is suffering that psychosis: if the identity is well-nigh refractory to direct intervention and the non-identitary narrative is practically non-existent, there is no way in at the individual level (Table 2a). On the other hand, family organization and mythology provide excellent opportunities for intervention

Table 2 Therapeutic intervention in psychosis

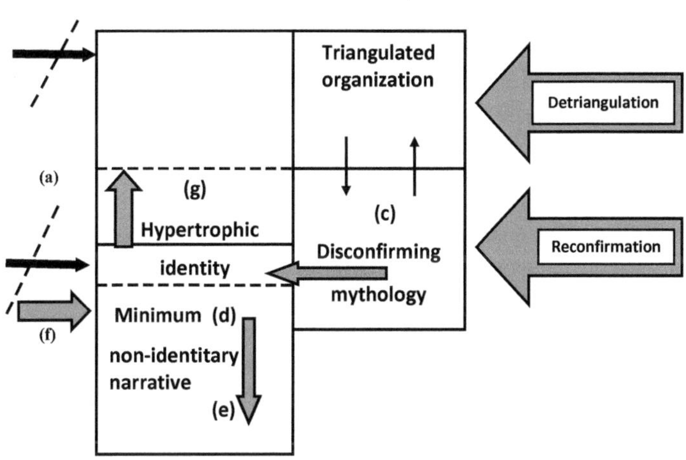

(Table 2b). Organizational and mythological changes influence each other (Table 2c) and are transmitted to the patient's individual narrative (Table 2d), also bringing about changes therein. What happens, basically, is that the non-identitary narrative expands (Table 2e) considerably, making an individual approach possible at last (Table 2f). Finally, without being subjected to direct confrontation, which it will hardly accept, the identity will tend to retract of its own accord until it reaches rather more reasonable dimensions (Table 2g).

> *To put it another way, if I am Napoleon, I will hardly be able to accept that I am not treated as such, and I shall refuse to talk about issues that exclude or contradict my imperial condition **(a)**. However, I shall agree to participate in a therapeutic process that challenges the way in which I have been triangulated and disconfirmed in my family **(b)**. This process will generate changes in the modus operandi of my family system **(c)**, that will make it more difficult for them to continue triangulating and disconfirming me. This will relax me **(d)**, allowing me to deal with other issues apart from defending tooth and nail my Napoleonic identity **(e)**. I will be able to talk about the weather, football, literature, philosophy or politics, without feeling that the essences of my sacred uniqueness are at stake, and this will allow me to take advantage of individual therapy sessions that beforehand I would have rejected **(f)**. Finally, as a result of a process that requires me to make less and less claim to an alternative identity, I shall progressively feel less Napoleon **(g)**.*

The first thing is to take care of the therapeutic relationship, which involves two equally important steps. The first is the construction of a therapeutic alliance with the patient that establishes a bond of trust. Psychotics are particularly sensitive to the perception of real help that is based on a personal commitment and not on bureaucratic relationships. The second step, equally necessary, is to legitimize this alliance with significant members of the family, who should perceive it as therapeutically coherent and useful for them, and not as a threat.

Family therapy of psychoses is essentially a process of reconfirmation, but given that triangulation, as we have seen, is the main vehicle for disconfirmation, during the evolution of the therapy special attention should be paid to neutralizing that vehicle through a process of detriangulation of the organization (Linares, 2006). Here are some pointers in this regard.

1. Development of multiple (the more the better) and fluid dyadic relations. The objective is that all the members of the family can relate with each other in a relaxed way, without awakening any individual's sensitivities. A good network of dyadic relations constitutes an excellent vaccine against triangulation. Here are a few pointers on how you can guide this work: hold sessions with each dyad, prescribe joint activities or simply reflect with them on the peculiarities of their relationship, reformulating these in a positive way.
2. Consolidation of subsystems: mainly the parental couple and the group of siblings. This is probably the most popular strategy in the field of family therapy, indeed it is doubtful that there is any other more proven intervention against triangulating dynamics. Strengthening the links between the parents, especially, is equivalent to neutralizing the stimuli that facilitate the intergenerational coalitions that are at the root of most triangulations. And, in addition, strengthening the relations of solidarity among the siblings by shattering the games that enthrone the prestigious sibling as opposed to the marginalization of the psychotic sibling.

3. Redefinition of the extended family by transforming the pseudo-parental roles. The existence of figures within the extended family who supplant and disqualify the parents, competing with them and usurping their functions with a hidden agenda of their own, is a source of triangulations that must be neutralized. The classic case of the grandmother that teams up with the granddaughter to embarrass her daughter, the child's mother. Far from being a healthy relationship for the former (probably the psychotic patient), it barely conceals her intention of demonstrating her own ability as an "authentic" mother.

By family mythology we understand that space in which the narratives of the individual members of the family converge. Proposals as simple as *Mary is rebellious and George is obedient* embody family myths that are imbued with cognitive dimensions (values and beliefs), affective dimensions (emotional climate) and pragmatic dimensions (rituals). In the family environment of the psychotic person, disconfirming mythology must inspire reconfirming strategies that target values and beliefs, the emotional climate and rituals.

"*It is a physical and genetic disease, in which the brain malfunctions, just as the pancreas of a diabetic malfunctions*". Here is myth number one, from the suprasystem (actually iatrogenic in nature) but one that the family can easily adopt. It is the so-called *myth of the cerebral pancreas*, under which it is impossible to carry out any psychotherapeutic activity. It must therefore be deconstructed at the very outset of the therapy, dedicating whatever time and effort is required to that end. The family and the patient should understand that, unlike diabetes, psychoses are complex phenomena in which there are psychological and relational factors of sufficient specific weight to justify psychotherapeutic interventions. The process is facilitated by the inclusion of medication control within the psychotherapeutic space, where it will be resized as one element among several others.

1. The values and beliefs that are specific to the family evolve over time while maintaining a common consistency. Thus, it is not uncommon to witness a succession of them, approximately in the following order:
   (a) "*The insignificant goody-goody*". Reflects the trend towards the self-absorption of the future psychotic, even as a child, when he or she begins to face disconfirming experiences. "*He always played on his own when he was small; he was so good that we sometimes forgot all about him…!*"
   (b) "*The disastrous weirdo*". This refers to bizarre behaviour that the future psychotic usually manifests as a final and desperate attempt to gain recognition, prior to the onset of delirium. For example, the son of semiliterate parents amasses a library of 3000 volumes; in a traditional farming family, a farmer puts himself forward as a healer; a young man goes on a 15-day silent strike. In all these cases, the reaction of the parents is to distance themselves in bewilderment, without showing any interest in understanding their son.
   (c) "*The unpredictable patient*". Once the psychosis has taken root, and with the aid of the "myth of the cerebral pancreas", the disease becomes a universal explanation of any manifestation by the patient that does not fit in with the family's expectations. "*Ummm! When he starts wanting to study again, there's a relapse on the way…*".

(d) "*The little opportunist tyrant*". This is a manifestation of chronicity, when the patient has effectively given up integrating himself into a normal life and does no more than vegetate, demanding from his now in most cases elderly parents, certain sad privileges such as money for tobacco or coffee. The atmosphere can become quite hostile.

These disconfirming values and beliefs must be replaced by other reconfirming ones. For example, the patient is someone important, someone worth knowing and treating. Their unpredictable behaviour is not necessarily the result of their psychosis, rather of their free, rebellious and creative spirit. He is not a heartless exploiter, rather a person who feels hurt and, by way of compensation, has become accustomed to living an easy life with as little effort as possible.

These reformulations must be communicated by the therapist and rigorously maintained throughout the therapeutic process, without incurring any contradictions or falling into the traps that the myriad of disconfirming agents can set, including the patient.

2. The disconfirming emotional climate coincides with what has been described by authors who have dealt with "*the emotions expressed*" (Leff, 2000). Among others, they highlight the following characteristics: a strong cohesion; high levels of conflict for relatively banal reasons, indifference to situations that should generate a more intense reaction; frequent expression of hostile emotions; important levels of criticism. Generally speaking, this is a quite inconsistent emotional atmosphere in which, in any case, negative emotions prevail.

   During therapy, the emotional climate must be transformed into one that is less conflictive, hostile and critical. In this way, psycho-educational techniques associated with the model of the expressed emotions can prove useful, provided that they are adequately contextualized as part of a psychotherapeutic strategy. It is as if each therapy could include a made-to-measure psycho-educational programme that helps the family to control their emotional negativity.

3. Disconfirming rituals can be developed in line with the detachment (in which case they will be exclusive rituals) or with the binding (and then they will be constrictive).

   Some examples:

   On Sundays, while having lunch with the family of the prestigious sibling, it is considered normal that the patient should remain locked in their room smoking. The parents do not go out together, rather they stay home to control the patient's movements.

   Disconfirming, exclusive and constrictive rituals must be replaced by others that are reconfirming, integrating and autotomizing, respectively. For example:

   (a) Rituals that make it possible to pay attention to the patient, such as inviting him to parties and celebrations. It will be necessary to make the effort to persuade the parents that it is necessary to forcefully communicate to the patient that without him or her the family is not the same and that there's no point in having the party.

(b) Rituals that convey expressions of affection (e.g. a good-night kiss). The psychotic tend not to be very fond of kisses, which they interpret as "the Kiss of Judas". That is why their parents have to convince them that a good-night kiss is now an expression of their genuine interest and affection.
(c) Rituals that consolidate a new relational organization (e.g. appropriate activities for the parental couple, different from those that correspond to the siblings).
(d) Rituals that combat the secondary benefits (e.g. redistribution of domestic tasks). It is important that these new rituals, which imply forgoing certain privileges and comforts, are implemented when the by now well-advanced therapy has generated patient's confidence towards the therapist. Otherwise, it is likely that the therapy will fail, as has happened so many times before.

Finally, in line with the philosophy of Table 2, when the changes in the family organization and mythology have begun to influence the individual non-identitary narrative of the patient, leading to its expansion, it will be possible to begin holding individual sessions. Our proposal is that for a while such sessions should alternate with family sessions and should then gradually relegate and replace them. The basic strategy behind this individual work will be the same: detriangulation (helping the patient not to be triangulated) and reconfirmation (helping him to believe in himself or herself). And this may receive a huge boost with an individual finale in which the patient communicates, to the world and to himself, that the therapy has been "his or hers".

References

Bowen, M. (1960). A family concept of schizophrenia. In D. D. Jackson (Ed.), *The etiology of schizophrenia*. New York: Basic Books.

Freud, S. (1915–17). *Vorlesungen zur Einführung in die Psychoanalyse*. Leipzig, Heller. (The standard edition of the complete psychological works. London. The Hogarth Press and the Institute of Psycho analisis. 1953–74).

Goldbeter, E. (2003). *Le deuil impossible. Familles et tiers pessants*. Bruxelles: De Boeck.

Guerin, P. J. (Ed.). (1976). *Family therapy: Theory and practice*. Gardner Press: New York.

Guerin, P. J., Fogarty, T., Fay, L. F., & Kautto, J. G. (2010). *Working with relational triangles: The one-two-three of psychotherapy*. New York: Guilford Press.

Haley, J. (1967). Towards a theory of pathological systems. In J. H. Zuk & I. Boszormenyi-Nagy (Eds.), *Family therapy and disturbed families*. Palo Alto: Science and Behavior Books.

Leff, J. (2000). Family work for schizophrenia: Practical applications. Acta Psichyatrica Scandinavica, 102, 78–82.

Linares, J. L. (2012). *Terapia familiar ultramoderna. La Inteligencia Terapéutica*. Barcelona: Herder.

Linares, J. L. (2006). Complex love as relational nurturing: An integrating ultramodern concept. *Family Process, 45*(1), 101–115.

Watzlawick, P., Bavelas, J. B., & Jackson, D. D. (1967). *Pragmatics of human communication*. New York: Norton.

Borderline Personality Disorder Storyboard from the Systemic Family Therapist's Perspective

Luigi Cancrini and Francesca Romana De Gregorio

Introduction

In her psychotherapeutic work with adults suffering from severe personality disorders, Lorna Smith Benjamin (1993, 2003) has effectively reconstructed the specific and unique circumstances of their childhoods. Exploring the interpersonal meaning of symptomatic behaviors which characterize the individual disorders, she was then able to connect these two sets of data. In fact, patients who suffer from a severe personality disorder will repeat, in their current adult significant relationships, those behavior patterns learned in childhood in relation to their important attachment figures. Thus, in these severely disordered situations, the adult patient is constantly superimposing to the current relationships—in other words, to the person who actually stands before him or her in the present—those figures or ghosts from whom these patterns originated. When faced with these ghosts, the patient will interact with the current figure either by (a) acting as he or she did in relation to the figure of the past; (b) acting the same way in which the ghost of the past did; or (c) by treating himself/herself as he/she was treated by that ghost (Benjamin, 1993).

What Benjamin did not verify is the actual reality of these reconstructions, which is what we did when in a later project, carried out in Rome and Cagliari, working with children who had been the victims of severe abuse, we were able to verify the validity of Benjamin's reconstructions and the possibility of constructing a typology of unhappy childhoods (Cancrini, 2013) which coincide with the different types of personality disorders. In fact, children living in these situations already display, albeit on a smaller scale and sometimes less conspicuously, the characteristic

L. Cancrini (✉)
Centro Studi di Terapia Relazionale, Rome, Italy
e-mail: info@cstfr.org

F. R. De Gregorio
Associazione Bambini nel Tempo Onlus, Rome, Italy

R. Pereira, J. L. Linares (eds.), *Clinical Interventions in Systemic Couple and Family Therapy*, European Family Therapy Association Series,
https://doi.org/10.1007/978-3-319-78521-9_2

behavior patterns of the adult disorder, with one important difference which is treatment possibility (Cancrini, 2017) because therapeutic work with children is certainly easier and more effective than what can be implemented when working with adolescents or adults who have not spoken out before.

The Borderline Childhood

In Benjamin's (1993) description, the childhood of a BPD presents the following four characteristics:

1. the family is pervaded by chaos with fights, conflict, and infidelity; partners, homes, and caregivers are constantly changing. Episodes of violence related to alcohol abuse and suicide attempts are ever present and take place—"as in a soap opera"—on a stage; the future (potential) BPD is forced to witness this and, often, to intervene.
2. the developmental history includes moments or phases of affectionate care followed by repeated experiences of neglect caused by the change of a key figure (a classic example may be that of a child who has to deal with mother's several boyfriends or with the different women that father brings home); or to isolation and loneliness determined by the fact that one or more caregivers disappears entirely for hours or days, without the child being able to understand why or for how long, without the adult providing an explanation for this (the child, in various ways, can feel he or she is to blame for these absences) and without there being any protective conditions to prevent abuse or ill-treatment of the child.
3. a developmental history in which the child was subjected to authentic yet discontinuous love and where he or she learned to be strongly attached to a key figure (to mother who was abandoned by her friends or to the alcoholic father) or to a family group which feels "betrayed" by the child's search for independence and especially by the child's search for support from figures outside of the family: harshly attacking, for example, the bond the child establishes with the operators of a community, with a special teacher, or with the child's foster parents.
4. a developmental history in which the child learns that "misery and illness attract love and concern": a dangerous thing to learn because later—as a child, a teenager, or an adult—he or she will expect that those who care for him or her (a lover, a therapist, or an educator) will provide more love and more caring if he or she is sick and suffering.

Diego's Case

Diego is 9 years old and the oldest of four siblings. From the reports and contact with services we learn that his two sisters are currently in the care of two aunts, while the younger brother is housed in another institute.

The precipitating episode, which led to the involvement of the Court and of family services, saw the child's mother throw a stick at him and hit him in the eye. This was done in the attempt to separate Diego from his sister as he was trying—in a fit of jealousy—to tie a rope around her neck. Despite a clumsy attempt to justify herself, mother admitted to having acted this way. The child initially claimed having fallen off his bicycle, and then described what really had happened, provoking the wrath of his father (who was already in conflict with mother), and the concern of his paternal relatives, who reported the incident to social service.

The family has been in the care of family services since Diego was 2 years old. Before the birth of the last two girls (about 4 years ago), the family was subjected to a court-mandated assessment of their parenting skills. This resulted in the suspension of parental responsibility for both parents.

The parental couple is highly contentious and there are frequent episodes of violence. In the past, the child's mother reported her husband for abuse and he was sentenced to jail.

The couple displayed severe lacks in parenting skills, as reported by home education services: the children are not provided with any system of rules, they eat at any time without being able to sit at the table, the parents have an unbalanced mode of relating and are ineffective in conveying affection to the children. Initially, the children were assigned to various families in the neighborhood, through a widespread custom in Sardinia which goes under the name of <<fill'e anima>> (child of the soul) which was then regularized, after family services took charge, through family support projects which saw Diego being hosted by one of these families for 3 days a week.

The children's father is portrayed as deeply ignorant and obtuse, still able to get by doing odd jobs and many illegal activities. His main activity is shepherding. He is described as particularly attentive to his physical form and with a morbid approach to sex. He comes from a family of eight children, an extremely severe and violent father, and a dependent and utterly male-dominated mother.

Diego's mother is described as immature, deceitful, impulsive. She reported being abused by her father when she was a child. According to services, she taught the children to lie. The court assigned educator who follows Diego in the home claims that he is no longer able to distinguish between falsehood and truth.

The bond between Diego and his mother is particularly strong. In his stories, the child talks about how much mother needs his protection and he introduces himself as her "boyfriend." She, in turn, is extremely jealous of their relatives who, after repeated and failed attempts, now refuse to intervene because of the bad relationship with mother. They describe her as aggressive and impulsive to the point, for example, of physically beating her sister-in-law who was helping her care for the children. Of the four children, Diego is the most damaged, the one who is most involved in the intense conflict between the parents, often an accomplice to mother in her attempts to catch father in the act of cheating. In the neuropsychiatric diagnosis, the term used is "oppositional defiant" disorder which manifested itself especially during the periods in which the child was entrusted to other families; after an initial phase of successful integration, mother would start to oppose all the projects with the foster families (Cancrini, 2017).

Therapeutic Intervention with the Borderline Childhood

The most salient feature of the situation experienced by these children is the chaotic discontinuity of affection and care provided them by the relevant figures: a discontinuity that does not, however, rule out authentic attachment. This creates the conditions which lead the pre-borderline child to alternate between anger and the search for other figures. These children tend to establish a strong emotional relationship with anyone who is involved in their caregiving; initially, this relationship will be disturbed by the child's constant expectation of abandonment; later it will be further complicated as the child feels that he or she is betraying the original figure that he or she has been separated from. When placed in a residential community or in a foster family, these children improve immediately, as they find the protection and caring they need. Problems will arise later in the process, when the child's emotional improvement will trigger feelings of guilt towards his or her family of origin and will activate a typical loyalty conflict.

The therapeutic goal in all these situations is, of course, to try to change this conflict; the first therapeutic interventions should be aimed directly at the family of origin. When the situation is critically disturbed and the child is exposed to severe risks (as was Diego's case), temporary or permanent removal from the family must be considered and the loyalty conflict must be addressed within a psychotherapeutic intervention carried out with the child.

As for Diego, he has been placed and is being treated in a childcare residential community. Child services have initiated a procedure for the forfeiture of parental authority and the child continues to meet both parents separately once a week. The educators' supportive actions are accompanied by psychotherapy interventions centering on the reconstruction of Diego's family history and on the drama of a child forced to play the inappropriate role of supporting and protecting mother from the violence of the parental couple's conflict. Father, distracted by other engagements and interests, soon disappears from the family visits and from Diego's life entirely. Mother continues to remain deeply attached to Diego. Described—by those who have dealt with the family for years—as immature, a liar, and extremely inconsistent in her ability to provide protection and affection, mother is in fact the leading character of Diego's love life (he introduces himself as "her boyfriend") and the protagonist of the therapeutic work carried out with great attention and care by Diego's therapist until the moment in which the Court made a final deliberation on the adoptability of the child. At this critical point, the therapist conducts a dramatic session in which the reality of detachment, at this point both unavoidable and impending, are dealt with and spoken of clearly. Mother is helped to express her love for him, a love that nothing and no one will ever question and will accompany him, regardless of all, into the family that will welcome him some day. In this session, the therapist speaks openly and clearly of the loyalty conflict, voicing Diego's fears and helping mother express, through her tears, her ultimate wish for her son's well-being. This is spoken of openly, with mother embracing her son who is, at this point, capable of dealing with the separation from her.

In our experience, the importance of an open discussion concerning the issues related to obvious loyalty conflicts is especially critical when it does not occur; in situations of adoption, such as Diego's, not addressing these issues early in the process can lead to adoptive crises which occur primarily during adolescence. Also, all the past attempts made by child services to place Diego in foster care underscore the importance of working on the loyalty conflict as these attempts failed because of his need to return to the mother who needed him so badly (the heroic interpretation) or that he had forgotten (the weak version).

In many other cases, in less critical situations, structural family therapy as proposed by Sal Minuchin (1967) and Jay Haley (1980) is the easiest form of intervention which can be implemented in this type of situation.

The patterns of the "peripheral father" or of the "absent grandmother" introduced for the first time in Minuchin's pioneering work (1967) are, in fact, frequently met with in those situations typical to the pre-borderline childhood and adolescence; it is to this type of young-adult pathology which Jay Haley (1980) refers to when discussing separation from the family. One can object that these authors do not use the term "borderline" in describing these cases; however, a careful perusal of the cases presented by them clearly reveals the strength and discontinuity of the bond that these teenagers and young adults experienced with their mothers and with other role models, and how therapy was centered on building relationships which acknowledged the fundamental importance of emotional bonds and to ensure the stability of these same bonds.

The Borderline Adolescence

Adolescents who were raised—and sometimes continue to live—in a context which is typical of the future BPD show clinical signs which resemble more and more those of the adult BPD although it is important to note the reversibility. Also demonstrated by longitudinal studies such as the Toronto Longitudinal Study (Golombek, Marton, Stein, & Korenblum, 1986), in fact, symptoms which are present at ages 13 or 15 are not predictive of a personality disorder at age 18, the reasons being that at this age environmental influences and context play a very important part: in practice, this means that at this stage the possibilities of effective therapeutic intervention are much higher than in later stages.

Returning to the clinical practice, the set of typical symptomatic borderline adolescent behaviors is still, as for the child, related to abandonment anxiety. In interpersonal terms, these behaviors manifest themselves as falling in love at first sight, instant idealizations, furious jealousy and/or dramatic and angry escapes when the other tries to set boundaries to a relationship which is perceived as exclusive and all-encompassing. From the clinical perspective, it is important to take into account the wide variety of symptomatic behaviors which this kind of psychopathological mechanism may generate in different family, social, and cultural contexts. The following table, drawn with some alterations from Kernberg (1984), proposes some of the most frequent behaviors.

At a time and in a culture in which access to drugs is particularly easy, addictions are in fact the most common manifestations of BPD during adolescence. The "honeymoon with heroin" described by Olivenstein (1981) corresponds in fact to a swift and all-encompassing idealization of the moods and sensations caused by a specific substance. From a different perspective, however, the act of seeking relief via dangerous substances which enable the user to not think, can be equated to those self-harming behaviors (cutting oneself) and those suicide attempts which are impulsive reactions that adolescents have when an idealized figure poses limits to their relationship. The risks involved in drug consumption (from overdosing to medical and legal problems) are particularly important, in fact, for this type of teenager: young addicts are characterized by uncontrolled impulsivity, or barely controllable behavior, instability of emotional bonds, and a continuous dramatization of events and of the emotions connected to them.

Marco's Case

Marco is 16 years old when we meet him for the first time; his mother and father have been together on and off for years, and have eventually entrusted him to the care of a loving grandmother who was always available and willing to take care of the child. When Marco began middle school, and following the birth of a second child that mother had with another man, his parents separated for good. Marco's anxiety soon became unmanageable, especially at school where he failed seventh grade for behavior problems and quit attending school for a few months in an attempt to go back and live with his grandmother. There were violent and painful conflicts between Marco and his mother and her new partner as both adults opposed his many absences from school. At this stage, Marco was very altered and the encounter with heroine had upon him an overwhelming effect. Heroine provided him with incredible moments of absolute well-being while at the same time starting an open conflict with his grandmother who was paralyzed by disappointment and fear. Marco's many rambling activities, his painful unrest, his defiance, all concur to suggest to those who meet him at this stage that this boy is desperately trying to fill a painful void from which he seeks refuge by injecting heroine: rehabilitation and detoxification can finally begin after we were able to implement a therapy project involving the family and centering on restoring the relationship with mother.

In different family and cultural contexts, the compulsive behaviors of the BPD adolescent may be different from those related to drug use. Some eating disorders of the bulimic type, pathological gambling and some forms of kleptomania, for example, present similar patterns to those of drug addiction. It is important to note that a diagnosis of BPD cannot be based exclusively on the presence of compulsive behaviors as these can also be associated to other psychopathological contexts such as PTSD; neurotic type disorders; or other personality disorders such as the narcissistic and antisocial, as we have previously observed based on our extensive and valued clinical experience in the field of addiction.

Returning to the BPD in adolescence, another common and important manifestation is linked to violent behaviors related due to lack of impulse control. As opposed to adolescents who suffer from an antisocial personality disorder, in the BPD adolescent these behaviors occur both within and without the family context, in response to an emotional stress connected to the intense fear of abandonment and are shortly followed by genuine and painful remorse.

Luca's Case

Luca is 17 when he is reported by his parents because he has "laid his hands" on his mother, has "wreaked havoc" and has stolen several times from his parents. These contrasts occur mainly in relation to the use and trafficking of hashish; with absences from school, and with the sudden discontinuity of the affection of a boy who went from being overly attached to his mother to running away from her. During the session, the violence of the emotions experienced by Luca becomes immediately evident. He cries, ashamed of what he did, while at the same time expressing anger towards his father of whom he recalls the painful betrayals and the physical abuse, towards himself and towards his mother when, for a long period during Luca's childhood father was a drunk. The parents are called together to take a firm stand towards Luca, enabling them to regain control of the situation at home, and this allows the therapist to shift the focus towards the conflict between the parental couple while Luca is helped to reflect on how the events experienced within his family have affected his difficulty in controlling emotions (and impulses) and on his difficulty in building an autonomous life project.

Another clinical variation of the BPD in adolescence is connected to the development of an anxiety disorder (panic attacks) or, more frequently, of a mood disorder. The alternation of more or less clearly anxiety-laden depressive phases to phases in which the adolescents' exaltation takes on an almost manic feature is very common in the BPD adolescent who is openly at war with his parents concerning issues of mild substance abuse, academic problems, rudeness, verbal violence, and engaging in dangerous activities. The resulting situation is that of a chaotic family which presents interesting similarities to that of the borderline childhood, and which makes it very difficult to see how the onset of symptoms and the frequency with which they recur can be linked to the strain of the affective relationships; this is especially true for those situations in which the initial help request is intercepted by psychiatrists who, not trained to think in terms of personality disorders (or axis II DSM-IV), propose a diagnosis of "bipolar disorder" or, less frequently, of "panic attacks."

Sudden mood changes are common in adolescence and later in adults with a personality disorder. In the course of therapy, it is possible to observe these changes from the patient's perspective and to connect these with little incidents to which the subjects ascribes, often without having a clear awareness, a significant interpersonal meaning. Fear of abandonment will rapidly transform the therapists' distraction or his/her (excessive) interest in someone else into blatant rejection, as typically happens to the child who, leaving the therapists cabinet, is painfully surprised to see another needy child in the waiting room. The BPD adolescent's relapses are often linked to the abrupt mood change suffered when a significant adult or the selfsame therapist—sometimes unaware—impose limits to their relationship. Lack of sensitivity and of psychotherapeutic knowledge often lead these displays to be labelled as "unexplained mood swings" or symptoms of a "bipolar disorder" when—to a more attentive therapist—they are nothing other than the expression of this patient's special fragility.

Therapeutic Interventions with the BPD Adolescent

Clinical work with the BPD adolescent is similar to that with the adult patient; however, its displays are less rigid and less stable and there are more possibilities of intervention, especially if the teenager is still living within the family. The most important difference regarding treatment is, in fact, the possibility of involving the family in the treatment plan, with which one can work within a well-established therapeutic strategy.

From a structural point of view, parents should be helped first and foremost to form a united front against the child's symptomatic behavior (Haley, 1980). This is easier to propose and to implement with cases in which the disorder is expressed via compulsive and violent behaviors which the adolescent should be helped-pushed-forced to control. Even when dealing with other cases, in which the pathology is expressed through forms of self-harm, anxiety crises, or depressive moments, the caregiver's attitude should reflect a clear distinction between who the child is or could be and what he or she does or feels during a given time or phase of his/her life. The best way to tackle these challenges is to convey that one fully understands and accepts the pain and suffering experienced by the child, but condemns the counterproductive ways in which they are expressed. One of the greatest challenges presented by many of these cases is a direct effect of the dramatic situation experienced by the family context. The therapist's observations and recommendations can be severely misunderstood or long-ignored altogether due to the chaotic, sorrowful, explosive, and rancorous atmosphere typical of these families which function in a way very similar to the one described for pre-borderline children. When this initial difficulty is overcome, however, the therapist's task suddenly becomes easier because the strength of the emotional involvement, which is also characteristic of these families, allows the teenager to experience the strength and authenticity of the affection within the family. Often, the symptomatic behavior which led to the initial help request, loses intensity and frequency. The therapist can then begin to deal with the subsequent and more structured intervention; on the one hand, favoring the designated child's differentiation and individuation, and on the other providing stability to the newly acquired family balance by addressing old unresolved problems within the parental couple, among siblings, or in relation to the extended family.

We have previously mentioned that the symptomatic behaviors we are discussing do not occur only in this type of family. What we would like to underscore at this point is that, while riddled with challenges, interventions with these families are usually easier and more productive than those with families characterized by an antisocial form of neglect. As already observed by Salvador Minuchin (1967) in one of his most beautiful books, written at the very beginning of family therapy, on his experience at Wiltwyck School for Delinquent Boys.

Minuchin describes "enmeshed" families, similar to our borderlines families, in which the discontinuity of affection does not impact its authenticity, the opportunity and the ability to work with parents and children still strongly entangled with each other. In these families, family therapy is understood as a path of activation and reorientation of emotional resources and it usually produces significant results in a relatively short time as opposed to the results obtained working with more antisocial families, which Minuchin described as "disengaged." The most remarkable feature of the disengaged family is it's emotional poverty; parents fail to recognize and express emotions, they are highly neglectful and remain distant from the adolescent child showing very little interest in his or her suffering.

As part of a research project on family and social factors of drug addiction among young people in Italy, at a time when drug abuse was severely punished and no addict would—of his own initiative—turn for help to health or social services, we worked together with a group of young colleagues and arranged for family interviews to be conducted within the homes of substance-abusing adolescents whom we managed to meet on the streets of Rome or in the local hospitals when medical conditions (the most frequent being hepatitis caused by infected syringes) or accidents forced the young addicts to seek medical attention. The interviews took place in the evening, they were open to as many family members who would participate, from both immediate and extended family. Interviews were conducted by a therapist, a young researcher, and a social worker. We soon realized we were facing two very distinct realities: the reality of the enmeshed families whose reactions were of immediate participation, becoming instantly and actively involved in their child's problems, even if they only learned about all the ongoing issues during the interview itself. Disengaged families presented another reality; family members did not want to participate in the interviews, and if so they did it unwillingly. When we attempted to underscore their child's need by describing the medical and psychological problems, their reactions ranged from detachment, to indifference, to violence.

The young addicts belonging to enmeshed families had a clearly borderline reaction, feeling repentant and remorseful in front of those parents who immediately assumed their share of responsibility. The substance abusers belonging to disengaged families reacted in a more antisocial manner, defying their parents who, in turn, could not show any real interest in their child.

Naturally, the development and implementation of a therapeutic project was greatly influenced by the type of family involved: easy, or—at least—easier with the enmeshed families; very challenging and requiring the use of paradox and counterparadox when working with the disengaged families (Albedo, 1984). The distinction between enmeshed and disengaged families is very important from a psyhological perspective: enmeshed families of adolescent drug-addicts are in fact closely related to borderline childhoods while the disengaged family seems more closely related to the pre-antisocial childhood. In these antisocial situations and in the more severe and consolidated cases of borderline addiction the systemic family therapists has to accept the idea that, family participation per se is not sufficient to grant recovery. Admission to a rehabilitation facility may be necessary, in fact, for those severe situations very much in the same way in which hospitalization can be useful when a severe form of obesity compromises treatment of bulimia. For cases in which the young addict is also involved in drug dealing and or violent behaviors, it may be necessary and productive to turn to the Juvenile Court. For all the above cases, it remains however essential that—alongside these specialized structures—the family actively participate in a treatment plan which affects the family as much as the individual; the young substance abuser might be the one to be hospitalized or sentenced to a court appointed program; however, he or she must always be regarded as the member a problematic family system as well as an individual whose individuation process is still incomplete (Cancrini & La Rosa, 1991). The psychodynamic meaning of this type of family intervention should be carefully assessed within an integrated vision of psychotherapeutic knowledge. The united front created by parents who oppose—for a sufficiently long time—the symptomatic behavior, allows the reconstruction of a situation in which the constant attentive but not intrusive presence of the maternal object allows the child to experiment both the sense of boundaries, connected to the fall of the emotional complicity within what Jay Haley called the "perverse triangle," and object constancy which is the natural antidote of abandonment anxiety.

The BPD Adult

We noted earlier that symptomatic behaviors of young adults and adults have remarkable similarities to those of the BPD adolescent. If untreated, towards the end of adolescence, the patient's disorder undergoes a form of "crystallization" (Zanarini, 2009) which tends to replicate and progressively strengthen the interpersonal mechanisms around which it is structured. After a long time during which moments of intense crisis alternate periods of apparent tranquility, the BPD goes from being a "troubled adolescent, with substance-abuse problems, mood swings, and impulse control issues" to consolidating a sort of new identity; there is a break with the family and with the previous life context and a new character is identified with, be it the "druggie," the "violent subject," or the "bipolar," or the "bulimic," or the sick criminal.

It is natural, based on the above considerations, that the diagnostic categories which are applied to the symptomatic behavior of the adult BPD when this is intercepted by health services or judicial structures is substantially similar to that of adolescents described in Table 1. Research conducted by Zanarini (2009) on a 7-year follow-up of the diagnosis of BPD within the hospital setting used—along

Table 1 Interpersonal summary of BPD

Childhood (and adolescence)	Adult symptoms
Chaotic lifestyle, need to adapt rapidly (impulsively) to the constant and unpredictable variability of affective and organizational references	Tendency to make quick decisions based on the prevailing emotion (impulsivity) and subsequent lack of constant affective relations
Repeated abandonment experiences	Fear of being abandoned manifested through intense and extreme emotional involvement; control; jealousy which may lead to violence; acting out—in front of a real or imaginary abandonment—of angry attacks and/or of self-punishing behaviors
Discontinuity and chaos do not exclude sincere affection bestowed on the child by the needy adults; bonds with attachment figures outside of the family are threatened and blamed and give rise to a characteristic loyalty conflict	When current positive relationships begin to consolidate and are in conflict with loyalty to the internalized figures, they are attacked
During the phase in which the child feels abandoned, being ill elicits care on behalf of the adult	Illness or discomfort is exaggerated (dramatized) to elicit care; frequently enacts self-harming behaviors (cutting self) and suicide attempts

side standard tests—as reference symptoms, other behaviors such as substance abuse, violent behaviors, suicide attempts, and the difficulty in impulse control, all of which are—in fact the most common expressions of this disorder. Differences are reported between adolescents and adults because in the latter, violent behavior is often related to alcohol abuse and is expressed within romantic relationships and social situations whereas adolescents are more likely to manifest these behaviors within the family of origin. Also in adults, bulimic conducts are less frequent and self-harming behaviors tend to be less demonstrative and more dangerous. The interactional logic underlying all of these symptoms is always related to the individual's origins which must be looked for in a specific and well-outlined type of "unhappy childhood" as is well represented by this interpersonal summary drawn, with some changes, from Lorna Smith Benjamin's (1993) outstanding work (Table 1).

Therapeutic Work with the BPD Adult

Therapeutic work with and adult BPD can begin, usually, only when the symptomatic behaviors are detected due to their severity: in other words, due to the gravity of the consequences that these behaviors have on the subjects' health (as classically happens in severe forms of addiction; after suicide attempts; or in the aggravation of psychic disorders of anxious, depressive, or manic type); on his/her interpersonal relationships (e.g., gender violence); or in social situations (implementing crimes, facilitated by alcohol and/or substance abuse, related to the difficulty of impulse control). This type of patient will, in fact, accept help with relative ease when going through a period of crisis ("I've lost everything"; "no one wants me anymore") or of true repentance for things he/she did ("it's my fault, I should never have acted that way") (Benjamin, 2003).

The psychopathological explanation for this "ease" is related to the fundamental movement of a child who experienced a borderline childhood. The search for a new relationship with the maternal figure represented by the therapist is merely the repetition of an ancient and natural dynamic. By investing a lot on the person who is offering to provide help, the borderline patient also demands a lot, and very quickly too, immediately giving rise to strong countertransference reactions in the therapist and generating important problems concerning boundary setting (Cancrini, 2006).

As already mentioned regarding the more severe situations with adolescents, it may be necessary to begin treatment by implementing important containment measures. When alcohol and/or substance abuse are the foremost concern, BPD patients often begin treatment within therapeutic communities or rehabilitation facilities because these places provide the BPD with the warm and caring environment they direly need. As opposed to addicts marked by antisocial or paranoid traits who openly reject care, BPD patients begin their process by adapting compliantly to the rules of community life and begin to create problems only at a later stage, when the fear of abandonment pushes them to seek for an exclusive and completely engrossing relationship with one or more staff members.

With the more severe psychiatric cases, presenting with repeated self-harming behaviors or severe depressive/anxious crises, it is usually necessary to begin treatment with a pharmaceutical regime and, sometimes, hospitalization. In a climate which is strongly characterized by medical and pharmacological interventions however, emotional investment is expressed more easily at the beginning of treatment, in terms of acceptance of care and of more or less openly seductive improvements. Later, there is usually a resentful recurrence of symptoms: a natural succession of facts with a clear relational meaning but which often leads the less experienced psychiatrist—unaware of his or her own countertransference of initial enthusiasm and later disappointment—to conclude that the patient's pathology is more severe than initially appraised and possibly untreatable.

In other circumstances, in which the symptomatic emergency is related to violent behavior, with or without alcohol and/or substance abuse, the required containment measures can be very different. In cases of domestic violence, it is often up to the spouse or to a close family member, to request the intervention of law enforcement or of a judge to whom this initial containment is entrusted. Here begins a process to which the BPD usually responds with repentance and apologies, but which must be further implemented with therapeutic interventions focusing on both the patients' difficulty in controlling impulses, and on the characteristics of the relationship in which the violent behavior occurred (Kowal & Simon, 2008).

This first step of behavior containment is always essential. It will, however, only have therapeutic significance if it is followed by a long-lasting psychotherapeutic intervention to be carried out, in our opinion, taking into account the stage of the life cycle that the person is experiencing. When faced with a young adult who is still developing, who has not yet built a significant couples' relationship or who has ended a relationship in a traumatic way, therapeutic interventions should be carried out directly with the subject. When the difficult situation takes place within a significant relationship, then the treatment setting should take this into account and possibly involve the significant other in the treatment plan.

Concerning individual therapy, the most effective and interesting approach for the systemic therapist is, in our opinion, Interpersonal Reconstructive Therapy (IRT) proposed by Lorna Smith Benjamin (2003). In their current behaviors and reactions, patients unwittingly and unwillingly, repeat patterns of interaction which they learned during childhood in relation to their caregivers. This is especially true for BPD subjects. Regarding couples' treatment, the timing and the ways of emotional involvement of these patients are often such as to make it very difficult to initiate a significant therapeutic relationship if the importance of that selfsame involvement is not recognized. Two examples can be useful to give an idea of how these seemingly different interventions are actually aimed at the same purpose and follow very similar paths.

Annalisa, a 28-year-old female, asks for help after a series of hospitalizations due to her self-harming behaviors. In discussing a childhood memory during her first session she remembers how—in order to fall asleep at night—she needed to feel her mother's hand under her cheek (mother had been abandoned by father), and the anguish she would feel waking up in the morning and mother, who had left early to go to work, was no longer there. For Annalisa it was both easy and useful, during therapy, to connect this memory to the fear of abandonment that had made it impossible for her to establish stable relationships until then: both for the violence of her emotional needs and for the way in which her need to control her made those same needs unstable and painful, generating in her a continuous crisis which expressed itself in self-harming behaviors.

Franco, a 33-year-old male, asks for help with his repeated binge-episodes of alcohol and cocaine abuse. During these binges, he disappears completely from a wife he does love very much. He quickly becomes aware of how, when his relationship with his wife is in trouble, he experiences an intense abandonment anxiety which forces him to return to the dramatic memory of loneliness, anger, and pain he felt when, after being left by his own wife, his father committed suicide. It was that father's behavior that he now, symbolically, repeated over and over again with his binges.

Concluding Remarks

In this work, we have adopted a perspective which differs greatly from the prevailing one used in today's psychiatric practice. We have considered the symptoms reported on Axis I of the DSM-IV and DSM-V as epiphenomena of the borderline personality disorder described in Axis II. It is important to underscore, yet again, that many similar symptoms can occur in subjects affected by other personality disorders, and that the most important definition—from a diagnostic and therapeutic perspective—is the one concerning the underlying personality disorder rather than the symptom itself.

The possibility of reconstructing those childhood situations which—if not recognized in time—give rise to the BPD, has a critical significance for prevention. To ask that childhood neuropsychiatrists, along with educators, and psychologists, learn to look beyond the surface of symptoms in order to intervene on the underlying situations which generate and support those same symptoms means asking that all of these professionals study and apply the observations of the most experienced psychoanalysts—from Anna Freud (1975) to Winnicott (1958) and/or of the systemic family therapists—when called upon to intervene on the causes of those symptoms.

The ability to identify the affective dynamics of the borderline disorder behind a significant variety of adolescent and adult symptomatic behaviors is equally important for the therapist who is not satisfied with mere symptom reduction. It is common—for these patients—to shift from one symptom to another; this is explained by the difficulty, also very common, to understand the complexity of the relationship between Axis I and Axis II disorders, which supports and explains the symptoms. When working with this type of patient, professional psychotherapeutic training goes hand in hand with the awareness of having to work on the underlying emotional difficulties in order to achieve a stable and enduring improvement.

Lastly, when called upon to intervene, therapists should be able to recognize and identify the life cycle phase which the patient is living; this is an acknowledgement of Milton Erickson's fundamental reflections on the need to choose the appropriate psychotherapeutic intervention moment by moment (Haley, 1985). The substantial continuity between early experiences (eventually suppressed in subsequent years) and symptomatic behaviors highlighted in adolescence or adulthood well demonstrates and supports the importance and relevance of Freud's fundamental discoveries; but the decision to work with the individual, the couple, or the family remains the first of the decisions which the therapist has to face in attempting to provide help, and the importance of this choice is proof of the need for a systemic approach to psychotherapy. Only a methodology based on the careful consideration of the life cycle and of the interpersonal context in which symptoms are manifested can enable the full use of all the available resources which the therapists disposes of when helping patients with these symptoms.

While remaining at times difficult and not acknowledged, the theoretical pathway leading to a constructive integration of the observations made by systemic family analysts and therapists is once again a fundamental goal for psychotherapy of our times.

References

Albedo, C. (Ed.). (1984). *Terapia familiare con tossicodipendenti*. Nuova Italia Scientifica: Roma.

Benjamin, L. S. (1993). *Interpersonal diagnosis and treatment of personality disorders*. New York: Guilford.

Benjamin, L. S. (2003). *Interpersonal reconstructive therapy*. New York: Guilford.

Cancrini, L. (2006). *L'oceano borderline. Racconti di viaggi*. Milano: Raffaello Cortina.
Cancrini, L. (2013). *La cura delle Infanzie Infelici*. Milano: Raffaello Cortina.
Cancrini, L. (2017). *Ascoltare i Bambini*. Milano: Raffaello Cortina.
Cancrini, L., & La Rosa, C. (1991). *Il vaso di pandora*. Roma: Nuova Italia Scientifica.
Freud, A. (1966/1975). *The writings of Anna Freud*. New York: International Universities Press.
Golombek, H., Marton, P., Stein, B., & Korenblum, M. (1986). A study of disturbed and non disturbed adolescents: The Toronto adolescent longitudinal study. I. *Canadian Journal of Psychiatry, 31*, 532–535.
Haley, J. (1980). *Leaving home: The therapy of disturbed young people*. Nw York: McGraw Hill.
Haley, J. (1985). *Conversations with Milton H. Erickson, M.D.: Changing individuals* (Vol. I). New York: Triangle Press.
Kernberg, O. (1984). *Borderline conditions and pathological narcissism*. Rowman & Littlefield.
Kowal, C., & Simon J. L. (2008). *Les enfants exposes aux violences conjugales*, Bruxelles: CVSE publications.
Minuchin, S. (1967). *The families of the slums*. New York: Basic Books.
Olivenstein, C. (1981). L'Infanzia del Tossicomane Arch. di Psicolog., Neurolog. e Psichiatria, XII pp. 201–227.
Winnicott, D. W. (1958). *Collected papers: Through pediatrics to psychoanalysis*. London: Tavistock.
Zanarini, M. C. (2009). The longitudinal course of broderline psychopatology: 6-year follow-up pf the phenomenology of borderline personality disorder. *American Journal of Psychiatry, 160* (2), 274–283.

Systemic Couple Therapy as a Tool to Approach Depressive Disorders

Carmen Campo

Introduction

Depressive disorders have almost always been studied and treated from a biological point of view, with psychotropic drugs, or from a psychological perspective, with an approach focused mainly on individual deficits. However, despite the extensive use of new-generation antidepressants, not every patient responds in a positive way, relapses are frequent and above all, many never manage to leave the healthcare system behind.

Many authors have proposed using couple therapy as a therapeutic method in cases involving patients suffering from depressive disorders, considering that the relationship between depression and the relational dynamic of the couple is relevant, (Barbato & D'Avanzo, 2008; Jones & Asen, 2004; Linares & Campo, 2000; Pettit & Joiner, 2006; Whisman & Beach, 2012).

The LDIT research (London Depression Intervention Trial) should be noted because it highlighted the greater efficacy of Systemic and Couple Therapy over that of antidepressant medication and Individual Cognitive Therapy, both at the end of the treatment and after 2 years (Jones & Asen, 2004). Other authors have also noted the usefulness of couple therapy as a factor in preventing future relapses, based on how it helps to improve how the relationship works, (Tilden, Gude, & Hoffart, 2010).

In our case, the experience of working with resistant and protracted depression patients has allowed us to demonstrate the usefulness of bearing in mind the relational context of such patients, both for refining the diagnostic criteria and for expanding the therapeutic resources.

Indeed, given that most patients with this pathology are usually in a relationship, considering the spouse to be the most significant figure from the outset, allowed us

C. Campo (✉)
Escuela de Terapia Familiar del Hospital de Sant Pau, Barcelona, Spain

R. Pereira, J. L. Linares (eds.), *Clinical Interventions in Systemic Couple and Family Therapy*, European Family Therapy Association Series,
https://doi.org/10.1007/978-3-319-78521-9_3

to incorporate a different perspective that on the one hand improved and completed the diagnosis, and on the other, became a new source of resources. The first evidence was the confirmation that, in most cases, there were signs of important difficulties in the relationship that had not been reflected in the data provided by the anamnesis that appeared in the clinical history of the patient. What is relevant is that these difficulties, which had remained masked until this point, were indeed significant insofar as they interfered with or regulated the symptomatic behaviour of the patient.

The second thing that became clear was that obtaining the collaboration of the spouse allowed us to expand our repertoire of possible therapeutic interventions, and at the same time it ensured that certain interventions performed with the patients at an individual level would not be neutralized by their clashing with the interests and expectations of the spouse, unknown to us until that moment.

In addition, focusing on the relationship turned out to be a useful instrument for preventing or resolving dysfunctional mechanisms which often put children at risk, such as triangulation and/or parentification.

The model we are presenting has been drawn up based on the clinical and teaching experience obtained from work carried out in the Psychotherapy Unit of the Psychiatry Service of the Hospital de Sant Pau in Barcelona. It responds to the need to respond to the inherent requirement of a public service to offer a psychotherapeutic approach that combines effectiveness with the lowest possible cost. And at the same time, to develop a useful and flexible methodology that meets the educational needs of students at the Family Therapy School, attached to said Service. It also aims to facilitate the study of recorded and transcribed cases, which when performed under a systematic procedure can be used for both qualitative and quantitative research.

Systemic Couple Therapy

The theoretical model used as a reference has been based on the main concepts that have been developed from the General Systems Theory and the Communication Theory. In this sense, working from a systemic perspective has meant, first and foremost, that we have broadened the focus of our observation and that we now observe both normal and pathological human behaviour in its relational context, and not in isolation (Hoffman, 1987). Considering, therefore, the tapestry of significant relationships in which the individual is immersed. Understanding by context, not something external that exists per se (commonly understood as environment or circumstances), rather something dynamic, in constant co-construction based on reciprocal interactions that are constantly being established.

When it comes to a child or a teenager, the most significant relational context is the family of origin. In the case of adults with a stable partner, even when the family of origin may have a specific weight, that partner is usually the most significant reference.

Having the systemic model as a reference has also made us consider that the behaviour of both spouses is reciprocally regulated in a circular manner, in such a way that either one influences the other. Thereby underlining the fact that every action can also be understood as a reaction in a loop of uninterrupted sequences of actions which are, at the same time, stimulus, response, and reinforcement. It is this circular vision of the facts that is going to facilitate the therapeutic interventions that are required if the spouses are to be aware that they both participate in constructing the relationship, and that each of them is influencing whether the relationship is satisfactory or not.

It has also been useful to differentiate the referential and conative levels that are found in any communication, (Watzlawick, Beavin, & Jackson, 1981). Differentiating between the content of the message and the implicit proposal as to the nature of the relationship has been crucial in understanding, above and beyond the anecdotal content, what it is that each spouse is actually proposing to the other insofar as the definition of the relationship is concerned.

Moreover, the analysis of the disagreements and conflicts observed within the relationship has demonstrated the importance of recognizing self-regulatory mechanisms that are used as brakes when such conflicts escalate. In this sense, it has been useful to differentiate between symmetrical escalations and complementary escalations. Symmetrical escalations can often lead the couple to consider breaking up, but they are also found at the root of the appearance of dysfunctional brake mechanisms, including symptomatic behaviour. In complementary escalations, however, the lack of alternation between the up/down positions and a disproportionate inequality insofar as positions of power are concerned, increase the risk of psycho-pathologies appearing. In both cases, it is useful to assess which dysfunctional braking mechanisms are in place and serve to maintain the pathology.

The fact that we have the systemic model as a theoretical framework has also led us to opt for a global perspective, a holistic epistemology, given that we take into account new scientific paradigms that highlight the interdependence of the phenomena and the complexity of the reality.

Relational Diagnosis

Without rejecting conventional clinical diagnosis (DSM-IV/DSM-V), which as a common platform of understanding remains a good formula for guiding cases, it is however extremely useful to complete and refine it based on an assessment of the symptomatic behaviour of the patient within their relational context. This means that one must understand that symptoms, like any other behaviour assessed in its context, form part of a sequence of interactions that are regulated by redundant interaction patterns. It also should be taken into account that symptomatic behaviour implies a message, even if it is not recognized as such, given that the subject tends to live out that behaviour in an involuntary way.

The fact that social context participates in and endorses such assessment, facilitates the tendency to mask its meaning, both for the patient and for the people around them. Symptoms, from that perspective, are a combination of power and weakness, insofar as they are a powerful inducer of behaviours, but, at the same time, they act as a brake for the possibilities of the subject, and a decrease of their self-esteem, given that their autonomy and their personal valuation are reduced.

When one of the spouses meets the criteria to be diagnosed according to DSM--IV/V, as in the case we are dealing with, it is also advisable to understand what aspects of vulnerability he or she presents. We should also understand what the initial conditions were, both individual and relational, that facilitated the development of the symptoms. At the same time, it is necessary to visualize the current aspects that are favouring their maintenance.

Therapeutic Process

The model of diagnosis and intervention that we use in couple therapy revolves around the two basic questions that can be asked: what is happening to them and how can we help?

Answering the first question involves understanding both the individual characteristics of each spouse, and the type of relationship they have established. That has brought us not only to an analysis of the situation happening at the time of the consultation, but also to take into account the past experiences, both relational and individual, that have led to the current situation.

Performing a diagnosis from the relational perspective (Linares, 2006) involves considering that human behaviour, both normal and pathological, is fundamentally constructed on past and present relational experiences. Relational experiences in the past determine each individual's inherent way of thinking, feeling, and acting, and these, at the same time, are regulated and limited by significant interactions experienced in the present. It is through this game between past and present, present and past, that human behaviour is configured.

From that perspective, knowing the most relevant past experiences of each spouse makes it possible to understand and legitimize each one's needs, the resources available to them, and the possible vulnerabilities they may have developed.

At the same time, working with both spouses allows the therapist to observe in real time how the interactions established between them regulate and facilitate how they both behave.

Understanding and categorizing the type of difficulties they present seems to us to be vital if we are to perform a good relational diagnosis.

Typology of Conflicts

Each couple makes up a world of great complexity, so it is not feasible to establish a typology of couples. However, on the contrary, it is useful to categorize the different conflicts that can be observed in couples that are going through difficulties.

Some problems can be defined explicitly by the couple, others may only be observed indirectly, through remarks or actions that highlight a number of disagreements. Those implicit conflicts are of great relevance, as they favour standby or stalemate situations in the relationship and generate helplessness and distress.

One of the differentiating characteristics of couples in which one of the spouses presents symptoms—especially when it comes to depressive pathology—is that the marital conflict they are going through remains masked for a long time, and very rarely does either one of them explicitly suggest a possible separation as an alternative to the distress. This is unlike what we usually find in requests for couple therapy without a concomitant pathology, in which the therapy is often initiated when the couple is about to break up. It is precisely the fact that there is a pathology that inhibits any movement that could involve changes and prioritizes taking care of the spouse as a patient, at opposed to any requirement that might be demanded of him or her as a partner.

The typology we use derives from the analysis and systematization of the distinct types of conflict that we have observed, grouped according to the different levels of difficulty they entail. This distinction seems basic because it allows us to make a prediction as to the difficulty of the case and to assess the viability of the couple, also taking into account the positive experience they might have been able to establish, something we refer to as their relational wealth.

Conflicts have been classified from lesser to greater difficulty, in three categories: (a) Those which derive from simple imbalances in the way they organize their coexistence, (b) Those which refer to difficulties in communication, and how each spouse resolves a conflict; and (c) Those that express different expectations as to the most basic aspects of the relationship, those that have to do with being a couple actually means for each partner. This last conflict category is the one that has turned out to be the most relevant in the cases we have studied with involving couples with a concomitant pathology.

In this last element, three great areas require sufficient consensus if the relationship they experience is to be deemed satisfactory: The type of amorous bond, what does it mean for each spouse to love and to be loved. The type of internal hierarchy, how does each member expect to organize how power is managed within the couple. And the basic projects, what do they expect to do together or individually, albeit with the acquiescence of the other member, both in the present and in the future.

Those expectations imply legitimate individual needs, and often they are not easily negotiable as they respond to aspects at the very heart of the individual's identity. That is why when the position of the spouses is highly polarized, a lack of consensus can lead to incompatibility of the relationship, and therefore the non-viability of the bond.

Disagreements as to what defines the relationship can arise from the outset or even after a long time of well-being and mutual accommodation. In the first case, such turbulences and destructive confrontations, not to mention the appearance of symptoms, often occur in an early stage of the relationship and they normally respond to a wrong choice, either due to haste brought on by diverse urgencies, or by having expectations of being able to change the other member. In the second case, they derive from the subsequent onset of different types of variables that have in common the fact that they have led to unilateral changes in one of the spouses, changes vis-à-vis the definition of the relationship that have not been agreed with the other spouse (Campo, 2010).

In the cases with depressive symptomatology that we have studied (Linares & Campo, 2000), differences usually prevail as to the internal hierarchy and the type of amorous bond proposed by each member of the couple although in some cases there are differences regarding the projects that, by definition, imply manifest incompatibility, such as deciding whether or not to assume parenthood, when that relates to identity aspects.

The detailed study of said cases highlighted differentiating relational characteristics in patients diagnosed with Dysthymia and Major Depressive Disorder (MDD) regarding the internal hierarchy, with a pattern of symmetry prevailing in dysthymic patients and a greater tendency to complementarity in those suffering major depression. Among the latter, the choice of partner tended to be influenced by a commitment to protection and priority emotional bonding on the part of the spouse occupying the up position in the relationship, as a formula by which to compensate basic emotional needs that were not covered by their family of origin, whereas in dysthymic patients, the expectation was to find an equal partner with whom to share life. In the majority of dysthymic cases, before symptoms emerged, symmetrical-type escalations had led to the possibility of separation while external situations (e.g. losing a job) had meant a loss of status and the failure of the equal spouse's expectations regarding power and of their affective closeness by which to overcome the loss. In the cases of major depression, what was observed was the failure of the protection promised by the up spouse, based on a number of unfavourable circumstances (greater dedication and responsibility at work, attention and care of his or her parents, etc.).

After the onset of the pathology, relevant changes happened in the patterns of marital relationships, including a notable stiffening of complementarity in MDD cases, as well as the establishment of an affectivity primarily characterized by "care eliciting" attitudes, based on their condition as patients. In the case of dysthymic patients, what was most significant was the role of the symptoms in slowing down symmetrical escalations, the change-inducing role in the behaviour of the spouse as a dysfunctional formula for rebalancing power, and the regulation of the demonstrations of attention and affection that they gave rise to. In both cases, when the disorder becomes chronic, the evolution is towards a resistant depression in which feelings of hopelessness and helplessness prevail, often translating into autolysis attempts of increasing severity.

Therapeutic Alliance

To answer the second question, how can they be helped, means that we must first of all take into consideration the contribution of second-order cybernetics, which alerts us to the fact that it is impossible to evaluate without intervening. And it implies taking into account from the very beginning, the importance of the type of relationship that is being established between the therapist and the spouses, and how being able to implement the necessary therapeutic interventions will depend on that relationship.

In that sense, the construction of a solid therapeutic alliance can be considered as the first necessary intervention to achieve therapeutic objectives.

The construction of the therapeutic alliance has been widely studied due to its relevance, and although much research has been focused on highlighting its importance as a predictor of change and success in individual therapy, (Horvath, Del Re, Fluckiger, & Symonds, 2011), various authors have also noted its importance in the results in family and couple therapy (Friedlander, Escudero, Heatherington, & Diamond, 2011; Horvath & Symonds, 1991; Montesano, 2015; Sprenkle & Blow, 2004). Highlighting how in couple therapy it is essential to maintain a balance in the alliances with each of the spouses to avoid potential drop-outs, (Anderson & Johnson, 2010; Mamodhoussen, Wright, Tremblay, & Poitras Wright, 2005). Others such as (Bergman, 1995; Mateu, Vilaregut, Campo, Artigas, & Escudero, 2014; Montesano & Izu, 2016), highlight the greater difficulty in the establishment of the therapeutic alliance when one of the spouses presents a long-term pathology, resistant to other treatments previously carried out, as well as an unresolved marital conflict, maintained over time.

Necessarily, when working with a couple, the construction of the therapeutic relationship implies greater complexity because it involves handling different relational levels, due to the multifocal nature of the bond. It is necessary to take into account not only the alliance of the therapist with each of the spouses, but also the alliance between the two spouses. In our experience, the latter, referred to as an intra-system alliance by scholars of the subject (Friedlander, Escudero, & Heatherington, 2009) is the most difficult to achieve when working with resistant depressive pathologies. In these cases, the alliance between both members vis-à-vis the therapy, i.e. the degree to which the couple shares its purpose, is usually a challenge for the therapist. It must not be forgotten that, in most cases, we are dealing with a type of relationship between the spouses that is dominated by hopelessness on the part of the patient, and in which, due to chronicity, negative interactions have been maintained over the years. It is necessary therefore to have enough time to establish the essential emotional bonds between the patient and the therapist, without this endangering the relationship with the spouse; at the same time, encouraging a collaborative alliance between the spouses, oriented towards their offering each other a new opportunity to establish a relationship that is satisfactory enough for them both.

Procedure

Although based on the idea that the differentiation between diagnosis and intervention relates only to methodological criteria, the procedure uses as this clear differentiation as a therapeutic strategy in two phases: an initial phase of consultation and assessment that is rounded off with feedback and a possible contract, and a second phase, subsequent to that contract, which is formulated as the actual therapy.

The first phase is presented to the couple as a necessary way to get to know them, to understand what the problem is, and to assess whether it is feasible to help them. It is designed to allow the necessary time for the construction of the therapeutic alliance with each of the spouses, and of the one between the spouses themselves—an essential alliance to promote a proactive and collaborative attitude. It also aims to reformulate and build a proper demand, certainly something very infrequent when working in this type of case. Normally, it is not the patient or the spouse who presents the request, rather the clinician who derives the case, or the therapist him or herself, if they have decided to reformulate a request for individual treatment into couple therapy, with increased efficacy in mind. In this case, it is essential that the other spouse should feel they are not alien to the difficulties that the patient presents, and that their collaboration can benefit them both (Campo, 2014).

The first phase of consultation and assessment consists of three semi-structured sessions that are conducted jointly with both spouses, plus an (optional) individual session with each of them and a feedback and explicit contract session, again with both spouses present.

These are semi-structured sessions with a common thread, but with a fluent and spontaneous conversation format to take advantage of all input that may naturally arise. The aim is that, through their questions and comments, the therapist can begin to facilitate a new perspective of both the individual and the relational reality, perhaps one that had not even been considered before then by either the patient or the spouse (Schlippe & Schweitzer, 2003), so that the couple begins to appreciate that it is possible to find new alternatives to the situation of hopelessness and stalemate they often find themselves in.

Personal data is collected, both from an individual and a relational point of view, with a perspective that is both synchronic and diachronic. In this sense, it is important to know the present, but also the past that has conditioned it. It is important to visualize how the different variables, both individual and relational, intertwine from a perspective of process.

It is a good idea to adapt the management of these first three pre-established interviews to the type of depressive pathology that the patient presents, and in this sense, it is helpful to take into account the differential characteristics between Dysthymia and Major Depression referred to above (Linares & Campo, 2000).

In the case of Dysthymias, and generally speaking, whenever a symmetrical relationship pattern prevails, asking the spouse to attend has to be done in a careful way, in order to neutralize as soon as possible the defensive attitude they tend to have. It is usually helpful to define them as collaborators of the therapist from the very beginning. In the first session, it is useful to collect information as to their concerns above and beyond the symptoms, but without sidestepping them. In this sense, these symptoms should be considered an objective of the therapy, not something beyond the remit of the therapist. It is also necessary not to initially force the association of symptoms with problem areas; questions on such issues should be raised only as a result of an interest of understanding the situation in a more complete way. Finally, the gathering of each partner's individual data (Age, Origin, Education, Work Environment and Health) becomes, at the end of the session, a privileged space of care and accommodation for each member of the couple. It is not only a question of gathering specific data, rather and above all the type of relational experiences that each area has meant for each partner.

In MDD cases, and in those in which a complementary relationship pattern prevails, the biggest initial difficulty in these early contacts is not in obtaining the collaboration of the spouse, who is probably used to maintaining a protective position which makes their presence easier at first, but rather in obtaining an attitude of proactive collaboration from the patient. They have to feel that it is not enough to be a disciplined patient when it comes to taking their medication; they have to give themselves another chance to begin to dissolve the feelings of hopelessness that grip them. To achieve this, accommodation needs to be extremely careful and in that sense, they need to feel listened to, respected and a subject, not an object, in whom the therapist is genuinely interested.

The second session explores the relationship of each of the spouses with their family of origin although it is much more than a mere genogram. It is mainly a matter of understanding what kind of relational experiences they have had with regard to affective bonding and rule learning. Experiences which are at the heart of the individual's style of response at a cognitive, emotional, and pragmatic level, essentially the traits that have conformed their personality. This is a session that usually provides information about the negative experiences that have ended up favouring the possibility of the patient presenting greater vulnerability, as well as the positive experiences that have endowed them with resources and resilience. During this second session, it is also useful to gather information as to the nature of the marital relationship of their parents and, therefore, the model of married life they have incorporated. Also, when said conjugal relationship was disharmonic, it is worthwhile knowing whether they have gone through the dysfunctional experience for a child of having been triangulated or, on the contrary, parentified. It is also a good moment to understand the nature of the past and present relationship each member of the couple has had with their partner's family, as this can provide information as to the expectations and possible conflicts that they have developed in that area.

Not only does all this exchange of information in the first two sessions make it possible to obtain greater mutual knowledge, it also, with the help of the therapist, facilitates the development of a mutual empathy with regard to the most significant experiences of the other spouse, which in turn favours a collaborative alliance between the two.

The purpose of the third session is to learn from a process perspective the history of the couple from its beginnings to the present situation. To understand up to what point the relationship progressed in a functional way and was considered satisfactory by both spouses. It is about calibrating for forecasting purposes, the total time of well-being they were able to enjoy, the "relational wealth" they have. It has an added advantage, and that is that asking how they met and how the relationship began tends to promote positive memories and a more relaxed attitude between the spouses (Bornstein & Bornstein, 1988).

It is a very beneficial session because it makes it possible to articulate the data collected individually up to that point from a relational point of view, making it easier to visualize the connections between the different variables and to better understand how they have come to the current situation.

It is also essential to gather information in this session as to the set of expectations and promises they had as far as their desired relationship is concerned (Sager, 1980), about that non-written individual contract that has sustained the relationship, as well as the different disagreements that might have arisen as time passed. Assessing in that case whether it is just a case of a number of imbalances or if their positions are so polarized as to imply incompatibility.

When either partner presents a pathology, as in the case that concerns us, it is also necessary to study at a chronological level the onset of the symptoms, the first consultations, relapses, suicide attempts, etc. In that sense, data gathered about the symptoms is especially significant insofar as it allows one to visualize the connections between the different variables that have facilitated its development and, above all, its maintenance.

After these three protocol interviews, it tends to be useful to perform individual sessions with each of the spouses although these are not essential. Their main purpose will be to strengthen the construction of the alliance with each of them, but it can also be useful for facilitating a more accurate diagnosis, for example, when there is a suspicion of infidelity, or resentment feelings have been detected, which could entail greater difficulty and the need for specific interventions to neutralize them.

After those first sessions, a feedback and contract session is held, which entails an intervention in itself. It is about being able to transmit the now informed opinion of the therapist, taking advantage of all the idiosyncratic information that both spouses have offered him or her. It is about giving a new meaning to both the individual experiences of each partner and to those that derive from their experience as a couple.

The aim is for them to be able to visualize from a global perspective how the different individual and relational variables intertwine because it is that interconnection that has given rise to the distress and, once it had emerged, to the symptoms that remained in place, once they had appeared on the scene. At the same time, it is necessary to formulate what alternatives might make them feel better.

In this feedback session, it is essential to highlight and amplify the individual resources that are going to enable the therapeutic process and ultimately, the therapeutic contract. To put it in a more colloquial way, the therapist's motives for deciding to go ahead and take responsibility for the case. At the same time, it is also necessary to convey that in order to be able to help them, the therapist is going to need a proactive collaboration throughout the therapeutic process.

On many occasions, especially when working with resistant depression patients, it is usually a useful strategy to provide the feedback in the form of a divided paradox that specifies the dilemma and the pros and cons the therapist has to weigh up when it comes to starting a psychotherapeutic work. To that end, the therapist can use the words of his or her team members, who are not in the session and no matter whether they exist or not, to express all the elements that might hinder any initiative towards a positive change, which, in such cases, are directly linked to feelings of hopelessness and resentment. On the contrary, transmitting with sufficient empathy (together with the co-therapist if there is one), why he or she believes it is worth helping them. It is a matter of expressing a message of hope, based on data obtained from reality, a message that says it is possible to search for new formulas, new alternatives, and ultimately, that they can give each other a new chance. On the other hand, the comments of the team, acting as representatives of the homeostasis, are going to emphasize the possibility that they might prefer to continue with the same established routines, and with the same feelings of bitterness and resentment they have cultivated until now. Using a paradoxical intervention of this type also has the advantage of allowing the therapist to explicitly express in a constructive way the contradictory feelings these patients often generate in the therapist, feelings that he or she can turn into something positive on the basis of the increased empathy and the improved alliance with the therapist that it usually entails.

This feedback normally makes it easier to formulate a contract that specifies the commitment of the therapist and the spouses to work together to achieve the agreed therapeutic objectives.

The second part of the process, now formally considered as therapy, begins after the contract has been signed. It is characterized by joint work with the spouses aimed at consolidating a context of goodwill in which positive interactions prevail, thereby favouring a more satisfactory relationship, more functional communication and the learning of new formulas for resolving conflicts.

During this phase, and especially when it has been possible to understand what contributions each of the spouses can make to generate well-being in the other, some individual sessions can prove useful to enhance and consolidate the new attitudes they will both have, attitudes that are going to facilitate a more functional and satisfactory interaction pattern.

During this second phase, when the depressive symptomatology has become resistant and a rigid complementary interaction pattern prevails, it is also worth arranging a few sessions with the patient on his or her own, duly agreed to by both spouses. The idea is to have an individual space, integrated within the therapeutic process and, if possible, led by the same therapist, to specifically develop strategies aimed at making it easier for the patient to both express their feelings and needs and to grow their self-esteem. In this regard, training in how to recognize needs and desires is useful, as these are so often blocked by an upbringing influenced by learning to use avoidance as a mechanism for resolving conflicts. As is learning new more assertive attitudes that allow flexibility in the up/down positions that characterize said pattern. It is not a matter of questioning the pattern, rather of making it more flexible, so it does not make it easier for the symptoms to be maintained.

Problems that might have happened in relation to the families of origin or their children will frequently need to be resolved in this second phase as well. In both cases, the aim will be to strengthen a team position between them that, without sidestepping the problems, will allow them to work together to resolve them.

In the case of the families of origin, it is interesting to note that the new perspective they both have as to each other's relational experiences promotes greater complicity in the resolution of difficulties. This new position can be very relevant, especially in the case of patients diagnosed with Major Depressive Disorder, because very often the previous alliance of the spouse with the patient's family of origin has conditioned the maintenance of symptoms, due to the increase of the latter's excessively down position.

In the case of the children, a new position of greater union and responsibility with regard to parenting is the best formula to keep children away from the marital dynamic, making it easier to thereby find a resolution of the dysfunctional mechanisms that often occur in these cases. Mechanisms associated with both triangulation experiences when there was symmetry between the spouses, and with parentification when the marital dynamic was led by a complementarity that was so rigid it prevented the patient from acting as a parent.

The total process requires around 20 sessions. These are normally held every fortnight although they can be progressively spread out more when the therapeutic objectives begin to be achieved but still need to be consolidated. It is also useful, responding not only to research criteria, to perform follow-up visits, in our case after 3, 6, 12 months, and 2 years, in which we were able to strengthen and consolidate the new relationship patterns that were developed, as well as to support the adequate handling of potential new difficulties, frequently associated in our experience to life cycles. An example of this are the changes that may occur in the family of origin in relation to an illness or death of the parents, and the consequent and necessary negotiation with the siblings, etc.

Given the chronicity of the cases, it is appropriate to close the therapeutic process when the therapeutic objectives have been reached, but always leaving the door open to any sporadic consultation that may prevent a possible relapse.

The analysis of relapses in the cases studied, which had been treated with the couple therapy model we have presented, highlighted that they usually responded to two different situations. When they occurred during the first phase of the therapeutic process, they were associated with the difficulty of addressing quickly enough the expectations of change that were generated in the patients when a good alliance was achieved, and the hopelessness they had felt until then was becoming neutralized. On the contrary, when the relapse happened during the second phase of the therapeutic process, it was usually associated with the exacerbation of certain latent conflicts, normally involving the family of origin, based on changes in the life cycle, or other areas such as sick leave from work, or handling all the paperwork to obtain a possible disability allowance prior to beginning the therapy.

Being aware of these two risks was useful when it came to exercising extreme caution as far as those variables were concerned and to intensifying the strategies needed to neutralize them.

The most useful therapeutic response for resolving and addressing relapses was to define them as valuable alarm signals, while at the same time giving them meaning by facilitating their connection with the difficulties the couple were going through, which could be revealed through a careful analysis of the situation.

References

Anderson, S., & Johnson, L. (2010). A Dyadic analysis of the between- and within-system alliances on distress. *Family Process, 49*, 220–235.

Barbato, A., & D'Avanzo, B. (2008). Efficacy of couple therapy as treatment for depression: A meta-analysis. *Psychiatric Quarterly, 79*, 121–132.

Bergman, J. (1995). *Pescando barracudas: pragmática de la terapia sistémica breve*. Barcelona: Paidós.

Bornstein, P. H., & Bornstein, M. T. (1988). *Terapia de pareja. Un enfoque conductual-sistémico.* Madrid: Pirámide.

Campo, C. (2010). Transformaciones del poder en las parejas: Cambios unilaterales en torno a la jerarquía interna. *Mosaico, 44*, 55–59.

Campo, C. (2014). La terapia de pareja en la práctica clínica: un modelo de diagnóstico e intervención. In R. Medina, E. Laso, & E. Hernández (Eds.), *Pensamiento Sistémico: Nuevas perspectivas y contextos de intervención* (pp. 251–278). México: Litteris Psicología.

Friedlander, M., Escudero, V., & Heatherington, L. (2009). *La alianza terapéutica en la terapia familiar y de pareja*. Barcelona: Paidos.

Friedlander, M. L., Escudero, V., Heatherington, L., & Diamond, D. (2011). Alliance in couple and family therapy. *Psychotherapy, 48*, 25–53.

Hoffman, L. (1987). *Fundamentos de la terapia familiar. Un marco conceptual para el cambio de sistemas*. México: Fondo de Cultura Económica.

Horvath, A., Del Re, A., Fluckiger, C., & Symonds, D. (2011). Alliance in individual psychotherapy. *Psychotherapy, 48*, 9–16.

Horvath, A., & Symonds, B. (1991). Relation between the working alliance and outcome in psychotherapy: A meta-analysis. *Journal of Counseling Psychology, 38*, 139–149.

Jones, E., & Asen, E. (2004). *Terapia sistémica de pareja y depresión*. Bilbao: Desclée de Brouwer.

Linares, J. L. (2006). Una visión relacional de los trastornos de personalidad. In S. A. Roizblatt (Ed.), *Terapia Familiar y de Pareja*. Santiago de Chile: Mediterráneo.

Linares, J. L., & Campo, C. (2000). *Tras la honorable fachada*. Barcelona: Paidós.

Mamodhoussen, S., Wright, J., Tremblay, N., & Poitras Wright, H. (2005). Impact of marital and psychological distress on therapeutic alliance in couples undergoing couple therapy. *Journal of Marital and Family Therapy, 31*, 159–169.

Mateu, C., Vilaregut, A., Campo, C., Artigas, L., & Escudero, V. (2014). Construcción de la alianza terapéutica en la terapia de pareja: estudio de un caso con dificultades de manejo terapéutico. *Anuario de Psicología, 44*(1), 95–115.

Montesano, A. (2015). Claves fundamentales en terapia de pareja: Una guía de navegación para la práctica. *Revista de Psicoterapia, 26*(102), 161–174.

Montesano, A., & Izu, S. (2016). Analysis of the therapeutic process in a case of couple therapy for depression: How to deal with a problematic within-system. *Studies in Psychology, 3*(2–3), 393–417.

Pettit, J. W., & Joiner, T. E. (2006). *Chronic depression. Interpersonal sources, therapeutic solutions*. Washington DC: American Psychological Association.
Sager, C. J. (1980). *Contrato matrimonial y terapia de pareja*. Buenos Aires: Amorrortu.
Schlippe, A., & Schweitzer, J. (2003). *Manual de terapia y asesoría sistémicas*. Barcelona: Herder.
Sprenkle, D. H., & Blow, A. J. (2004). Common factors and out sacred models. *Journal of Marital and Family Therapy, 30*, 113–129.
Tilden, T., Gude, T., & Hoffart, A. (2010). The course of dyadic adjustment and depressive symptoms during and after couples therapy: A prospective follow-up study of inpatient treatment. *Journal of Marital and Family Therapy, 36*(1), 43–58.
Watzlawick, P., Beavin, J., & Jackson, D. (1981). *Teoria de la comunicación humana. Interacciones, patologías y paradojas*. Barcelona: Herder.
Whisman, M. A., & Beach, S. R. (2012). Couple therapy for depression. *Journal of Clinical Psychology, 68*(5), 526–535.

The Hungry Brain: A Revision of the Concept of Anorexia Nervosa and a New Direction for Systemic Therapy

Jorge De Vega and José Soriano

Background

The authors of this chapter have been working for over 20 years with serious cases of Anorexia Nervosa in teenagers and adults in two clinical units, one specifically relating to eating disorders in Barcelona (José Soriano) and the other for acute psychiatric cases in Las Palmas de Gran Canaria (Jorge de Vega). Over that time, they have attended around 900 patients so under-nurtured that their lives were in danger. The doctors work both with the patients and their families when the person is in hospital and continue their work once the patients are discharged for several months longer and even, on occasions, for years. The focus of their therapy is designed to take advantage of the influence of purely organic factors on the triggering and persistence of the problem to generate a therapeutic alliance with the patient that helps them to tackle the problem.

Stories of Anorexia

María is 22 and has been overweight since she was 15. She remembers having been the target of ridicule and insults at school and her parents urging her to "look after her figure" and to diet. This she did for years without any results until one day, the boy that she was mad about and who she had never dared to even approach, began to go out with one of her friends. That was when María decided once and for all to

J. De Vega (✉)
Rayuela Family Therapy School, Las Palmas de Gran Canaria, Spain
e-mail: vegarayu@cop.es

J. Soriano
Universidad Autónoma de Barcelona, Barcelona, Spain

R. Pereira, J. L. Linares (eds.), *Clinical Interventions in Systemic Couple and Family Therapy*, European Family Therapy Association Series,
https://doi.org/10.1007/978-3-319-78521-9_4

lose weight but she wanted results immediately so she moved on to a diet of an "apple a day". The weight loss was dramatic indeed and was celebrated by her family, friends and above all, by María. However, soon the weight loss became alarming and her parents began to tell her that things had gone too far. Far from paying attention to them, their comments irritated her since she considered she still had not lost enough weight. Soon, her parents were distraught as María faded into skin and bones. They took her to the doctor where her body mass index (BMI) was calculated at 17 when it had stood previously at 30-. The doctor tried to calm the family and took blood samples that proved to be completely normal. He recommended that María put on a few kilos. María quite naturally did not agree with this recommendation. She maintained that her blood samples proved that she was "perfectly OK" and complained that she was still not satisfied with her physical aspect, that she needed to lose "a little more weight".

The story of Ana is quite different in nature. Ana was always thin (BMI 19) as were all her family. She had never been concerned with her weight nor had to worry about what she did or did not eat. She was an excellent student and got great grades for University. Her parents decided to reward her by giving her a summer course in England. She hated the food they gave her in the residence where she was boarding. Nevertheless, she had a great time but came home four kilos lighter. This did not concern either Ana or her parents at first but weeks went by and not only did Ana not make up the lost weight but she continued to lose more. After a few months, her state was critical and everybody recommended that she try to put on weight. However, much to everyone's surprise, Ana said she needed to lose "a little more", that she was dissatisfied with her looks.

Inés is 43 and works as a clinical auxiliary worker. She is married and has two daughters. She always weighed less than the average but was within normal parameters (BMI 22). However, she began to suffer severe pain in the knees that the doctor diagnosed as rheumatism. When she checked it out on the Internet, she saw that patients who had the same as her had managed to relieve their pain by losing weight. Her surfing on the web produced an obsession with "healthy eating" and she followed vegetarian and vegan diets of all kinds, began to lose faith in gluten, went macrobiotic and so on. It did not take long for Inés to get to the same stage as Ana and María and she was taken into hospital with them into the eating disorder unit with a BMI of 13 and the same diagnosis as her hospital companions Ana and María, of Anorexia Nervosa.

Clinical Aspects

Anorexia is a highly disconcerting disorder where a person, usually young, begins to reduce weight for many different reasons and instead of stopping at a more or less reasonable or aesthetically desirable weight decides to continue ending up literally as little more than skin and bones. They put their lives at risk or die.

Although there is no common family trait or life story, nor experience nor reason for their losing weight, they end up sharing the same fate. When the BMI falls below 17, all initial differences fade and independent of status, family, intelligence, culture or level of studies, they fall into the exact same mould.

So, is there any common characteristic? First of all, the fact that they are female as occurs in 90% of the cases. In our opinion, any such explanation as exists for this fact has not been sufficiently investigated as of yet. Almost all of the cases reveal some kind of obsessive personality—they may be perfectionists, highly self-demanding and are considered by most to be intelligent, with excellent academic performance. These characteristics that by no means are given in all of the cases are a kind of natural "lifestyle requisite" for any serious disorder to fully bloom. By this we mean that legions of people, both men and women, embark upon diets which most abandon after a short period, some, the most motivated among them, because they have reached their goals. The most consistent of these manage to keep their weight down and only the truly obsessed members of this group go beyond what is a reasonable weight loss, most of them initially to avoid "sliding back up the scale". Intelligence is important here in that many intelligent people use their skills to avoid being recognized for their considerable weight loss and to escape the controls of their social environment to continue to lose weight. From the perspective of academic performance, people who are highly intelligent and who are self-demanding usually shine in their studies. However, as we have seen from our cases, once the disorder has taken control, academic performance is adversely affected and it is not unusual for the patients to abandon their studies.

That is where we find the first coincidence of cause and effect. One of the main characteristics of malnutrition is that it accentuates the obsessive features of a personality in particular with respect to food and all other aspects of eating (Brozek, 1953; Franklin, Schiele, Brožek, & Keys, 1948; Keys, Brozek, Henschel, Mickelsen, & Taylor, 1950; Schiele & Brozek, 1948). The DSM-5 highlights this aspect when it says: "Our observation of behaviours associated with other forms of hunger suggest that obsessions and compulsions relating to food can become exacerbated by malnutrition" (2014, p. 341).

The whole range of symptoms described in the literature for Anorexia Nervosa (referred to from here on as NA) is vast and largely inconsistent. The DSM-5 offers three criteria for diagnosis of NA:

(a) "Restriction of energy intake with respect to physical needs that leads to a body weight significantly inferior to what is healthy for the age, gender and course of development of the individual affected
(b) Extreme fear of gaining weight and persistent behaviour interfering with any weight gain even when the individual is extremely low in weight
(c) Alteration of the way the individual conceives of his/her own weight and constitution, with an imbalanced influence of the weight and body image in the person's self-evaluation and an obstinate lack of recognition of the serious nature and effect of the low body weight on health" (DSM 5 vol. 1, 2014, pp. 338–339)

ICD 10 highlights with respect to the disease that it is an "endocrinal disorder affecting the hypothalamus, pituitary glands and gonads", something not mentioned by the DSM-5 (1992, p. 220) and also that it produces "distortion of the body image and excessive obsession and panic of fatness or flabbiness, leading the patient to self-impose a restrictive diet that keeps them well below their necessary BMI".

Criterion C of the DSM-5, as it is dated, seems to "downplay" the importance of this "distortion of the body image". Both manuals underline excessive physical exercise as a common feature of patients trying to lose weight yet neither of the classifications mention a central symptom to classic descriptions of the syndrome, that is hyperactivity (Gull, 1874) in the sense of perceived need to be permanently active without any clear end in sight (i.e. not as a conscious and voluntary manoeuvre to lose weight).

Both the ICD and the DSM-5 allude to the fact that anorexic patients may present the symptoms of self-provoked vomiting and/or abuse of laxatives and diuretics. The DSM-5 divides the patients between restrictive intake and gorgers/purgers, a distinction not made in ICD 10. The distinction in DSM-5 is temporary however, considering the restrictive intake category to be permanent and gorgers/purgers to disappear if and when "there is no recurrent gorging/purging of the individual over a period of three months" (2014, p. 339).

Both manuals consider that any one anorexic person may alternate between phases of bulimia and restrictive intake over time and that it is extremely uncommon to find "pure" cases of one or the other. Most bulimic patients have periods of being purely restrictive and some restrictive patients make recourse to vomiting to avoid putting on weight, especially if they are taken into hospital and submitted to processes of forced feeding. It is clear, however that the patients who are mainly restrictive are obsessively fixed in their habits, with a trend toward excessive self-control, perfectionism and extremely self-demanding whereas gorgers/purgers tend to be more impulsive and emotionally unstable. These aspects should be borne in mind when planning the psycho-therapeutical treatment and care.

Outside the symptoms described in the manuals, we have found in our practice that patients may present the following:

- Irritability with self and others and aggressive with nearest and dearest. This irritability is most noticeable when sitting down to eat. Often the individual will try to avoid eating with the rest of the family and/or in the places established as common areas of the house
- Significant deterioration of relationships with friends and relatives and a tendency toward isolation
- Scarce or no interest in establishing romantic relationships
- Obsessive behaviour of all types, not only with food but also with order, cleanliness and silence in the home among others
- Organic symptoms such as loss of period and hypothermia
- Hyperactivity, as mentioned previously, understood as excessive activity to no specific end

- Tendency to self-inflicted pain and damage: scratches and/or cuts on the thighs, abdomen and breasts (this symptom is almost exclusive to patients who are mainly gorgers/purgers)
- Serious cognitive alterations related to feeding and food with unreal and inconsistent distinctions made between good/bad food or, to be more precise, between “dangerous” and “less dangerous” foodstuffs
- Absurd ideas with respect to getting fat and thin

From all this, we can see that the pivot of the serious nature of the disorder is “the panic associated with gaining weight or getting fat”. This panic explains all the other symptoms and beliefs. It is panic that makes patients continue to lose weight when they are already below normal levels of nutrition.

“Teresa, who is 1.60 tall and weighs 23 kilos (a BMI of 9) and on the verge of death due to starvation tells us that she fears if she “relaxes” and eats, her weight will go up to 80 kilos in a week. Teresa is perfectly aware that she is very thin and a far cry from reaching 80 kilos but for her an increase of 100 g in weight tomorrow means the start of a giddy and inevitable ascent toward 80 kilos. What is worse still is that when her weight remains constant over several days at 23 kilos, she feels panic that she may step on the scales and find that she has gone up 100 g unwittingly. She no longer wants to reduce further weight but the only thing that can reassure her and dispel her panic is the fact that she gets onto the scales and finds that she weighs “a little less: 22.900”.

So anorexic patients once they are in a state of malnutrition “are not trying to be thinner but to avoid getting fatter”. This concept is central to the therapy. Moreover, the DSM-5 indicates that *“The intense fear of getting fat is not relieved by weight loss but rather intensified”* (2014, p. 340) (underlining is our own). This is something that defies all logic, a total paradox, it seems, but is what we find time and time again in our clinical practice.

This panic reaches such an extent that patients will manifest openly that they are more afraid of going up in weight than of dying. One of the risks entailed therefore in this disorder is that of suicide attempts, a risk that is significantly increased after situations of forced feeding.

Uncollaborative Patients

One of the main obstacles in the treatment of anorexic patients is the lack of collaboration on the part of the person being treated to acknowledge his/her problem and accept treatment. They oscillate between being falsely charming at times, openly challenging at others and untrusting always. Many professionals consider that they are lacking in self-awareness and responsibility, or knowledge or maturity. This is exacerbated when they hear comments such as “I can’t drink water or I’ll put on weight” or “If I eat everything today, tomorrow I’ll weigh four kilos more”. Eventually, they may consider them as totally superficial, given their excessive obsession with body shape. So many professionals write them off stereotypically as "stupid kids who want to be models" and treat them as such. They do not make the slightest attempt to search for the collaboration of the patient, something summed up in the words of one professional when he assured the family: "I save lives, I don't change mindsets".

It is our belief that our patients do not collaborate for the same reason that they have come to the serious state of malnutrition they find themselves in: due to panic of putting on weight. When they are admitted to hospital, they see our attempts to force-feed them not as a way of saving their lives but rather of taking it away from them.

By understanding the panic, we can see how other symptoms respond to the same pattern, such as the irritability with the family when they try to make them eat properly and the progressive social isolation. A large part of our community relations are organized around food. Someone who is afraid of eating stops going to family reunions, celebrations or any congregation where food is involved or could be such as meetings with friends since at some time there may be an invitation to eat. Being with people stresses these patients out significantly because friends usually make references to the other's physical appearance, under normal circumstances, these can be tolerated or may cause upsetting but anorexics receive them, whatever they may be, either good or bad, with anguish. For the same reason, they find it significantly stressful to have relations with the other people and most patients avoid any type of intimate contact, for fear of references to their physical status. It is extremely disagreeable for someone who rejects their body or feels permanently insecure with respect to it to hear comments from another person on their physique. When we take this into account, we should never use one of the most trotted out arguments to our patients that "you're far too thin and men prefer curves".

Excessive physical exercise, indulged in out of panic of getting fat, takes on a whole new significance. Even the distortion of the body image as proposed by Hilde Bruch (1957) and which has been embraced by a large part of the professionals in the area can be seen as the only "logical" way of justifying further attempts to continue losing weight when below minimum levels of nutrition. There are authors that consider that this distorted vision is the result and not the cause of the diet and excessive exercise (Zanker, 2009), but whichever way, once it is established in the head of the patient, it represents an extremely powerful force of motivation and also of future relapse (Halmi et al., 2002).

The most worrying aspect of this symptom is that some professionals consider it to be a by-product of the psychotic disorder and treat it with neuroleptics.

Passing Symptoms

We said before that, paradoxically, the fear of putting on weight increases as the patient becomes more and more undernourished and likewise, most of the symptoms described disappear when the patient begins to eat again normally. However, this is true paradoxical as it seems, explaining why most of the hospital programmes focus on forced feeding. After all, most of the central symptoms of NA are, in reality, symptoms of malnutrition (Bergh & Södersten, 1998; Epling, Pierce, & Stefan, 1983; Zandian, Ioakimidis, Bergh, & Södersten, 2007) and so we act on this front to avoid errors caused by applying psycho-therapeutical procedures when what is needed is to bring the person up to their normal weight and vice versa.

One of the earliest references on this respect is to be found in the pages of the "Proceedings of the Royal Society of Medicine" in a paper presented by Ryle on the 24th January 1939. Arthur Hurst commented in reply to the intervention of Ryle's that "The patient is made to realize that the physician fully understands her difficulties. She is told that in spite of her nausea, loathing of food and discomfort on eating she must eat, as it is only by eating that she can re-educate her appetite. It was lost by fasting; it will be restored by eating. The process will be uncomfortable, but it can and must be carried through. After one long conversation a full meal is given, and the patient is not left until the whole of it has been consumed. There must be no time limit for this first meal; resistance is often extreme, but it can always be overcome with patience and good temper. After success with the first meal progress is generally uninterrupted. Resistance still occurs in many cases, but it becomes rapidly and progressively less. In a severe case, it may be necessary for the physician to be present at one meal a day for the first week or fortnight, but the management of the remaining meals may be left to an experienced nurse.

When the appetite is returning and the patient is eating full meals without difficulty, the psychological problems which led to the anorexia may be discussed, but this is not always necessary, as in many instances they have been forgotten in the severity of the illness that followed or they have solved themselves by the time the patient has come under treatment. A few straightforward conversations are sufficient to reveal and straighten out most mental tangles. No form of deep analysis is ever required" (Hurst, 1939, p. 744).

A Psychosomatic Disorder

We prefer to contemplate NA as a psychosomatic disorder in the strictest sense and that is how we explain it to the patient, their family and the other professionals in charge of the case. It is a disorder with a psychological component that can condition its onset and that will condition its development once the patient has reached severe malnutrition (with a BMI equal to or below 17), creating an eminently organic downhill crisis that "takes control of the situation". The main characteristic of this somatic collapse related to the malnutrition is that the need to lose weight escapes the control of the patient at the same time as the panic of "putting on weight" and "becoming deformed" exacerbates the most absurd and incomprehensible symptoms of the disorder.

Once this point has been reached, there is little that can be done by the patient to resume control of the situation nor by the professionals to help them until such time as the patient has recovered sufficient levels of nutrition.

Some authors have seen a parallel between NA and drug addiction (Huebner, 1993; Nardone, Verbitz, & Milanese, 1999; Selekman & Beyebach, 2013). The reasons that lead people to dabble with drugs are many and diverse but the reason that makes them addicts is single: a neurochemical process takes place in the brain when the person consumes a given substance for a given time.

Many NA patients refer to the first "addictive hook" and the sensations produced by severe hunger or how after a first stage of self-provoked vomiting, such becomes uncontrollable and they feel the vital need to purge themselves, much the same as to gorge themselves.

All professionals who work with addicts know how little use it is to try psychotherapy with a patient who is high. The day after a magnificent exchange full of emotion, revelations and insights, the addict will have forgotten almost the whole of the conversation or may even have forgotten the whole event. Much the same occurs with the patient of NA. No efficient psychotherapy can be carried out with a patient suffering severe malnutrition. It is an uphill struggle for the professional. No matter what cognitive or emotional input has been processed, the next day their fears, mental blocks and lack of confidence will go back to the same levels as they were in days previous. The most we can aspire to at that time is to gain their confidence by setting their minds at ease, letting them see that despite their panic, we are resisting like them and not attacking or menacing. It is vital that we be patient and reply repeatedly and coherently all the insistent questions of the patient who, like a police officer, is trying to find consistencies and inconsistencies in our replies, and any signal, either verbal or non-verbal that can allow them to decide to trust in us or, on the contrary, to maintain themselves on the alert for danger.

At this juncture in the process, we can advance positively, however, with the psychotherapeutic work with the family members, with or without the patient. Our main objective is to reduce the levels of emotion expressed, above all, in critical or hostile comments, with excessive emotional commitment (Rienecke, Accurso, Lock, & Le Grange, 2016). This is not necessarily designed to make the patient look at putting on weight again but rather to reduce the possible reasons for which the patient justifies his/her refusal to eat and a possible relapse. The idea is to reinforce levels of positive comments and "warmth" in the relationship.

Activity-Based Anorexia

For some years now, we have been familiar with an analogous animal model for NA, that is, activity-based anorexia (ABA) (Epling et al., 1983).

Experiments consist in reducing the access of an animal to food to only 1 h and a half a day while giving them free access to an activity wheel. When the food diminished, the rat begins to increase its activity and runs endlessly round the wheel.

Curiously, the more it runs, the less it seems to be interested in eating. After a few days, if the experiment is not suspended, the animals can die.

There are various different explanations for this behaviour that is clearly similar to the behaviour of many NA patients. One of the least experimented but most widely assumed is that we have a "reflex search" behaviour genetically implanted that moves all animals to search out food in other places once it becomes scarce where they live. Gutiérrez (Gutierrez, Vázquez, & Boakes, 2002) offers an alternative hypothesis: in his opinion, both undernourished rats and people increase their activity by way of reflex to generate and maintain body heat. One of the sources of his inspiration was an accidental discovery (Lambert, 1993; Lambert & Noakes, 1990, quoted in Gutierrez et al., 2002). Lambert tried to reproduce the ABA conditions but the rats did not increase their activity nor did they lose weight. When he tried to work out why his experiment was not working, he found that the only variable that had escaped his control was the temperature in the room where the cages were. The thermostat was broken and the room temperature was around 25.6 °C instead of 21 °C, the standard temperature for this type of experiment.

Gutiérrez replicated the ABA experiment but altered the temperature in the cage to beyond 30°. He saw how the increase in temperature impeded excessive activity, reduced ingestion and extreme loss of weight (Gutierrez, Baysari, Carrera, Whitford, & Boakes, 2006). This occurred even when the animals had gone below the weight loss limit (Cerrato, Carrera, Vázquez, Echevarria, & Gutiérrez, 2012; Gutiérrez, Cerrato, Carrera, & Vázquez, 2008).

In William Gull's classic study of NA (1874), the famous English doctor prescribed heat for his three anorexic patients. Gull was using research by Chossat (1843) who investigated the symptoms of malnutrition in chicken where they had observed that severely famished birds, when given food, hardly appeared to have enough energy even to consume it, apart from those birds who were offered heat from a sunray lamp.

Gutiérrez, Vazquez, and Beumont (2002) proposes taking all this information into account when dealing with anorexic patients and has even invited them to take sauna sessions regularly with highly promising results (Gutierrez & Vazquez, 2001). Other authors have found that submitting depressed patients to high temperature sessions improves their condition significantly (Janssen et al., 2016; Masuda, Nakazato, Kihara, Minagoe, & Tei, 2005).

The phenomenon of ABA and the data compiled from these studies prove to us anew that there is something evidently organic behind NA that escapes the control of the patients.

So Why Women?

Our Society dictates that the ideal figure for a woman is extremely thin. The media bombard us with images of "perfect women" submitting all women to intolerable pressure to conform to the ideal. Is this a sufficiently strong argument to justify the anorexic figures for women standing at 90% of the total population of patients? To be totally honest, our answer must be “No”. We consider that there are many more factors that account for the nine to one proportion, too many to cover in this one chapter, but some of which we explain here:

The aesthetic ideal is slimness, true, but it is the ideal both for women and for men. So would it be correct to say that women feel the social pressure to conform to a social ideal nine times more intensely than men?

A difference is made in that it is seen attractive for men to also have some muscle tone whereas most women consider it somewhat anti-aesthetic to have marked muscles. This may mean that men when trying to lose weight decide to develop their muscles in the gym whereas women prefer to go on controlled calorie diets. So do nine times more men than women go to the gym? We doubt it, There are many women who go to gyms and sports facilities looking to exercise to lose weight. Then again, if we consider that one of the strategies anorexic patients adopt to lose weight is to submit to excessive programmes of exercise in order to burn calories, why are there hardly any anorexic patients in the gyms?

If we accept that the risk of gaining muscular mass doing gym is something of a dissuading factor for an anorexic then what about long distance running? Marathon champions tend to be extremely thin with BMIs of around 18 and running has become something of a mass phenomenon. However, there are no women with symptoms of malnutrition among the thousands that participate in races. Likewise, hardly any of our patients have reported going regularly to a gym or running marathons.

When our patients describe their “excessive exercise” what they do, how and when, it is more than clear that it is a counter-panic manoeuvre more than a planned, structured process designed to achieve a goal in the mid- or long-term. The need to do exercise is felt almost immediately after eating and often is carried out in private. So they will do half an hour of abdominal exercises as a way of reducing the panic felt as a result of eating and perhaps putting on weight. The patients cannot see the point of doing exercise 3 h after eating since for them it makes no sense since “the damage is already done”.

Another key symptom should be observed parallel to this: hyperactivity is not physical activity directed at burning up calories to avoid getting fat after having eaten but rather, in the words of our patients, due to a feeling of general unease at all times. Is the hyperactivity perhaps a reflex organic reaction to combat the hypothermia that occurs due to a significant loss of body fat? (Gutierrez et al., 2002).

The last reason why women suffer anorexia in such a high proportion as compared to men, in our opinion, is still to be discovered and it is possible again that the reason has more to do with organic aspects relating to the neuro-endocrine system and metabolism that may influence in baseline body temperature and/or in the different distribution of body fat in men and women (Karastergiou, Smith, Greenberg, & Fried, 2012; Wells, 2007) than with the psychological and social aspects which are commonly attributed as factors explaining the imbalanced proportion of women anorexics.

To Recapitulate

We suspect, on the one hand, that a substantial part of the clinical symptoms of NA may have an organic root and we know, on the other hand, that most of these signs disappear once the patient has achieved a normal level of nutrition. Therefore, it would seem obvious that when talking of hospital admissions, our first priority should be to re-establish correct levels of nutrition. In that sense, we are no different from other food disorder treatment units. However, it does come as some surprise to us that with so much evidence that we are dealing with a phenomenon proved to have a high level of organic components and the suspicion that patients who are suffering malnutrition have lost total control of the situation and are no longer acting voluntarily or premeditatedly, that nevertheless many therapists still consider chronic anorexics to be devious manipulators and liars and as such, totally lacking in collaboration.

Our respect for the organic side of the problem, together with the attention we give to the panic experienced at the thought of putting on weight has led us to adopt a posture where we offer help while understanding their reticence to accept it, avoiding all criticism, imposition and threats. We believe that a therapist should be able, even in a context of coercion, to achieve some kind of partnership in the therapy and that is our challenge.

If eating food for a patient in a chronic state of malnutrition is physically and psychologically traumatic, forced feeding is even more so. We do not consider that it is correct to adopt rigid therapeutic stances that increase suffering and the perception of ill-treatment.

We consider it is a mistake for a therapist to work on the premise of total lack of collaboration on the part of the patient or that considers it useless to even try negotiating with them. When we began work with these patients, we also used behavioural strategies of increased privileges (Attia & Walsh, 2009) as rewards as defended by Minuchin as a method to commence recuperating weight with our patients in admissions and previous to the sessions of psychotherapy in the family (Minuchin, Rosman, & Baker, 1978). In this set-up, it is typical for the patient to be forbidden visits of and calls to family members and is obliged to respect total repose. Only when the weight begins to increase will they be "rewarded" by being allowed to get out of bed, to watch the TV, to receive calls and to walk about. It was also usual in the initial days for patients to be fed under the direct supervision of our staff who also encourage them or insist upon them finishing their meals.

Our initial experiences with these strategies in the treatment of NA were as disagreeable as they were unproductive. Most of the patients recovered weight, it is true, and could be released but with hardly any change in their cognition. The level of suffering was marked and the hostility toward the professionals even more so but what was most detrimental about the whole cycle was that the percentage of readmissions was high (over 40%).

We could have simply considered this to be inevitable and to have adopted as our own the words formerly alluded to: "We save lives, we don't change mindsets".

However, we refused to accept the inevitability of the situation and, instead, tried to help our patients to "change their mindsets" through the therapeutic techniques we are proposing here.

Our Therapeutic Strategy

We have evolved in our practice over the years as we observed how rigid strategies and premises gave rise to inefficient, unproductive and painful results. Little by little, therefore, we became more flexible in our attitudes to try and avoid conflicts and achieve a greater level of cooperation and partnership between the family and the patient. In essence, what we were trying to do was to bring down the emotional stress and tension between patient and therapy team at the same time as we were achieving a similar situation between the patient and the family. One of the obvious tools that we have employed over the years to this end are the Psycho-Educational Models used primarily in treatment of schizophrenics (Vaughn & Leff, 1981). The information thereby afforded by family and patients allows us to considerably reduce emotional tension. We try to achieve a "horizontal" therapeutic relationship, something that is difficult in a hospital context that revolves around power status and roles stereotypically and rigidly defined for patients and therapists.

It is important for us to hold a family interview on the first day of admission where we briefly explain our view of the problem: "The reasons that lead a person to lose weight are multiple and diverse but once a state of malnutrition has been reached, the patient loses all control over the process and successive loss of weight is to a large extent both involuntary and undesired, degenerating into a vital need in order to avoid the growing panic of getting fat".

We explain that we are talking about an organic process for which exist many different explanations and for which there is no other cure but to get weight back up to a normal level of nutrition. We tell them in advance that they will see that once the patient has recovered to a "normal" weight, the symptoms will gradually disappear one by one and that paradoxically the more weight they gain the less will be the panic of putting on weight. By normalizing their weight, we will normalize their lives, giving them back control over their future and facilitating their discharge from hospital. The bad part about the whole process is that the patient will be forced to face their illness and all the fears associated with the same.

It is at this point that Jorge de Vega introduces a tale that is deliberately slightly repulsive and is a cross between psycho-educational information and a fable with moral in the purest style of Rosen on Milton Erickson (Rosen, 1986), externalization techniques (White, 1994; White & Epston, 1993), and provocative metaphor (Andolfi, Angelo, Menghi, & Nicolo-Corigliano, 1982). It is to be the "theme" on which the psychotherapy pivots and is called "A Tale of a Tick". It goes like this: "When I was a kid, I used to spend the summer in the village where my father was born, a little village in Salamanca. There was a whole gang of us, boys and dogs together. We knew all the dogs by name and character. We gave them food and learnt how to tend to their basic needs. We knew that when a dog was really thin and you could see its bones, it did not mean that it did not want to eat but rather that it was full of ticks. If we looked behind its ears, we would find gorged ticks, full of blood. The thinner the dog, the bigger the ticks. We learnt how to play vets and get rid of the ticks without hurting the dog."

When I see a really thin person, I remember these scrawny dogs. I can't help but think that Anorexia is a tick that gets inside the brain, sometimes through the eyes, when you looked in the mirror and decided you were fat and had to slim, or through your ears when you heard someone comment on how fat you were. It gets inside you and sticks its sting into your brain, sucking up your body and occupying more and more space until it takes over your brain, only leaving you a tiny part to yourself. But the tick is an insect and so your brain becomes obsessed with "insect thoughts" that have no logic and fill you with panic, things that make no sense like: "If I eat a doughnut, I'll weigh 3 kilos more tomorrow" or "Doing a thousand abs will only help me lose weight if I do them immediately after eating" or "I should control my intake of water because water makes you fat", things like that.

You can get rid of the tick and get your brain back for yourself but only when you manage to eat enough to recover from malnutrition. On the way you'll see how when you do, the tick will start to die and will take up less and less space in your brain. We're here to help you understand how your tick works and to get rid of it once and for all.

The story is an attempt to relieve the patient of their guilt and to extend bridges for them to form a partnership with the therapist and their family at the same time as the disorder is attacked head on. So the public enemy number one is the anorexia and not the patient.

The first family interview is also when the patient is weighed and their BMI calculated. We talk about normal and abnormal BMIs and propose we move toward reaching a BMI of 18 in order to be able to allow the patient out of hospital. Usually when they hear this, the patient's anguish is immense. The proposed weight gain seems to them to be disproportionate, independent of whether it is in fact less than what they weighed when they considered themselves thin, or less than the weight they originally wanted to reach when they were losing weight. We explain to the patient and his/her family that, in our experience, patients can stay stable once discharged with BMIs equal to or above 18 but that those who leave with lower BMIs tend to be readmitted soon afterwards.

We give both the patient and his/her family a personalized sheet of paper with information with respect to BMI and normal weights.

We finish the first interview explaining the norms to be followed during hospitalization and finish with two sentences that sum up our therapeutic process:

(a) "You will only be discharged from hospital when you have reached the weight we have agreed upon. We decide when you leave but nobody is going to force you to eat or to put on weight so you'll decide how long you're going to stay".
(b) "We don't want our patients to get fat, we want them to regain control of their lives".

The Hospital Routine

We also give a written list of basic norms when the patient is admitted, both to them and to their families. We tell them the norms are there for their safety and as strategies to help regain control of their lives.

The first information the patient receives is the staff's instructions. We ask the staff not to pressure the patients for them to eat or for them to eat fast. They must avoid any comment with respect to quantity or quality of food or to the physical aspect of the patient. The patient is to be weighed every day before breakfast in pyjama. They may see their weight.

They will get their food in the dining room with the rest of the patients (In the Chronic Psychiatric Unit this means eating with patients who suffer serious mental disorders. Surprisingly, this causes them less anxiety than eating with other patients with food disorders since the latter produces comparisons, criticism and tension).

The patient is offered a normal diet. With the sole exception of intolerance or allergy, no negotiation is allowed as to diet. Since the patient does not have to eat everything, they can therefore decide themselves upon their diets.

To control possible vomiting, independent of the fact of whether the patient has made recourse to this in the past or not, the bathroom is locked while the patient is eating and when they need to use it, they must be accompanied by a member of staff. A rest period of an hour after breakfast and snacks and 2 h after lunch and dinner is established where the patients go to the common room (for occupational therapy, TV, reading and general entertainment) and on no account may visit the bathroom, not even accompanied.

When first admitted, the patient must pass full repose time in the common room. As they recover their body weight, they are allowed to stroll around the Unit except for repose periods after meals. Water intake is controlled (a habitual and potentially dangerous strategy is for some patients to drink large quantities of water, even up to 5 L, in order to distort their weight). The patient is authorized visits and calls from Day 1 of admission into hospital. As they are capable of feeding themselves normally and recovering their weight levels, controls are relaxed and we allow them to stroll around the Unit, to go to the bathroom on their own, to have their bathroom permanently open, to rest in their rooms and even to go out with the family or to spend some time at home.

The usual routine is that after a few days of hesitation and testing the patience of both family and team members, looking for ways of discharge without the necessary weight recovery, patients begin to eat, little by little, with a great deal of fear and enormous feelings of guilt. It is not unusual for them to continue to drop in weight over the first few days of admission to see if there is widespread alarm or tightening of procedures, something that simply does not occur. Once they decide that they are to face their phobias because there is no other way out, they discover an objective fact which is disconcerting for them at the daily weigh-in: that putting on weight is actually much more difficult than they thought.

We said before that psychotherapeutic treatment with patients who are in a chronic state of malnutrition does not appear to us to be useful. Their phobia will still "occupy too much space in their heads" for them to devote attention to anything else. If we accepted speaking about subjects that they proposed at that time, we would spend day after day talking about food, quality, quantity, variety, healthiness and of the changes they notice in their bodies. We politely refuse to talk about any of this but rather focus on the "tick thoughts" that worry at the patient's brain continually and that are lacking in all logic (even for them). We have already given some examples but others are: "Why is it that the more I reduce in weight, the more dissatisfied I feel and the more I need to continue to lose weight?" or "Why do I think that if I put on weight, my family won't love me anymore?" or "Why do I think that drinking water makes me put on weight?" This is an interesting work but can only be done when the therapists have seen a positive evolution in weight just as it is to compare with the patient their fear that "I'll go up dramatically in weight because yesterday I ate" with the objective data offered by the daily weigh-in.

Once the patient begins to put on weight, their rigid obsession with their illogical phobia disappears and we can begin to talk about other subjects: family relations, friendships, interests, ambitions, their life stories and the possible reasons for having begun to get thin among others. We also experience the trigger for recovery, that is, the surprise they feel when they discover against all odds that as they recover weight, they feel much happier with themselves. This point is key in the therapeutic partnership since it is a turning point when the patient sees that what we promised was true and that we were not trying to deceive them.

We also incorporate helpful information as the patient asks us questions, now that they are in a position to retain the answers and make sense of them. We talk for example of the basic needs of the metabolism that is the calories used by our bodies when we are in complete repose. It is amazing to see how even patients with training in clinical science find it enormously difficult to digest this fact when for them the body will only use calories when involved in activities (another "tick thought").

All the time, we alternate between individual interviews on a daily basis and family interviews twice a week. In the latter, we meet up first with the family then incorporate the patient. The first part allows the family to give free rein to their feelings and their worries, things that they do not dare to broach with the patient. We try to encourage them at the end of this part to share this information with the patient in the second part of the interview. The joint interview is like any family session where the therapist alternates between the roles of "go-between", "stage director" and "spectator". What the therapist is trying to do as we have repeated throughout this chapter is to produce and consolidate the therapeutic partnership and to reduce the negative feelings produced within the family. We give information with respect to the progress of the patient and any changes in norms. We propose and organize when fit temporary outings from the

Unit. The patient talks about their present difficulties and fears but also about their hopes and their achievements, together with their plans for the future.

A reduced percentage of patients take psycho-pharmacological drugs normally sedatives (sleeping in a hospital with the noise, the lights, the nurses' rounds is more difficult than at home) and to a lesser extent anti-depressants. We try to avoid anti-anxiety pills but a small number of patients ask for them. When the patient takes medication, we talk to them and to the family about dosage, changes, effects, side effects and prohibitions.

Once the patient is close to the goal agreed upon, conversations in the family group are led toward subjects of a relational nature, such as relevant aspects of the patient's personal or family history, difficulties and conflicts to be resolved, together with short- and mid-term plans and long-term goals. We draw up the schedule for out-patient treatment where we refer to subjects that require attention such as control strategies when faced with problems.

Monitoring After Discharge

When the patient is discharged, it is normally because most of the symptoms have disappeared. The "Tick has been neutralized" and its influence on the life of the patient has decreased although many of their and their families' fears may reawaken when faced with the necessary changes of timetables, diets and activities once they resume normal life.

For us it is important that the low levels of hostility, criticism and emotional involvement in the family are maintained and our first instructions are to do everything possible to avoid conflict. One useful strategy is for the patient and the family to commit to continuing the daily weigh-in. Every day the patient weighs himself/herself in the presence of a family member who jots down the values and brings that information to the therapist in the consultancy. We propose that after discharges the BMI should reach 20 and not advance or decrease more than 2 kilos from that value as a kind of "buffer zone".

If these commitments are respected and if there are no further alterations nor new symptoms relating to the eating disorder (behaviour changes, aggressiveness, vomiting or abuse of laxatives), we understand that there is no reason for critical comments or arguments and we try to get everyone's agreement on that point. Another important point is that if the patient falls below BMI 18, they must be readmitted before they lose more. Normally in such cases we recommend discharge with a BMI of 20 although it is not obligatory.

The initial monitoring consists in consultancy every fortnight, alternating individual and family interviews flexibly, according to the subjects to be dealt with. The content of the consultancies is highly varied and depends upon the evolution of each case.

Conclusions

In this chapter, we have given a brief overview of how we work with anorexic patients and their families and the underlying principles upon which our work is inspired. We consider our results to be promising with only 10% of the cases being readmitted, of which 20% tend toward chronic cases and over 70% with substantial improvements in their original condition. The average monitoring period is 2 years from discharge and the relationship between patients and staff is highly cordial.

References

Andolfi, M., Angelo, C., Menghi, P., & Nicolo-Corigliano, A. M. (1982). *Detrás de la máscara familiar; La familia rígida, un modelo de psicoterapia relacional.* Buenos Aires: Amorrortu.

Attia, E., & Walsh, B. T. (2009). Behavioral management for anorexia nervosa. *New England Journal of Medicine, 360*, 500–506.

Bergh, C., & Södersten, P. (1998). Anorexia nervosa: Rediscovery of a disorder. *Lancet, 351*, 1427–1429.

Brozek, J. (1953). Semistarvation and nutritional rehabilitation. A qualitative case study, with emphasis on behavior. *American Journal of Clinical Nutrition, 1*, 107–118.

Bruch, H. (1957). *Weight disturbances and schizophrenic development* (Vol. II). Zurich. Congress Report of II International Congress For Psychiatry.

Cerrato, M., Carrera, O., Vázquez, R., Echevarria, E., & Gutiérrez, E. (2012). Heat makes a difference in activity-based Anorexia: A translational approach to treatment development in Anorexia Nervosa. *International Journal of Eating Disorders, 45*, 26–35.

Chossat, C. (1843). Recherches expérimentales sur l'inanition. *Sciences Mathématiques et Psysiques, 8*, 438–640.

Epling, W. F., Pierce, W. D., & Stefan, L. (1983). A theory of activity-based anorexia. *International Journal of Eating Disorders, 3*, 27–46.

Franklin, J. C., Schiele, B. C., Brožek, J., & Keys, A. (1948). Observations of human behavior in experimental semistarvation and rehabilitation. *Journal of Clinical Psychology, 4*, 28–45.

Gull, W. (1874). Anorexia nervosa (apepsia hysterica, anorexia hysterica). *Transactions of the Clinical Society of London, 7*, 22–28.

Gutierrez, E., Baysari, M., Carrera, O., Whitford, T., & Boakes, R. (2006). High ambient temperature reduces rate of body-weight loss produced by increased activity. *Quarterly Journal of Experimental Psychology, 59*, 1196–1211.

Gutiérrez, E., Cerrato, M., Carrera, O., & Vázquez, R. (2008). Heat reversal of activity–based anorexia: Implications for the treatment of anorexia nervosa. *International Journal of Eating Disorders, 41*, 594–601.

Gutierrez, E., Vazquez, R., & Beumont, P. J. (2002). Do people with anorexia nervosa use sauna baths? A reconsideration of heat-treatment in anorexia nervosa. *Eating Behaviors, 3*, 133–142.

Gutierrez, E., & Vazquez, R. (2001). Heat in the treatment of anorexia nervosa patients. *Eating and Weight Disorders, 6*, 49–52.

Gutierrez, E., Vázquez, R., & Boakes, R. (2002). Activity-based anorexia: Ambient temperature has been a Neglected factor. *Psychonomic Bulletin & Review, 9*, 239–249.

Halmi, K. A., Agras, W. S., Mitchell, J., Wilson, G. T., Crow, S., & Bryson, S. W. (2002). Relapse predictors of patients with bulimia nervosa who achieved abstinence through cognitive behavioral therapy. *Archives of General Psychiatry, 59*(12), 1105–1109.

Huebner, H. F. (1993). *Endorphins, eating disorders, and other addictive behaviors*. New York: Norton.

Hurst, A. (1939). Discussion on anorexia nervosa. *Proceedings of the Royal Society of Medicine, 32*, 744–745.

Janssen, C., Lowry, C., Mehl, M., Allen, J., Kelly, K., Gartner, D., et al. (2016). Whole-body hyperthermia for the treatment of major depressive disorder: A randomized clinical trial. *JAMA Psychiatry, 73*, 789–795.

Karastergiou, K., Smith, S., Greenberg, A., & Fried, S. (2012). Sex differences in human adipose tissues—The biology of pear shape. *Biology of Sex Differences, 3*, 13. Retrieved from http://www.bsd-journal.com/content/3/1/13

Keys, A., Brozek, J., Henschel, A., Mickelsen, O., & Taylor, H. L. (1950). *The biology of human starvation*. Minneapolis: University of Minnesota Press.

Lambert, K. G. (1993). The activity-stress paradigm: Possible mechanisms and applications. *Journal of General Psychology, 120*, 21–32.

Lambert, M., & Noakes T. J. (1990). Spontaneus running increases VO2max and running performance in rats. *Appl Physiol, 1*, 400–403.

Masuda, A., Nakazato, M., Kihara, T., Minagoe, S., & Tei, C. (2005). Repeated thermal therapy diminishes appetite loss and subjective complaints in mildly depressed patients. *Psychosomatic Medicine, 67*, 643–647.

Minuchin, S., Rosman, B. L., & Baker, L. (1978). *Psychosomatic families: Anorexia nervosa in context*. Cambridge, MA: Harvard University Press.

Nardone, G., Verbitz, T., & Milanese, R. (1999). *The prisons of food: Strategic solution-oriented research and treatment of eating disorders*. London: Karnac.

Rienecke, R., Accurso, E., Lock, J., & Le Grange, D. (2016). Expressed emotion, family functioning, and treatment outcome for adolescents with anorexia nervosa. *European Eating Disorders Review, 24*(1), 43–51.

Rosen, S. (1986). *Mi voz ira contigo; Los cuentos didácticos de Milton H. Erickson*. B. Aires: Paidós.

Schiele, B., & Brozek, J. (1948). Experimental neurosis resulting from semistarvation in man. *Psychosomatic Medicine, 10*, 31–50.

Selekman, M., & Beyebach, M. (2013). *Changing self-destructive habits*. New York: Routledge.

Vaughn, C., & Leff, J. (1981). Patterns of emotional response in relatives of Schizophrenic Patients. *Schizophrenia Bulletin, 7*(1), 43–44.

Wells, J. (2007). Sexual dimorphism of body composition. *Best Practice & Research Clinical Endocrinology & Metabolism, 21*(3), 415–430.

White, M. (1994). *Guías para una terapia familiar sistémica*. Barcelona: Gedisa.

White, M., & Epston, D. (1993). *Medios narrativos para fines terapéuticos*. Barcelona: Paidós.

Zandian, M., Ioakimidis, I., Bergh, C., & Södersten, P. (2007). Cause and treatment of anorexia nervosa. *Physiology & Behavior, 92*, 283–290.

Zanker, C. (2009). Anorexia nervosa and the body image myth. *Eating Disorders Review, 17*, 327–330.

A Challenge to Borderline Personality Diagnosis: Investigating Post-traumatic Personality Disorders. Connecting Personality Traits to Development in Family

Matteo Selvini

Systemic Model and Attachment Theory

The pioneers of family therapy didn't consider personality disorders. The first experiences in the 50s to 70s only point out psychopathology that is the first axis of DSM IV: Bateson with schizophrenia and double bind, Cancrini (Cancrini, 2006) with drug addictions, Selvini Palazzoli with anorexia. Therapy is focused on the dissipation of illness through the systemic work of "depathologizing," prescriptions, rituals, provocation, and so on.

The first systemic manual written in 1967 by Paul Watzlawick et al. Pragmatics of human communication, an edit of the complex and subtle thought of Gregory Bateson, strongly leans on the here and now. In contrast to psychoanalysis, it asserts that the focus of the clinical work has to be shifted from past to present, with the observation of the dynamics and communications within the families that for the first time in the history of psychiatry/psychoanalysis are called to participate all together. Therefore, the systemic model rises ignoring the models of developmental psychology (see the opposition to the attachment theory since dyadic), focusing on disruptive interventions that can change families in short term (see the structural interventions of Minuchin, the strategic ones of Haley, the paradoxes of Selvini Palazzoli).

The generation successive to the pioneers, since the 80s, will realize the systemic extremism limits: a too simple theory that risks feeding mechanical, provocative, and executive attitudes in the therapists.

A renewal is produced by the division of the family therapy movement in two currents: post-modern constructivism draws the attention on the therapist and her/his creativity, where the development of the personality focus is replaced with the

M. Selvini (✉)
Selvini Palazzoli Psychotherapy School, Milan, Italy
e-mail: matteoselvini@scuolamaraselvini.it

R. Pereira, J. L. Linares (eds.), *Clinical Interventions in Systemic Couple and Family Therapy*, European Family Therapy Association Series,
https://doi.org/10.1007/978-3-319-78521-9_5

badly defined theme of "narration." Selvini Palazzoli's lead remains instead focused on psychopathology and families, but is open to the concepts of evolutionary psychology: the attachment theory becomes crucial.

It is the systemic trend that could be called "integrative of suffering" because talking mainly of homeostatic function of the symptom, "power tactics," "failed release," the dimension of pain was to be partially blurred or forgotten.

Cirillo and his research group start to deal with trauma and personality in "The addict's family" (Cirillo, Berrini, Cambiaso, & Mazza, 2016); immediately after the last work of Mara Selvini Palazzoli "Anorexic and bulimic girls" (Selvini Palazzoli, Cirillo, Selvini, & Sorrentino, 1998) in which the authors theorize four types of personalities of the anorexic-bulimic patients: dependent, borderline obsessive-compulsive, and narcissistic (p. 175–195) which today we prefer to rename as post-traumatic personality (subject-parentified, seductive, autarkic, and punitive-tyrannical) in reference to the reorganizations of attachment which I will discuss in the next section.

There is a transition from a pure relational model to an individual-familiar pattern, where the dimension of trauma has to be recovered, both as specific trauma and traumatic development (also in the sense of deficiency).

The Development Contexts as Learning Matrix of Individual Functioning

In dealing with the causes of personality disorders, the same dilemma that arises in relation to psychopathology recurs: is the search for the family/relational "causes" correct? The dominant biological psychiatry replies adversely to this question, referring to genetic and biochemical factors. The second axis of the DSM IV only describes personality disorders, without any reference to their etiopathogenesis.

In the literature of psychotherapy, you can find instead hypothesis linking a personality disorder to a matrix or a relational context, for example, a reference author such as Lorna Benjamin (1993) speaks of the chaotic family, "a disaster a day" of the borderline.

On the other hand, scholars of personality (Oldham, Skodol, & Bender, 2009) strongly emphasize that family can "mould" only part of the infant, who always has an active role and brings its genetic (beauty, health, etc.) and temperamental specificity.

Personality disorder is the result of a complex path of development, an interactive path where both specific trauma and developmental trauma, linked to family difficulties, can have a very considerable impact.

Especially the moment of birth seems to leave an outstanding imprinting to the character: for example, a very good mother can fall, for reasons often not easy to decipher, in a post-partum depression that inevitably has consequences on the baby, in the sense of a disorganized attachment.

Later this woman will recover, her husband will be a good father and husband, but their son, who we may meet in adolescence, will carry the memory of that original drama in his body (Van der Kolk, 2014).

For this reason, it would be a mistake to think that in the family that we meet today, we can always find that the relational dysfunction that caused the symptom or the dysfunctional personality trait is still active and unchanged. This was one of the major limitations of systemic purism. That child could have also been a difficult child and the family could have activated responses either not at all or only partially reparative.

See in our recent Entrare in terapia (Cirillo, Selvini, & Sorrentino, 2016, p. 145) the reflection on the developmental systemic dimension: it is often severely incorrect to connect a symptom to the way in which the system acts in the present.

Our work has to be both individual and relational: we don't focus primarily on the families but on the development of our patients, trying to understand if their reference figures have been adequate in the past and if they are in the present.

We know that families can be dysfunctional: distorted reality (Selvini, 1993) first of all means that a parent sees his child in an unrealistic/deformed way. We have to be careful not to take for granted that families are always dysfunctional. The emblematic conception of Boszormenyi-Nagy and Framo (1965) that "When there is some disorder in children there is always some trouble in the marriage, even if not all troubled marriages produce disturbed children" granted as an axiom of truth by the pioneers of family therapy has favored judgmental and hypercritical attitudes: our goodwill towards families is a crucial therapeutic factor, whereas blaming and demonizing families, typical of the Freudian culture, is dangerously toxic and harmful.

When in a first session with a teenager and his parents (Selvini, 2014a, 2014b) I see a chillingly sadistic father in action, I observe a helpless mother and I am perturbed by the fury of their son's reactions, I can certainly speculate that this type of system has worked in this way since the birth of the child, and surely I will have to try to understand the causes of the drama (cross-generational reflections on father's story, story of the couple, etc.,) but the clinician must also wonder what may have been the active role of the child, for what reasons and in what stage of its growth.

Even a relationship or a nonfamilial event could have had a negative impact, especially if none of the family have been aware of it. The acknowledgment of the trauma is the first phase of resilience (Selvini, Sorrentino, & Gritti, 2012).

The individual/systemic model has to be a procedural and circular pattern of reciprocal influences between the specificity of child development and family relations (Canevaro, 2009).

The Five Reorganization Strategies

In the study of personality disorders, that is, the most unsuccessful developmental paths, the concept of disorganized attachment is crucial: the child is subject to an impact with a reference adult that is frightened, frightening, hostile, or helpless

(Lyons-Ruth, Dutra, Schuder, & Bianchi, 2009). Recent research on non-clinical populations calculate approximately 15–20% are subjects with a disorganized attachment; this percentage rises to 50–80% in populations of patients in treatment. It is therefore highly likely that a large portion of our patients present this matrix in their development history.

Liotti and Monticelli (Monticelli, Panchieri, Armovidi, Liotti, 2008), then Lyons-Ruth et al. (2009) conceive disorganization as a fracture, that is a high anxiety subjective state of being in the dilemma of fear/need of the reference figures: a type of distressed ambivalence impossible to bear. The historic concepts of defense can be reinterpreted as the need to find a way out from unbearable live experiences. Lyons-Ruth and other attachment researchers identified two key strategies to regain control that is to reorganize the disorganization:

Protective: the savior. This is the classic role reversal, where the child becomes grandfather of himself, acting as the parent of his parent/reference figure. It is evident that the prevalence of this existential choice will lead to the identity (or subidentity in typical disorganized patterns) of the parentified type.

Punitive-tyrannical: the tormentor/executioner. The child becomes tyrannical/dominant towards the reference figure. We find this reorganization especially in the borderline types (the "persecutor/rescuer" vertex of the dramatic triangle) but is also likely to be one of the matrices of antisocial, paranoid, and narcissistic personalities.

Liotti suggests to study three other reorganization strategies:

Submission: the victim. The child may learn that to control the figure of reference, and therefore to make it less threatening and more predictable, being completely "under his command," in a state of utter complacency/subjugation works well. This idea struck me because it solves a big contradiction that had tormented me in the description of the "dependent-symbiotic" type. In the mentioned book (Selvini Palazzoli et al., 1998) describing the dependent type, we put together symbiotic traits (the difficulty to act independently and to think with one's own head) with reversal of roles traits (protective). As we will see later, it is the frequent combination of two reorganizations, but it appeared a confused type when looking for matches in the development history. In fact, in dealing with subjects that in the DSM IV could be classified as "dependent," the clinical experience didn't confirm at all the presence of a hyper-protective learning environment. On the contrary, we encountered case stories with severe deficiencies, almost abusive stories; in parallel, in literature we can also find reference to an authoritarian style in parenthood (Bornstein, 1998). I can therefore assume the existence of two types of dependent personalities, so different from each other as to raise the doubt of whether it is a good idea to apply the identical term. In fact, this submissive child seems more easily led to the genesis of a masochist tract or a passive aggressive one that is precisely to an identity based on the submission to the will of the reference figure. We must therefore distinguish carefully between the inability to think and do only on the basis of an infantilism caused by a caregiver being anxiously overprotective and the same inability built on the strategy of submission to a reference that is unreliable/threatening.

Seductive: the manipulator. We come here to a classic theme of the history of psychotherapy: the famous Freud's hysterical subjects now renamed histrionic: girls scared by not being acknowledged who try to exist with active hyper caregiver involvement strategies (using precisely seduction and discomfort and illness). These children run the greatest risk of sexual abuse. Putting into focus this type of reorganization helps us to hypothesize their active part, precisely on the grounds of excessive attention seeking.

Autarkic: the self-sufficient. Liotti calls this reorganization "unplug the attachment plug," that is, the highly avoidant attachments that lead to the origins of the obsessive, schizoid, or paranoid personalities, but that we often meet as precariously present in border and psychotic outlines: if my caregiver frightens me, I will delete it, I'll manage without this person.

The connection between these strategies and many trust disorders appears obvious. The attachment phobia requires activation of other motivational systems, matrices of reorganizations.

This simple reorganization model is very useful to rethink in the light of developmental psychology the classical concept of defense and to understand the development pathways that lead to personality disorders.

Abolishing Stigmatizing Borderline and Masochistic Diagnosis

It is unlikely that our patients will show a single reorganization: the divided self of post-traumatic patients is precisely characterized by different parts of the same person that swing from one to the other (see the historical concept of dramatic triangle Karpman, 1968). To set up a treatment program, it's important to identify first the insecure attachment area (ambivalent or avoidant) and subsequently the prevailing reorganization: this gives direction to the approach and the prognosis.

We start from the protective reorganization (ambivalent attachment area), which is the one that presents the best prognosis, to the point of not being considered in the II axis of the DSM IV. They require a more directive approach, a guide, as does the entire area of ambivalent attachment. They struggle to accept the therapy because they have difficulties in taking care of their needs since they are tuned to those of the other. We find traces of this functioning in the psychodynamic diagnosis of oral dependent (Johnson, 1994). These people are particularly exposed to the risk of overload (hyper-responsibility), with the consequent anxious and depressive symptoms. These people will very easily choose the helping professions. Miller (1978) has defined these personalities as neurotic narcissistic. Others, including the author, have called it parentified personality (Selvini, 2008).

With the punitive reorganization, in the avoidant attachment area, we move to the opposite pole of the worst prognosis: the tyrant child will trigger a lot of negativity in his reference figures that can reach actual abuse. Development paths open that start with a fight reaction to stress/trauma and lead to the diagnosis of narcissistic, antisocial, and paranoid personality disorders. Here the approach should be welcoming, as throughout all the avoidance area, but with important initial cautions: the narcissist confuse empathy with commiseration and often responds more positively to a good-natured challenge seen as being more respectful.

The submission (in the ambivalent attachment area) is instead connected to a post-traumatic frozen (freezing/dulling/depression) reaction that has a bad prognosis although better than the tyrannical one. Indeed, we have a "good boy" although a bit "detached." The trajectory towards personality disorders leads to masochist, border-dependent subtype, passive-aggressive diagnosis. The key point of therapy is to lead the patient to the changing experience of having an active, effective, and fulfilling role.

The seductive reorganization (in the ambivalent attachment area) seems to be more clearly linked to a relational context where the experience of invisibility feeds fear. Hence two major subtypes: the seducer-resuscitator (with better prognosis) and that of the sick patient (e.g., hysterical paralysis cured by Freud). Here too, the post-traumatic reaction seems predominantly "fight" but more mixed with dissociative/flight aspects, therefore the risk that the body speaks instead of the person itself. The DSM IV diagnosis will be that of the histrionic personality. In therapies we will work to understand and satisfy that need of visibility and to prevent acting-out and self-injurious behaviors (fatuous exhibitionism, promiscuity, etc.).

Finally, the autarkic reorganization (in the avoidant attachment area) is engaged on post-traumatic dissociative/flight. It presents an intermediate prognosis gravity similar to the seductive one, and leads, in order of severity, towards schizoid, obsessive, and avoidant personality disorder diagnosis. The challenge of these treatments is entering in a truly authentic contact with these patients, helping them to do the same with the other (enlargements).

As correctly suggested by Herman (1992), the diagnoses of borderline and masochistic personality have become severely stigmatizing for patients. Diagnosis of personality that favor the recognition of the distortions of the development path and then help an empath/positive attitude towards patients are much more useful. My proposal is to abolish the borderline and masochistic labels and replace them with definitions related to the reorganizations:

1. Submissive/parentified post-traumatic personality
2. Seductive post-traumatic personality
3. Punitive-tyrannical post-traumatic personality
4. Autarkic post-traumatic personality

I suggest to integrate two of the reorganizations because clinical experience shows that they are almost always combined together, although with different specific gravities, as we anticipated in anorexic and bulimic girls (Selvini Palazzoli et al., 1998) even only intuitively.

Clinical research has demonstrated the presence of severe trauma in almost all patients receiving psychiatric diagnoses in general, and especially in subjects with borderline and masochistic diagnosis. The diagnosis of borderline is however still used for too many people although greatly different among themselves. Hence the need for clinical research to identify more homogeneous groups of patients to assess the major/minor effectiveness of different treatment strategies.

Organizing a Classification of Personality Disorders

I followed the criterion of continuity between normality and pathology: the same trait can be classified as a style, a neurosis, or a disorder (Johnson, 1994). If we take, for example, narcissism, we have the benign narcissism style of the basically well-functioning person, aware of the risk of his tendency to feel superior, his being contemptuous, his difficulty in seeing his limitations, sometimes insensitive to the feelings of others. Then we have the neuroses of those who are only partially aware of their narcissistic functioning, and finally the real disorder, that is the malignant narcissism of the person entirely ego syntonic with its dysfunctions.

The diagnosis of personality has no clinical utility without a simultaneous assessment of the severity of the disorder.

As ordering criteria of the whole range of the personalities, we have used the attachment theory and, therefore, the range of ambivalent/disorganized/avoidant attachment.

Even Solomon (1989) proposed a similar contribution that Cirillo (2013) adopted as a starting point for a classification of personality disorders, ranging from excess of dependency to excess of autonomy.

Therefore, the following 14 personality types:

Ambivalent area

1. dependent
2. parentified
3. histrionic
4. passive-aggressive

Ambivalent versus disorganized area (that is borderline personality disorder)

5. protective-submissive post-traumatic
6. seductive post-traumatic

Avoidant versus disorganized area (that is narcissist, antisocial, paranoid, schizoid, and schizotypal disorders)

7. tyrannical-punitive post-traumatic
8. autarkic post-traumatic

Avoidant area

9. avoidant

10. obsessive
11. narcissistic
12. antisocial
13. paranoid
14. schizoid

This vertical classification has nothing to do with severity assessments which are preferably to be read horizontally on all types (style-neuroses-disorder). In my article of 2008, I placed the borderline disorder in the area of disorganized ambivalent attachment. If instead we cancel the borderline diagnosis to replace it with that of post-traumatic personality, they should be placed in the avoidant disorganized area.

This classification is similar to that of Benjamin's regarding the belonging-detachment axis, but it is detached from the three clusters of DSM IV because these gather areas of opposite attachment: for example, the dependent of the ambivalent area and the obsessive of the avoidant area, are joint in the anxious cluster. It is inevitable that following a development criterion a purely descriptive classification will clash. Our diagnosis will be both categorical and dimensional. They will be categorical because in a minority of cases we will meet people who embody the prototype of a certain type or personality trait. But they will especially be dimensional because more often we will see people who embody and combine different traits.

The more complex and decisive differential diagnosis is therefore that between a primary or organized personality disorder and a disorganized personality disorder as post-traumatic. For example, a child who grows up with a stable avoidant attachment and is simultaneously exalted for exceptional natural gifts may develop an organized narcissistic disorder, which has similarities with the traits of people with a post-traumatic story of punitive reorganization. The two personality structures, and therefore treatments and prognosis, however, will be completely different. The same problem arises for other differential diagnosis: for example, a paranoid will be so structurally perched in response to a negative environment or will he be presenting a main reorganization that conceals others, more accessible to the therapeutic relationship?

Connecting Personality Traits to Stories of Development in the Family

In the mid-90s, while preparing our book anorexic and bulimic girls (Selvini Palazzoli et al., 1998) we started to research these correlations and to study the related literature.

In the clinical work, it was important to verify that the expected links overlapped: for example, with a narcissistic trait we expected that that child had been exalted/obeyed and very often it was just what we found in the family history. However, when the hypothesis was not confirmed, this was still very interesting, because it brought to light other subtypes of personality, such as revenge narcissism

(Di Maggio & Semerari, 2003). Similarly, it was very interesting to study the cases where the dependent trait did not fit a family history of infantilism/overprotection. This made it possible to better identify the submission reorganization.

I'll try now to synthesize in a table the main correlations.

Personality traits	Development story of the family
Dependent/infantile/ symbiotic	Overprotection
Parentified	Role reversal
Histrionic	Only seen if ill or seductive
Passive aggressive	Humbled and overwhelmed
Protective-submissive post-traumatic	Neglect, abuse, parental fragility in emotional context
Seductive post-traumatic	Unpredictable alternation of acceptance/abandonment in an emotional context, but a lack of visibility
Punitive-tyrannical post-traumatic	Alternation of exultation/aggression in an unpredictable/hostile environment, lack of affection
Autarkic post-traumatic	Unpredictable alternation of presence/absence of fragile parents in a rejecting and cold context
Avoidant	Aloofness and hypercriticism in a formally adequate context
Obsessive	Aloofness and hyper-responsibility in a formally adequate context
Narcissistic	Lack of caregiving and quality magnification unrelated to the merits
Antisocial	Lack of caregiving and manipulation in a stress context
Paranoid	Deficiency and aggression in a lack of affection context
Schizoid	Inaccessibility to attachment figures

With this scheme I suggest a distinction between trauma and lack of caregiving. Deficiency leads to developmental deficits linked to organized insecure attachment, ambivalent, or avoidant. Development trauma refers to attachment disorganization.

Treatment Strategies

The existing literature, both on personality disorders and on post-traumatic disorders, two fields that tend to overlap a lot, tends to ignore the work with families, only focusing on individual psychotherapy.

The clinical experience of my group, tested mainly on the restrictive anorexia ground (Cirillo, Selvini, & Sorrentino, 2011) where girls with post-traumatic personality, dominated by autarkic, submissive, and protective reorganizations, but all five are present, although with different prevalence, showed the effectiveness of a multimodal teamwork that integrates individual therapy with family therapy.

Family therapy is crucial both in the first phase of the personality disorders treatment: the impact of the acknowledgment of the trauma (Selvini et al., 2012) or of the lack of caregiving, but also in the next phase in which the family is prepared to share the trauma that the patient has never revealed and is willing to support him in the elaboration process.

We must stop the multigenerational chain: it can often be noted that a post-traumatic patient has at least one post-traumatic parent.

Here a dramatic example of tyrannical reorganization. We are contacted by the father of Marco, a 15 years old boy, very concerned about his eldest son's poor school performance, of the violent tensions at home with his mother, the physical ill treatment towards his sister. In the first meeting, we invite Marco with his parents: he appears very challenging, provocative, and very intelligent. The mother worries us even more than him: her hostility towards the boy is fierce, unstoppable. We are immediately forced to split the formats: Cirillo sees the parents, with me behind the mirror, and I see in parallel the boy alone. The parents tell a typical chaotic history, one of "a disaster a day." The mother comes from a very wealthy family, her father died in an accident when she was a teenager, she became the black sheep of the family, in perpetual conflict with her mother who takes over her late husband's well-established activity, the favorite daughter seems to be her sister. She has no professional achievements and an unstable love life until her marriage to an employee of the family business. They go and live in a luxury apartment in the center of Milan. But also, this union is plagued by continuous conflicts: the woman has severed relations even with her husband's family. When asked about her relationship with Marco she leaves us shocked: "He has always hated me, from birth, he refused my milk, he has never noticed me." The father very feebly tries to mediate, overwhelmed by the incitement/intolerance of his wife and the provocation of the boy, he loses his temper and hits his son. Marco, in individual therapy, with a typical but nevertheless surprising change, stops despising me and starts an overflow of revelations and thoughts. On WhatsApp, he sends me at least 40 hyper distressing pictures of bleeding wounds, he hands me a series of cutters. The parents are totally unaware of the self-harm problem, which has been going on periodically for several years. Marco in a dramatic individual session reveals, with a cold and detached attitude, his projects to exterminate his family, his experiments, his enjoyment when he sees them suffer...

Through a complicated negotiation with the boy, we manage to relocate the boy (relative's foster family) and this safety measure produces immediate improvements. We manage to convince his mother to start a personal therapy and we discuss with the parents how to contact the social services (we are in the private context). In separated parallel sessions with Marco and his parents, we agree to resume contacts between the mother and the boy, that had been interrupted for a few weeks.

This case very clearly shows the unavoidable need of simultaneous family and individual therapy in taking charge of personality disorders. In fact, this child and then boy had been sent to various psychotherapists and had always been seen individually, with insignificant results, most likely iatrogenic.

In the first sessions with a patient with a personality disorder, the recognition of trauma is crucial: "We need to understand what has terribly frightened Marco when he was very young. Marco defended himself from the fear by becoming very domineering: being a bad boy gives him security for a while, until the consequences of his bad behavior turn upon him, frightening him to death! We have to get out of this tragic vicious circle."

The psychoeducation on the causes of personality disorders, through the theory of reorganization, is a decisive tool for family and individual personality disorders therapy. At a later stage of processing, family support installs a sense of security in the patient who can consequently remember and elaborate: the best part of family therapy is that of sharing the suffering to allow a reconciliation that is prerequisite to a healthy sense of belonging.

Conclusions

The work of classification of personality disorders is very important, especially in the still not well-defined area of post-traumatic personality, just to be able to set up a systematic research in which treatment protocols can be more effective. In this area where psychiatry reveals its utter helplessness, systemic psychotherapy can really prove its social utility: a scientific challenge taking its first steps.

References

Benjamin, L. S. (1993). *Interpersonal diagnosis and treatment of personality disorder*. New York: Guilford Press.

Bornstein, R. F. (1998). Depathologizing dependency. *Journal of Nervous and Mental Disease, 186*, 67–73.

Boszormenyi-Nagy, I., & Framo, J. L. (1965). Rationale and techniques of intensive family therapy. In I. Boszormenyi-Nagy & J. Framo (Eds.), *Intensive family therapy: Theoretical and practical aspects*. New York: Harper & Row.

Cancrini, L. (2006). *L'oceano borderline. Racconti di viaggi*. Milano: Raffaello Cortina Editore.

Canevaro, A. (2009). *Quando volano i cormorani*. Roma: Borla.

Cirillo, S. (2013). Autonomia e dipendenza: Due termini che di oppongono? *Terapia Familiare, 102*, 15–34.

Cirillo, S., Berrini, R., Cambiaso, G., & Mazza, R. (2016). *La famiglia del tossicodipendente, Nuova edizione*. Milano: Raffaello Cortina Editore.

Cirillo, S., Selvini, M., & Sorrentino, A. M. (2011). Anoressia Restrittiva: Una ricerca su 34 casi. In P. Chianura, L. Chianura, E. Fuxa, & S. Mazzoni (Eds.), *Manuale clinico di terapia familiare*. Milano: Società Italiana di Psicologia e Psicoterapia relazionale, Franco Angeli.

Cirillo, S., Selvini, M., & Sorrentino, A. M. (2016). *Entrare in terapia. Le sette porte della terapia sistemica*. Raffaello Cortina Editore: Milano.

Herman, J. (1992). *Trauma and recovery: The aftermath of violence—From domestic abuse to political terror*. New York: Basic Books.

Johnson, S. (1994). *Character styles*. New York: Norton.

Karpman, S. B. (1968). Fairy tales and script drama analysis. *Transactional Analysis Bulletin, VII*(26), 39–43.

Liotti, G., & Monticelli, F. (Eds.). (2008). *I sistemi motivazionali nel dialogo clinico*. Milano: Raffaello Cortina Editore.

Lyons-Ruth, K., Dutra, L., Schuder, M. R., & Bianchi, I. (2009). From infant attachment disorganization to adult dissociation: Relational adaptations or traumatic experiences? *Psychiatric Clinics of North America, 29*, 63–86.

Di Maggio, G., & Semerari, A. (2003). *I disturbi di personalità. Modelli e trattamento*. Laterza: Bari.

Miller, A. (1978). *The drama of the gifted child: The search for the true self, revised edition paperback*. New York: The Perseus Books Group BASIC BOOKS.

Monticelli, F., Panchieri, L., Armovidi, C., & Liotti, G. (2008). Dinamiche motivazionali e psicopatologia. In L. Monticelli (Ed.), *I sistemi motivazionali nel dialogo clinico*. Milano: Raffaello Cortina Editore.

Oldham, J. M., Skodol, A. E., & Bender, D. S. (2009). *Essentials of personality disorders*. Washington, DC: American Psychiatric Publishing.

Selvini, M. (1993). Severe mental disorders and distorted reality (English Trans.). *American Journal of Family Therapy, 24*(2), 107/116.

Selvini, M. (2008). Undici tipi di personalità. L'integrazione della diagnosi di personalità nel pensiero sistemico complesso. *Ecologia della Mente, 31*, 29–55.

Selvini, M. (2014a). Coinvolgere adolescenti riluttanti. L'efficacia di un primo incontro familiare. *Terapia Familiare, 105*, 55–78.

Selvini, M. (2014b). L'integrazione della diagnosi di personalità e dei funzionamenti non-traumatici nel pensiero sistemico. *Ecologia della Mente, 37*(1), 49–59.

Selvini, M., Sorrentino, A. M., & Gritti, M. C. (2012). Promuovere la resilienza "individuale-sistemica": Un modello a sei fasi. *Psicobiettivo, 32*, 32–51.

Selvini Palazzoli, M., Cirillo, S., Selvini, M., & Sorrentino, A. M. (1998). *Ragazze anoressiche e bulimiche*. Milano: Raffaello Cortina.

Solomon, M. (1989). *Narcissism and intimacy*. New York: Norton.

Van der Kolk, B. (2014). *The body keeps the score: Brain, mind, and body in the healing of trauma*. New York: Penguin Press Viking.

Watzlawick, P., Beavin, J. H., & Jackson, D. D. (1967). Pragmatics of human communication. In *A study of interactional patterns, pathologies, and paradoxes*. New York: Norton.

Part II
New Resources in Systemic Therapy

The Importance of Being Siblings

Rodolfo de Bernart

Introduction

In the tradition of family therapy, the therapeutic intervention is usually focused on the subsystem of parents. Sometimes this subsystem doesn't exist or doesn't like to be involved in therapy; in these cases, it's better to have other resources, inside and outside the nuclear family.

In these clinical situations, our interest for siblings subsystem was born. This "siblings resource" seems very important for the special quality that exists between members of the same family and on the same generational level. Every one of them shares the family history when talking about emotions, feelings, and events, but may read this reality in an individual, sometimes even conflicting reconstruction. All this material can be used in a therapeutic family setting, where differences are important in order to build up alternative readings to the ones which family brings in during therapy.

Working with all these alternative readings it's possible to start again the process of a vital cycle of the family. Dunn and Plomin say (1990, 1991) that a brother or a sister uses environmental factors different one from the others for his/her growth, while shared experiences are not important for his/her growth.

R. de Bernart (✉)
Instituto di Terapia Familiare di Firenze, Firenze, Italy
e-mail: ITFF@itff.it

R. Pereira, J. L. Linares (eds.), *Clinical Interventions in Systemic Couple and Family Therapy*, European Family Therapy Association Series,
https://doi.org/10.1007/978-3-319-78521-9_6

Siblings in a Normal Family

Papers about this subject are few and usually available only in the English language. (Ascoli, 1988; Bank & Kahn, 1982; de Bernart, 1989, 1991a, 1991b; Dunn, 1986; Dunn & Kendrick, 1987; Dunn & Plomin, 1990, 1991; Kahn & Lewis, 1998; Pecchioli, 1987).

In a family, siblings work as a subsystem: Minuchin (1976) says that this is the first social laboratory, in which siblings can experiment with relationships with peers. Siblings can help one another, can get isolated, can work together or accuse one another. In this "Peers World," they learn how to work, negotiate, cooperate, and compete.

Every brother and sister has his/her own function which is largely decided by his/her role and identity received during years in his/her family life.

Before a baby is born his/her parents anticipate what will be his/her identity and they are already deciding their role. When a baby is born, this event is full of individual processes and adaptation processes to find new modalities of functions inside the family. Individual and familial expectations, feelings, and sensations are tied to events that happened during the pregnancy, or at the birth or in the first period after the birth, or because of similarities and identifications between parents and children. Even the order of birth is to be considered: if a baby is born first or second is important (1976), not only because the birth of a first child is a new event for a parent but because, as Bank and Kahn say, only one subject can occupy a certain psychological space during a certain period of time. Which means that first born child can have a prelation on a determined functional position that can't be occupied by the second brother if the first brother didn't leave that open. The other children will have to become something else in the family.

The parents too have the power to decide the role of their children. A positive functional assignment can be reinforced by parents until it becomes a positive identity (the good, the clever).

On the contrary, a negative assignment can become heavy for the child's development and can affect the child in a negative way.

In "healthy families," these roles are assigned and modified in a flexible way and this guarantees the development of everybody. But if a functional position is becoming stable and stuck because a parent or both parents need it, with the complicity of the siblings, then the space for a symptom is taking place.

In the movie "The Family" by E. Scola, 1987, the first son, Carlo is described by his father as "honest and sincere" while the second son Giulio is defined "liar and mean" and this will sign the life of the two brothers permanently.

Carlo will become a professor, married to a wise woman and with a large family.

Giulio after a disastrous military experience, will marry the housemaid, and will try numerous jobs always failing.

Only after turning 70 Carlo will realize to have underestimated his brother: 30 years ago he had considered Carlo's very good book ugly and superficial, without even reading it, "basing his judgment on the author."

But Giulio too trusted the brother's judgement only on the basis of the parents' definition "Carlo is sincere and honest."

So he did not even try to propose his book to an editing company and lost the "occasion of his life"

Not only parents can influence a child, but children can be influenced by the birth of a sibling. The need to defend their role in the family can bring them to significant, symptomatic behaviors.

Silvia, 8 years old, stopped eating after a gastroenteritis. Nobody can explain her attitude. On the second meeting the psychiatrist and the supervisor ask her to create a fantasy about her little sister, who the mother lost due to a miscarriage. Luisa (this was supposed to be the name of the new little girl) is replaced in the fantasy by Silvia, who sits on her mother's lap with a small bear puppet representing Silvia. When asked, she said that in order to stay on mom's lap she had to stay little, which requires not eating. After that, Silvia started to eat again and her mother could "afford" another pregnancy (De Bernart, 1984, 1989).

Silvia's symptoms can be caused by many factors: not growing up, not losing the place on mom's lap but also punish herself for having desired the death of the little sister.

And it's clear that it isn't the simple verbalization of the symptom that made Silvia get over it. It's impossible to write the intense emotion built in the session by the therapist, through the use of sculpture and of metaphorical objects which brings the little girl to live her conflicts and fears through a couple of instants, during an intense resolving experience.

The experience is giving back freedom to the parents too. They later become able to afford another pregnancy, without asking the daughter, like they did the first time.

Eugenia Scabini (1987) says that family ties are bound and they have a limited amount of freedom, they are hierarchically structured and defined by attachment and loyalty. The meaning of these two concepts is of course the one defined by Bowlby (1969) and Boszormenyi-Nagy and Spark (1973).

Bank and Kahn (1982) define the bond between two siblings as "a connection between two identities, on both the public and the intimate level, an adaptation of personal identities." We could say that these two bonds are strongly ambivalent: together with love and feelings of need are usually present feelings of hatred, rivalry, and jealousy.

The emotional bond between siblings depends on the level of access and is divided by Bank and Kahn (1982) into two categories: low access and high access.

These have some characteristics like: they have an age gap of 8–10 years or more, so they act like members of different generations; they have shared little time, space, or personal stories, they've never been to the same schools, they don't have the common friends and they had "different parents" (parents are different at different ages) they lack—at least partially—a shared history, often they don't even need one another.

When the age gap is little or they have the same sex, they also have common life experiences and an easier access; while different ages and different sex limit their access. The highest access, of course, is the one of twins, obviously (1989); the lowest one is the one of siblings who grew up living separately (e.g., because they lived with different families).

High access siblings have an intense bond. This can also happen because parents didn't give them enough attention. In this case, siblings build a strong bond of loyalty which touches powerful emotions, take years to be developed and influences their identity in a stable way. Loyalty between siblings can be reciprocal or only in one direction. The reciprocal one can be characterized by a special code, private, that only siblings can understand, for their relationship: these siblings are devastated when separated.

This language differentiates them from other family members or friends: they protect themselves from strangers and from their physical or psychological attacks. They cooperate, resolve their conflicts, and contain aggressive emotions and behaviors into acceptable limits. They develop rituals of forgiveness and understanding.

The harmony of the group gets over the importance of every individual search for personal advantage; they are compatible and complementary about their roles and their identities. In the case of the one direction loyalty, the sibling, usually a girl, takes responsibility for her brothers or sisters during childhood and even during adulthood. The caretaker gives to others without expecting anything back; his/her role and identity are rigid and closed; the warmth that usually a group of reciprocal brotherhood have is lacking. This missing part has long-lasting negative effects both on who gives and on who gets.

When parents are available and present, they don't teach specific strategies to siblings in order to act as siblings. But there are many different indirect ways in order to influence relationships among siblings. For example, all the members of the family are touched by what Bowen (1979) calls "multigenerational family influence." This heritage influences how members of a family act to each other or create and maintain relationships in the family. This happens also through the siblings' heritage: children hear their parents talking in explicit or indirect way about their experiences as siblings and they try to act like them or sometimes in a completely different way, in order to avoid the same mistakes their parents did or to protect themselves from the same traumas.

Siblings in Therapy

As we said in another occasion (1991), we use to work with the subsystem of siblings every time it is necessary, every time the resources for changing offered by the parental subsystem are insufficient or absent. The way to operate changes of course when we have children, adolescents or adult siblings.

I have already spoken about children siblings in a workshop during the Conference "Children and their system": I can just say that we use them as experts in the diagnostic phase. It's clear that children depend on their parents, so they can't have resources in order to help alone their problematic sibling. This situation changes very much when we work with the subsystem of teen siblings, who can build what we will call the “Mind of Siblings,” which is able to act significant operations toward change.

This “Mind of Siblings” can be initially organized through practical homework, which pushes all siblings to help the one with difficulties.

For example with a family of six siblings in which the second child, Daniel, had a heavy suicidal depression, we asked the siblings to organize a sort of “watch” where one of them was always staying with Daniel in order to prevent suicide. Siblings had to get together during the interval between therapy sessions to talk about the mental state of Daniel and their relationship with him. The results of these meetings of the “Siblings Mind” were then reported during therapy sessions.

When the “Mind of Siblings” is built and stabilized, the therapist can start to give more complex homework which has the target of finding new readings of the family situation and of the relationship with parents. These themes are discussed during therapy, then at home, during “Mind of Siblings sessions” and results are later shared with the therapist, who becomes a consultant of the elaboration and redefinition work made at home by the “Mind of Siblings.”

This reframing is helped by the fact that siblings can share the individual readings about their family life, but come to conclusions which are different from the ones which were created before and which reinforced the symptom. The change takes place on the cognitive side, but not only on that side. The functions of each sibling, which before weren’t interchangeable, can now rotate or be distributed in different ways among the members of the subsystem.

This allows a new level of freedom for everybody, the end of the symptomatic behavior, and can avoid and prevent relapses in the identified patient or migrations of the symptom or building of different symptoms in other siblings when the identified patient gets better.

Let’s see this aspect while watching Daniele’s family. In a different phase we make the hypothesis that the father is trying to get a more significant role in the family, which he never had, being quite peripheric; while the mother had a more important presence in the family.

Therapist: “Which one of you thinks your father will have a problem to get connected with him/her? I think it’s Daniele but I could be wrong…for Daniele it could be difficult to have a relationship with father and reduce the one with mother.”

Daniele: “It happened to me many times to need the help of my father but it’s difficult for me to ask for help, as it’s like admitting I am not able to handle myself.”

Therapy: “It’s not the same thing, you can ask for help with a symptom in a generic way but if you ask for help directly you need an answer which means a relationship. But balance is necessary too. In order to allow Daniele to have a good relationship with the father, Francesco (2nd child), who has a strong bond with father, how much will he have to connect with the mother?”

Francesco, Daniele and the other siblings look each other in silence, not talking but understanding.

Therapist (continuing after a pause): “The Mind of Siblings” can be used to verify different possibilities, agreed among you all and not one against the other.”

This “experimental” situation gets all the siblings to have a different relationship with the two parents. It may be that later they will come back to the situation from which they started. But nothing will be the same again because everyone will have a bigger and more varied experience, from which to start. And we should consider also the changes that happened in the parent's subsystem.

Siblings are assigned a homework in order to understand that the identified patient is not the only one having difficulties, the contrary of the concept expressed by the whole family during the sessions in therapy. Siblings need to recognize and redistribute fragile, aggressive, and depressive parts among themselves, with a double target: sustain the identified patient and avoid possible migration of the symptom to other siblings.

The need of completing this task is important to the siblings not only in order to resolve Daniele's difficulties but also because every one of them was touched by this crisis.

For example Francesco is examining his own difficulty to put borders to his wife's family, Sandro becomes aware of a serious of problem in his couple life, Giovanna can find a balance between the distance and the proximity of her parents.

Siblings are reconsidering their roles and their functions in the family and are establishing direct relationships among themselves. There is no more need to pass through the mother, who before was always a go-between among them.

In the near future this will establish an emotional and intensive exchange of feelings.

This work with the subsystem of siblings is not new in the structural family therapy. We used to divide families in subsystems giving them different homework in and out of therapy sessions to different groups. What makes this therapeutic modality different is, instead, the optic with which we consider the subsystem of siblings.

The "Mind of Siblings" is built with the precise task to read in a different way the history of family relationships. Even if the homework are more practical at the beginning, we think that later this capacity of "re-reading" the real situation of the family is possible and leads to a successive change.

Everything is possible of course only if the siblings can establish an intensive bond of trust and desire of collaboration among themselves. During our work, we had sometimes difficulties in building the "Mind of Siblings." In these different situations, we realized that we took for granted that the siblings subsystem existed even in cases in which there was a very big emotional distance. In other words, we realized that there was another category of "low access" siblings.

In this case, the anagraphic distance or living far away from one another wasn't the reason for the "low access." On the contrary, the cause of "low access" was the increasing strong rivalry, jealousy, and rancor, which normally exist among siblings but became stronger in these specific clinical cases (De Bernart, 1991a). Bank and Kahn (1982) called the temporal and spatial access the first kind. I named this new kind "Emotional Access."

Susanna and Sara are two sisters of 20 and 18 years old both showing anorexia and bulimarexia.

According to Bank and Kahn they should be "high access" sisters because the age gap is just 18 months and they always lived together and shared the same friends and schools until teen age when Susanna started to show the first symptoms.

When she was 12 years old Susanna after a weird sickness stopped eating and started to lose weight.

She started to be treated in individual psychotherapy.

For a quite long period the situation went on and Susanna was worried about Sara's health, specifically controlling the quality and quantity of her food (Sara had to finish everything in her dish otherwise Susanna would start crying).

Parents were impotent to resolve the situation and they accepted Susanna's request to keep her quiet. When she was 14 years old Sara as well started refusing food, the situation became more dramatic and the mother too started taking big doses of benzodiazepine until she needed to go to the rehab.

In the first meeting in which the sisters are alone, after some family sessions, the therapist talks about rancor and jealousy.

Asked by the therapist, Sara confirms she had jealousy and difficulties to get her parents attention which was all for Susanna because of her sickness.

Even during the worst part of Sara's anorexia the parents were still worried about Susanna, who was so closed in herself, that they didn't even know what she was thinking.

Therapist (to Sara): "tell me the first time you were mad at your sister and why"

Sara: "She used to put food in my plate and I had to eat it"

Therapist: "and what were your parents doing?"

Sara: "Dad was indifferent. Mom was divided between being worried for Susanna who didn't eat and got mad at me because I was sick anyway"

Susanna: "For me the rage was born when Sara started doing what she wanted!"

In this case, the "Mind of Siblings" must be built after the elaboration of jealousy and rancor made before by the therapist in session and later at home. This need of elaboration is signaled by the resistance that siblings show to do the task of reading the family system and their functions.

Sara: "Susanna didn't want the "Mind of Sibling" meeting in order to talk about our fears and how to get out together from the family. I'm very angry!"

Therapist: "you didn't understand: either you get out together, or one of you will get out and the other has to sacrifices herself!"

Sara: "Than I get out."

Susanna: "What? Do you think that I want to sacrifice myself? I had to work to get out, but Sara can't do this on her own. Maybe we can work together."

Therapist: "Yes! But first of all you must trust one another…Up to now Mom and Dad always make you fighting between you and increasing your jealousy to avoid alliances. If you don't agree one will have to stay home or you both have to stay home."

If you want to overcome this situation where you are both prisoners you must go home and restart the reunion.

This time: talk about your fears and decide how to get out.

But before, tell one another your jealousies but not the once you already know. The secret ones, the ones you never told each other.

In the next session the sisters report a satisfying result; followed by a short stasis; then the siblings sub system starts to work and a differentiation from the parents starts, expressed by a period of fights against the parents themselves.

When this phase of elaboration of jealousy and rancor is over, it's possible to make a structure of the "Mind of Siblings" and continuing as we said before. The trust that they create and the bond of loyalty are what siblings need to have in order to use the sibling's resource.

When this is done, it will work forever but not in a stable way. We noticed that a characteristic of the sibling bond is to work in an alternate manner. When there is no need it stops, even for long periods. But when needed again it starts rapidly and lasts until the need or the problem is resolved.

The therapist function is to be just a catalyzer, but it's hard to think that siblings could work on jealousy and rancor just because this is asked by a "wise" therapist. Before, the therapist should build a strong therapeutic relationship with the siblings as individuals and as a system.

But this is not specific: a good therapeutic relationship is important in every intervention. So, I will not write on this subject here.

Conclusion

Therapeutic work with siblings is still experimental, but the number of cases is increasing every year.

Anyway it's good to say that siblings resource is always useful because it is proved that the migration of the symptom from a sibling to another and the insurgence of new symptoms is reduced in a significant number.

It is also clear that it's important for a patient who wants to build a new presentation of the family reality. The siblings are our "horizontal roots" and keep for us possible alternative readings of our family history even when the "vertical roots" (parents, grandparents, uncles, and aunts) disappear.

There are thus two risks and counterindications:

The first is the risk of starting too quickly the separation of the subsystem of siblings from the entire family when the collaboration and the loyalty is not yet started. In this case, the mistake is shown by the return of the symptom which just disappeared. The remedy is easy: go back to the entire family and check if the symptom disappears again.

The second counterindication is represented by a very deep and long emotional distance between the siblings. To get close again for them sometimes can be very difficult. A special kind of this situation happens with adopted children. If this emotional distance is not rapidly filled, it's better to come back to the family system again or you can risk to lose the family.

The research in this field is very interesting but it's difficult because the families have now very frequently an only child, at least in my country (Italy), mostly, but not only, for economical reasons.

This change in the composition of many families is not only a present problem but also a future losing of important resources for the family system. The disappearing of siblings causes a disappearing of uncles, aunts, and cousins too, which are important resources for the family.

This model of intervention in family therapy can appear as pedagogic and prescriptive modality.

Actually, this intervention should be considered as phases of a more complex therapeutic process, which can be completed later with a deeper work with individuals with a systemic and sometimes psychodynamic approach.

The two clinical examples ended in two different ways. The first through an individual therapy. The second only through the "Mind of Siblings" phase.

References

Ascoli, M. (1988). *Fratelli: Funzione, relazione e crescita normale.* Tesi di Laurea in Psicologia, Università di Roma.

Bank, S. P., & Kahn, M. D. (1982). *The sibling bond.* New York: Basic Books.

Boszormenyi-Nagy, I., & Spark, G. M. (1973). *Invisible loyalties.* New York: Harper and Row.

Bowen, M. (1979). *Dalla famiglia all'individuo.* Roma: Astrolabio.

Bowlby, J. (1969). *Attachment and loss (1, loss).* London: Hoghart Press.

De Bernart, R. (1984). *Anoressia Mentale: La Prospettiva Relazionale.* Bibliografia Famiglia, anno 1, 2, Aprile-Giugno, pp. 1–4.

De Bernart, R. (1989). L'Anoressia come aspetto comunicativo fra fratelli. *Atti del Convegno: "Disturbi del comportamento alimentare"*, 21–25 Giugno, Módena.

De Bernart, R. (1991a). Le Risorse della Gelosia: Appartenenza e Separazione nel Sottosistema Fratelli. Atti del V Incontro degli Operatori dei servizi Pubblici sull'applicazione delle Tecniche Relazionali "Appartenenza e Separazione: Teoria, Psicoterapia". *Etruria Medica, 1*, 99–105.

De Bernart, R. (1991b). Introduzione e presentazione a: Dunn J., Plomin R. "Il Significato delle differenze nell'esperienza dei fratelli all'interno della famiglia". *Terapia Familiare, 37*, 5–7.

Dunn, J. (1986). *Sorelle e Fratelli.* Roma: Armando.

Dunn, J., & Kendrick, C. (1987). *Fratelli.* Bologna: Il Mulino.

Dunn, J., & Plomin, R. (1990). *Separate lives. Why siblings are so different.* New York: Basic Books.

Dunn, J., & Plomin, R. (1991). Why are siblings so different ? The significance of differences in sibling experiences within the family. *Family Process, 30*(3), 271–283.

Kahn, M., & Lewis, K. G. (Eds.). (1998). *Siblings in therapy.* New York: Norton.

Minuchin, S. (1976). *Famiglia e Terapia della Famiglia.* Roma: Astrolabio.

Pecchioli, S. (1987). *L'importanza di essere fratelli.* Tesi di Specializzazione in Psichiatria, Università di Firenze, (su materiali clinici di R. de Bernart).

Scabini, E. (1987). *L'organizzazione Famiglia tra crisi e sviluppo.* Milano: Angeli.

References

[illegible]

What If There Is Another Person in His/ Her Life? Infidelity in Couple Therapy

Annette Kreuz

Introduction

Human couples are complex dual systems in an ever-changing social context. Divorce rates continue to rise in all Western countries, and especially in Europe. Infidelity is the main reason for breakup, ahead of personal incompatibility, heartbreak, and violence. Happy, satisfying, and long-term relationships are rare, with only 5–10% of marriages lasting "till death do us part." It goes without saying that staying in a relationship is as good a predictor of it being a happy one as school attendance is for learning. Research data shows that many relationships continue in spite of an extramarital affair that has been revealed or discovered, even though the experience leads to considerable suffering and conflict. Many couples search for professional help and therapy to breach the gap in confidence and restore mutual trust. We know why couples do not separate, even though their relationship has ceased to be a romantic one of mutual confirmation. In these cases, it is children, money, relatives, and religion that glue people together despite their lack of intimacy. The key question for therapists is whether there is an effective way to overcome infidelity, and how to plan their intervention so that it can be efficient and effective.

Leaving infidelity behind implies the reconstruction of the intimate couple relationship and complete repair of the damage. This is crucial for both members of the couple to be able to invest fully in their intimate relationship. As in every other traumatic life event, it would be much healthier to do preventive work instead of repairing the damage, and there is no doubt that there are ways to strengthen the couple bond and make the relationship a safe place, which is affair-proof and

A. Kreuz (✉)
"Centro Fase 2" for Family and Couples Therapy, Training and Clinical Practice, Valencia, Spain
e-mail: fasedos@ctff-fasedos.com

R. Pereira, J. L. Linares (eds.), *Clinical Interventions in Systemic Couple and Family Therapy*, European Family Therapy Association Series,
https://doi.org/10.1007/978-3-319-78521-9_7

immune to disturbances and intrusions from "third persons." The following pages mainly center on creating the secure functioning of a couple in a primary relationship and present a working model to achieve this therapeutic goal.

What Do We Mean by a "Couple"?

A couple is a dual system formed by two persons that consider each other as belonging to the same generation. We can form couple relationships from adolescence onwards until we die. In our cultural context, the relation starts with mutual attraction and positive regard on a voluntary basis, and both partners commit to make it last. The "partner" is considered to be the closest person in the world, with the highest degree of emotional, psychological, and physical intimacy, as well as communication patterns that include regular sexual contact. Regular sexual contact is what distinguishes the primary attachment partner from a best friend.

It is true that the basic subsystem of a family is more often than not a heterosexual couple, but romantic love as the starting point of the family is a recent achievement and has only existed for around 250 years. The mutual commitment in the couple relationship generally excludes other "equals," and is exclusive. There are some famous examples of "couples" that included three people, for example, Lady Di, Prince Charles, and Camilla Parker Bowles, who ended up becoming the current wife of Britain's future king. Yet the perception of these triadic relationships is that they are wrong and are a prototype of cheating. With the exception of polyamorous people who consider themselves to be non-monogamous with the informed consent of everybody involved, the human couple aspires to be a unique and exclusive twosome.

It is perfectly true that each couple forms an unrepeatable system with unique mutual adjustment patterns in the different aspects of intimacy. Research shows that there is no difference between heterosexual and homosexual couples with regard to most of the patterns of interaction and emotional bonding, leading to psychological, social, and biological intimacy in exactly the same way. This also means that both types of couples struggle with the same problems in terms of the maladaptive patterns of couple interaction.

In this chapter, we shall employ the term "romantic partner" or "intimate partner" in a generic way to refer to both parties in this special, emotional, and loving bond that exists between two people who recognize each other as their primary attachment figure in adult life. We use these terms instead of the more traditional words "spouse," "wife," or "husband."

Similarly, many couples are parents with children of different ages. It is obvious that not all couples have children. In fact, there are even more and more couples who choose not to live together on a permanent basis, yet they consider themselves to be each other's romantic partner. There are also adults who live in remarried families, where they are parents with an ex-spouse, and romantic partners with a new person. All these different ways of bonding do not affect the essence of the relationship: the romantic partner is the primary attachment figure in adult life; he or she confirms the identity of the other partner in their bio-psycho-social aspects.

The Model of Intimacy: Romantic Partners Confirm Each Other's Bio-psycho-social Identity

Most adults still consider that starting and maintaining an intimate, romantic couple relationship is one of their vital projects in adult life. Most people prefer the idea of sharing a lifetime with somebody as opposed to being alone. Today, the search for one's "significant other" employs new methods, including special apps for dating on cell phones or on the Internet. The target population is segmented according to the preferences of those involved, and the programs are user friendly and easy to download. However, a closer analysis reveals that it is only the means that have changed. When it comes to falling in love and bonding with another person as our romantic partner, we do it in a very specific manner: the other person starts to be our primary attachment person, a "job" that instantly transforms him or her into the most vital ingredient in our identity and well-being. Being a couple means synchronizing our lives and is far more than daily routines and chores. Couples in romantic relationships depend on each other to regulate their nervous systems, in much the same way as occurs with the primary attachment figures in the early stages of child development. Romantic partners need each other for excitement and relaxation, and the relationship in itself is (or should be) the secure base in their world. When we (one or both partners) fall in love, the person we fall in love with turns out to be our favorite drug, psychologically and physiologically speaking. The bliss and mystery come from an altered state in our brain chemistry that is transformed into clearly altered states of consciousness, which seem to last for a limited period of time. All these incredible dynamics serve only one purpose: to convert a total stranger into "family," make him or her the closest person on earth and, if possible, the mother or father of our children. The (mutual) sense of belonging and the continuity of the relationship in itself are perceived as vital and inseparable. We want to have these feelings every day for the rest of our lives.

Being the primary attachment figure in adulthood for somebody means confirming the identity of this person in three dimensions: bio-physiological aspects (confirmation and skin-to-skin contact), cognitive confirmation (contact and confirmation on a cognitive or mental level), and social confirmation (contact and confirmation in and by the social context). The main reason to be in a couple relationship is mutual support and confirmation throughout the entire adult life cycle. If one or both partners fail to confirm the other one in one or more of the three dimensions, the couple relationship becomes unstable and its continuity is endangered (Figs. 1 and 2).

Each couple co-creates the complex rules that regulate the distance and proximity between them. The most profound fear we have is to lose our identity, our sense of "self." Our romantic partner confirms our own sense of who we are in the world.

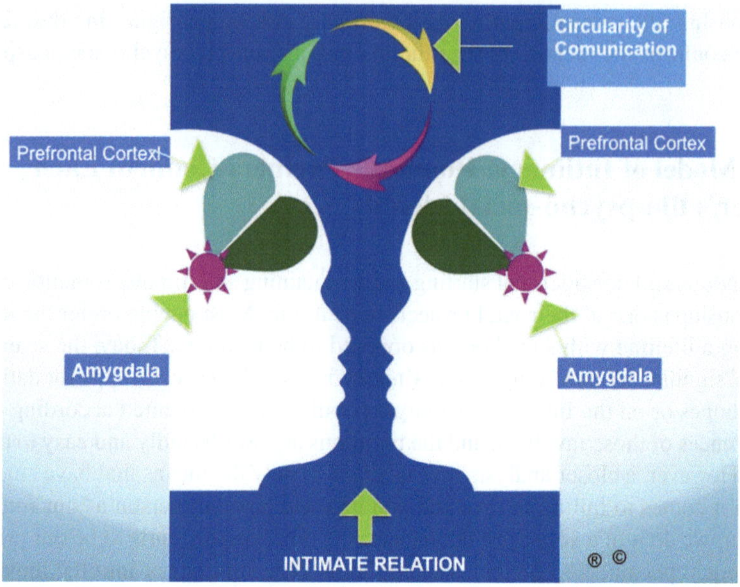

Fig. 1 The intimate couple relationship: the blue vase in the middle represents a harmonious relationship in total synchronicity. Both partners (profiles) are at the perfect distance to look into each other's eyes and read their faces. The multicolor circle symbolizes the constant circularity of all interaction patterns between both partners: all the actions are both an effect and a stimulus of the pattern itself. What seems to be a two-colored heart symbolizes our brain with both its hemispheres, whilst the purple star represents the amygdala, the most important structure in our brains that regulates our emotions. All these components form a complex dual system of interaction that is based on constant feedback processes that modulate a continuous "dance" of proximity and distance of the partners

In the couple, each of us is the "MAGIC MIRROR" of our partner: our loving gaze enables the other to reach his or her best version. The romantic partner is the person who perceives all the potential capacities, but is also the one who protects us from the danger of overstepping our limits. There are two main ways in which the sense of identity in a relationship is lost:

1. There is too much intrusiveness (closeness). The instinctive reaction is to distance ourselves.
2. There is too much distance (separateness). The instinctive reaction is to move closer and even become clingy.

The interpersonal distance that is perceived as being optimum emerges from the biological outfit and personal (especially early childhood) experiences of attachment. In intimate couple relationships, each partner has to be the best advocate of the other: he or she knows exactly who the partner is, where he or she is coming from, what his or her needs are and what motivates him/her. The strengths and flaws

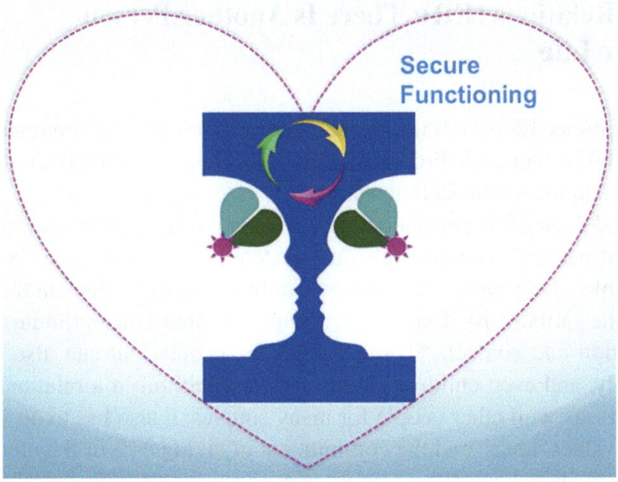

Fig. 2 The secure, functioning couple: both partners are in what we call the "couple bubble," (here heart-shaped) that prevents any other "third party" from getting between them

of one another are familiar, and their projects, wishes, and fears are all well known. The other one is the first person each one goes to when it comes to talking about something important. Successful couples are able to limit and modulate states of activation and relaxation in their interactions. They do so by visual contact, physical contact, speaking and verbal interactions that express recognition, positive regard and appreciation. They avoid getting emotionally overwhelmed, especially in situations of conflict and anger. They are good at coming to an agreement, and especially at agreeing to disagree. They maintain a high level of emotional connection, friendship, and goodwill. They know and take care of the specific and vital needs of their partner, biologically, psychologically, and socially. They repair whatever harm there is to the relationship or to the other person immediately and adequately, and they put the relationship first.

As we mentioned before, the couple relationship has a purpose: it constitutes mutual confirmation throughout the life cycle of each partner, including any changes that may take place. If one or both members fail to confirm the other sufficiently in one of the three biological, psychological, or social dimensions, the relationship becomes unstable and endangered. The necessary and sufficient confirmation has to be conceptualized in the same way as we think of the "good enough" pictures of the human body in child development. It means confirmation of the essential parts. What is essential depends on the developmental stage of the relationship itself and the needs of the persons involved. Yet we must be aware that confirmation is very much like pixels in a photograph: the more the better, better confirmation improves recognition and makes identification easier thanks to the existence of more information.

External Relations (ER): There Is Another Person in His/Her Life

External Relations (ER) or Affairs are an Emotional Solution to Emotional Problems. Their Probability Increases Proportionally to the Lack of Mutual Confirmation in Both Partners in the Stable Relationship.

In our model, an ER is considered to be a special form of what we call "management of third parties." The couple's dual system has to create clear boundaries, a "couple bubble" that protects the dual system from any third element that might get in between the partners. By doing so, the couple maintains the optimum distance for communication and contact. "Thirds" might be people, but can also be work, a hobby, family, and even children. Being true and faithful in a relationship means more than no sex with other people for many couples: it also has to do with loyalty to common values, ideas, and the commitment of taking care of the other. An extra relationship is an indicator that the couple needs "something more" or "less of something" or "something different" in their interactional patterns and/or their life in general. An ER is a problematic way of regulating distance or proximity and covers a need in the relationship. There are ERs that start as a way to regain personal space when there is too much closeness, whilst others begin as the opposite, i.e., there is too much distance bio-psycho-socially. This means that an ER is a symptomatic behavior. Maintaining this behavior is always a sign that something is wrong and has to change in the stable intimate relationship if the couple does not want to head towards failure and separation. External relations based on mutual consent or open relationships are an exception to this because they do not meet the requirements of what is termed infidelity, strictly speaking:

(a) The relationship is with a different person, outside the stable habitual relationship
(b) There is an intense sexual and/or emotional involvement, or a very different kind of relationship
(c) It is socially TOTALLY SECRET, regarding the quality, intensity, and duration

An ER (infidelity) is like an earthquake hitting the "building" of the stable romantic relationship. There are earthquakes with a capital E, and earthquakes with a small e. Whether large or small, each one affects the couple in ways that are impossible to foresee. These effects will have short-, medium-, and long-term impacts. Some ERs are innocuous in the long term (the building in the relationship is earthquake-proof), but others may cause immediate and severe damage to the stability of the couple. This means that they will need instant and skilful help to repair the relationship. A little more than half of all relationships involving infidelity that is found out finally break up and, exactly as occurs in the physical world, it is the replicas that cause the definitive collapse and the most devastating damage. Some ERs help to renovate an obsolete structure of interactional patterns in a relationship, and serve to rebuild the relational building as a safe one, offering protection from "thirds." In this sense, they can benefit couple that previously had deficiencies in the way they confirmed each other biologically, psychologically, or socially. On the majority of occasions, starting and continuing an ER occurs when the stable relationship is experienced as being flawed, empty or painful, and there is considerable anger and resentment towards the partner because of his or her lack of responsiveness to emotional, social and/or sexual demands.

Without any doubt, opportunity not only makes the thief, it also makes the lover. Clinical research seems to agree on the description of occasional infidelity (one-night stands). Generally speaking, when discovered, the involved person is left feeling guilt-ridden and remorseful. Therapeutic management of this single episode as a "mistake" is relatively easy, even though it might be experienced as an earthquake for the relationship. Some of the reasons put forward by people when asked why they gave into temptation or looked for an opportunity, are as follows:

Lack of sexual experience (both or one partner wants to know what it is like with another person)
Simple curiosity (what would it be like with this person?)
Kindness (saying "no" would have been rude)
Luck (an "Angelina Jolie" or "Brad Pitt"-type hits on you with an indecent proposal)
Pity (to help the other person overcome problems)
To upkeep their status (I am still able to hook up with somebody)
Craziness (falling in love)
Longing (missing certain important aspects in the stable relationship)

We agree with Rafael Manrique (1996, p. 333) when he says: "the most important desire we experience is to be the desire of another person." In loving relationships, we aspire to be the object of desire of our partner, and this aspiration aims for completeness and exclusiveness. However, desire others will not stop simply by marriage. Sexual exclusiveness is the closest metaphor for feeling the bliss of being unique for the loved one.

ERs imply many different sensations, emotions, and feelings: excitement, hope, desire, but also fear, pain, guilt, deception, and deceiving. I totally agree with Moultrup (2005), yet would add "in our cultural background," when he says, "There is virtually no way to maintain a healthy stable couple relationship in the long run in spite of the impact of other intimate relations with different people. By definition, an ER provokes a deficit in at least one level of intimacy that will be unhealthy and imply a profound and negative impact on the individuals, the marriage and the children of the family" (p. 17).

ERs as a Result of a Lack of Biological/Sexual Confirmation

Returning to our model, sexual ERs may be a direct consequence of the lack of mutual confirmation in everything related to eroticism, sensuality, and sexuality. Sex is a non-specific, non-verbal language which is very complex and very powerful. And as in all languages, we have to learn and practice its interaction. It is very important to know that complaints about sex account for 60% of the dissatisfaction in bad couple relationships, but only 20% of the happiness in happy couples (Pinsof, 2002).

Psychological intimacy and social confirmation are extremely important, and if they fail, this lack of confirmation leads directly to bad sex. The three dimensions of mutual confirmation form an interdependent system of extreme complexity, with possible effects that might compensate or worsen shortcomings. If we look at the data regarding the use of social media and gender differences, there seems to be a clear and curious bias regarding sexual and psychological intimacy for men and women. For women, psychological intimacy seems to precede erotic sexual encounters, whereas in men, the sequence is often reversed: sexual intimacy comes before psychological closeness. Unfortunately, this initial desynchronization is the reason of infinite power struggles in many couples. If we start communicating, whether erotically or verbally, we have to face one simple fact: to be understood by your partner, you have to speak his or her language.

It is obvious that there are certain moments in the life cycle of the family which entail more problems in synchronizing sexual desire in the couple, regardless of natural differences in sex drive, preferences in the type of contact, and the frequency and intensity of encounters. Whenever there is a loss or mourning process, this affects sexual desire and the probability of ERs increases. Pregnancy, the death of a child or a parent, a midlife crisis, an empty nest, and retirement are all crises that occur as a result of fundamental and structural changes that alter the psychological and physical balance with a possible depressive reaction and the consequent loss of libido.

We also have to mention some of the pathological conditions that alter sexual behavior. Some neurological conditions may lead to the inappropriate expression of sexual behavior, with the loss of decorum or distance and open sexual harassment, for example, in the late stages of alcoholism, or the cerebral deterioration in Pick's disease. In these cases, it is the family that brings the person to therapy because of their lack of insight into his or her behavior. Another specific situation is the manic episodes of bipolar patients, or sex binges as a consequence of cocaine addiction.

Some authors describe compulsive sexual behavior as "sex addiction." Behaving like Don Juan is a form of infidelity. Men are much more likely to behave in this way, and there seem to be transgenerational patterns running through families. A famous case is the Kennedy clan. The sex-addicted person needs to constantly seduce possible new partners and/or use orgasmic discharge as a way to autoregulate anxiety or discomfort. The sexual encounter transitionally satisfies the need for attention and calmness and removes intense emotional states like pain and emptiness. In many cases, these people have a history of parental abandonment and neglect in their early childhood. In their family, sex has been a central theme, either because it has been a totally taboo subject, or because of sexual overstimulation (physically and psychologically) which has been completely out of sync with the developmental situation of the child. This is exactly what we mean by a lack of confirmation of the real needs of a child. The treatment requires individual attention over and above that required by the couple to restore trust in the couple relationship.

ER as the Result of a Lack of Psychological Confirmation

Both men and women in couples start therapy with one clear statement. "You just don't understand me." The sentence is an all-round disqualification and, at times, the excuse for starting an ER. A lack of empathy is at the base of many estranged and distant couples and their desynchronization. Of course, all couples have to face conflict. Gottman, in his research (2015) shows that only 40% of all conflicts in couples are resolved, whilst the rest stay as they are, or disperse over time. The classical models of couple therapy are conflict based and use conflict resolution strategies and language as one of the main therapeutic tools to relieve distress. Validation and appreciation as part of the psychological confirmation, active listening, negotiation, and conflict resolution are important and valuable tools. Understanding the internal world of the partner (mentalization) include being able to represent the relationship as it is in the eyes of the romantic partner, understanding what he or she likes and dislikes or misses. It is crucial to differentiate between adequate conflict resolution and an appropriate expression of upset, distress, or anger as part of open conflict. If the expression of anger and open conflict strategies are dysfunctional, the conflicts will never end. The resulting lack of bio-psycho-social confirmation will put both partners at risk in terms of starting an ER.

Long-term couples that present a clear deficit in the expression of anger and conflict are named "conflict avoiders." They deny their differences and try to be too nice to each other. The result of these dysfunctional interaction patterns are superficial relationships. There is an accumulation of resentment and dissatisfaction. ERs are a means to create the necessary closeness in a different intimate relationship, as the ongoing unresolved conflicts in the stable couple make adequate sexual and psychological intimacy impossible. When the ER is discovered or disclosed, it constitutes a big wake-up call by the actively involved partner towards the other one. ERs in conflict-avoidant couples are usually short lived and come with lots of guilt. They have a good prognosis in therapy terms.

The second type of couples is "intimacy-avoidant couples." They behave exactly in the opposite way with no control over their expressions of anger and conflict. Their fights are ferocious and symmetrical in ongoing accusations and attacks. The problem for these couples is that they need to take the risk of expressing their most vulnerable and loving sides. Unfortunately, the intense fighting builds up vicious cycles of interaction with an unhealthy form of confirmation, at the expense of real, positive, psychological, and social confirmation. If make-up sex is added to this explosive cocktail, this ends up as the full desperate picture of intense relational suffering. As a result of the constant hurt and deception, these couples often indulge in ERs on both sides, with mutual suspicions, or affairs that are known but not admitted. Couple therapy is sought because of the verbal and sometimes physical abuse during conflicts. Therapists are able to help with positive results by pushing partners beyond anger and making them open up to each other to express their real needs and longings. This disclosure of vulnerability is necessary for a healthy life together and for mutual bio-psycho-social confirmation.

External relations modify the complex fluctuating balance at the core of a relationship, which has often been unconsciously established at the very beginning. We have already mentioned several times in this article that ERs modulate interpersonal distance. ERs radically change the power structure of the couple; there is a "before," "during," and "after." A positive stable romantic relationship should be the closest, most intimate scenario for both of the partners, i.e., the secure base in the couple bubble, as we said before. As soon as one of the partners gets involved in an ER, the distance from his or her stable romantic partner increases. At the same time, greater proximity with the lover is generated. There are situations in which lover and stable partner might switch places totally regarding sexual, psychological, or social confirmation.

Therapeutic intervention aims to improve the stable romantic relationship and therefore, initially has to focus on the lack of mutual confirmation, highlighting the deficits. Considerable work has always been done around interpersonal conflict and mutual understanding. Our model broadens the techniques for the therapist through "bottom-up" interventions. This is especially important because in high-conflict couples, given their high level of arousal, "top-down methods" simply do not work. In a hostile and aggressive environment, people get easily out of their "window of tolerance" for social interaction. This means they lose the ability to stay in the range of social contact and their thinking and speaking becomes compromised. We are only able to think and talk lucidly and coherently when we do not feel threatened as a person or in the relationship. In the presence of an ER (disclosed or discovered) with all the pain and suffering, eye-to-eye contact is often a mine field for dysregulation in one or both partners. Subcortical functioning takes over with fight-flight and freeze responses. In its psychobiological part, our model works with self-regulation and mutual regulation to rebuild the secure base for talking and negotiating appropriately (Tatkin, 2011, 2013; Tatkin et al., 2014).

ER due to the Lack of Social Confirmation

Healthy couples confirm each other socially and confirm their relation socially. The couple is identified as such in the social context, which nowadays often includes modern social media. This is especially true in the respective families of both partners, in their former families in remarried couples, with friends, in the workplace, with parents of their children's friends, etc. Modern life with migration includes different aspects of social isolation, with long distances to parents and siblings, lack of leisure time activities that promote social contact, and professional secrecy. All in all, this makes social confirmation of the couple difficult. Facebook can be a perfect antidote. Every society has its myths about what is possible or not in stable long-term relationships and, of course, there are all kinds of myths about affairs. In Western society, there is little hope of enjoying a romantic and passionate long-term relationship, and often putting the couple relationship first is perceived as being potentially detrimental to the parenting of the children. We would like to point out that, in our view, the secure well-functioning couple is the basis of the emotional climate in the household, and is the best investment a couple who are also parents can make for their children. Scheinkman (2005), Perel (2017) and other authors consider that the enormous increase of ERs has to do with the mythical expectations that people place in marriage or long-term committed relationships. Others blame the consumer society, with its maximum expression in consumer sex (sex tourism) and the idea of utility, exchangeability and use, and throw away extended to the partner. Modern relations are "liquid" (Bauman, 2005). Social confirmation that is deficient face-to-face may become even more complex with modern social media and virtual realities that are constantly present and demand attention. It is by no means a surprise to find that episodes of ERs with porn (men) and chats (women) are at the top of discovered affairs.

Steps for Intervention: Some Considerations

Discovering that your partner is having an ER, or being told by your partner that he has been involved in an ER, is always traumatic for the betrayed party. It is considered to be an emotional shock with a catastrophic impact. The degree of damage will be related to the depth and extension to which the betrayed partner felt involved and confirmed in the relationship before finding out about the affair. The worst experiences of infidelity are therefore situations where more than one area of confirmation is involved. In clinical practice, the most devastating effects relate to couples where one considers the other person to be his or her "soul mate." These couples have a high amount of psychological intimacy and companionship with social confirmation.

Losing a primary attachment figure can trigger what is called anaclitic depression or broken heart syndrome. In its extreme form, this is known as Takotsubo or miocardic stress syndrome. A romantic breakup may cause this syndrome, and it is a very real form of having one's heart broken. The person that has been involved in the ER has to be aware of the fact that his or her partner has to overcome a trauma, and that the recovery process will need time, and most of all, repair. Even when there has been an emotional divorce before finding out about the affair, (the partner had already lost the primary connection), the effects of the ER are traumatic, even though to a lesser extent.

In his book "Private Lies," Pittman (2003) describes the normal process in a relationship after an affair has been discovered. We consider this process highly probable:

1. Betrayal (one or both partners have an ER)
2. The battle (has there or has there not been an ER and who is to blame)
3. Defense: it was not my fault
4. Incongruence: emotional desynchronization between the actively involved partner and the betrayed party

5. Awakening of the betrayed partner
6. Human sacrifice (normally the third person falls by the wayside)
7. The return of the cheater (with or without the proposal to include the third person)
8. Mourning of the lost relationship

Reversing the process for mutual bio-psycho-social confirmation of the couple needs courage and special skills on the part of the therapist. The therapist can act as a catalyst for positive processes of social, mutual, and self-regulation, and (re)establish the profound attachment of the couple in favorable conditions.

Couple therapists divide themselves into two categories: those who believe that it is possible to work with an ongoing ER (disclosed or secret) and those who do not. The majority of therapists will insist that the affair stops at the start of the therapy and ask the involved party to totally break off the relationship with the third person(s). Even though this might be the best solution, it is often also very true that people simply cannot or will not do it and they therefore lie. This introduces considerable additional complexity into the system and requires extreme sensitivity and comprehension on the therapist's part. We consider that the therapeutic situation mirrors the multiverse of the people involved, where lies and secrets are the possible reasons for interactional patterns. The question is how to repair the damage caused by these behaviors (including damage to the therapeutic relationship).

Personally, I prefer to work without secrets as it is much easier, and I try to set the ground for this in the initial interviews. Nevertheless, there are exceptions, with special contexts. In particular, there are three specific situations to consider. The first one implies probable violent reactions of the partner, physical, and/or emotional reactions, and the abusive use of information against other people (lover, children, dependent parents, etc.). When facing a possible violent reaction, individual assessment is a must in the initial phase of the treatment, as are psychometric diagnostics where indicated, and a full history of psycho-medical data to assess risk factors like alcoholism, drug abuse, and the possession of weapons. Jealousy is still, after all, the second most frequent reason for homicides, and impending or recent separation may trigger suicide (attempts). In the case of extreme violence (self-inflicted or against another person), there is often excessive rumination regarding the ER (not only in the initial phase, where this is normal) together with other factors like emotional fragility, impulsiveness, a history of abandonment and substance abuse.

The second exception has to do with what is called an "out-of-the-door affair." The person involved in the ER is totally sure about wanting to leave the stable relationship. In this case, the therapeutic task is to actively help in the separation. Forcing the partner to disclose the ER may imply them quitting the therapy and may deviate energy and attention from its main focus.

The third type of exceptions are situations that we call "request for absolution." In these cases, there has often been a casual, unplanned, short sexual contact that may have even happened years ago. The couple has a crisis for a different reason (e.g., the death of a child, serious illness) and the actively involved partner expresses an urge to "tell the truth" to redeem his/her strong feelings of guilt. Often, there is a hidden agenda of latent aggressiveness that can be detected in the ER itself and in the fact that the disclosure is late and occurs in a crisis situation. A therapeutic contract would focus first on the main problem and dedicate time and work to crisis management and conflict resolution. A possible disclosure would be discussed optionally at the final stage of therapy.

Working through the complex personal and relational issues that arise when there is an ER needs time. The phase of intimacy (Kreuz & Gammer, 1989) is supposed to last between 15 and 40 sessions in general, with or without "thirds" and triangles. Other therapists speak about 2 years of treatment to overcome the crisis and regain confidence in the relationship. Being able to trust your partner needs lots of repair and confirmation on a day-to-day basis, not only in therapy sessions. The new balance regarding the "give and take" in the relationship usually implies a considerable dosage of confrontation for both partners. Giving and receiving forgiveness, which is totally necessary to overcome an ER, needs many previous steps.

When a secret ER is revealed, the therapist needs to help the couple fill out a general agenda that might be as follows:

1. Speak about the main details of the ER.

   Since when, and until when?
   With whom?
   Is the affair ongoing or is there any contact?
   Who knows about it?
   Was there any sexual contact at home?
   How was it discovered?

2. Leave space and time for the betrayed partner to express their feelings, especially anger, disappointment and drifting apart, and help the involved partner deal with it.
3. Other secrets and misbehavior, (i.e., secret individual therapy sessions, money issues)
4. Redefining the ER as an emotional solution to an emotional problem arising from the lack of confirmation.

The reframing of the couples' problems make it clear that speaking about the affair is the first step to repair and getting back into a healthy relationship. If both partners decide to continue, the re-establishment of the secure base without the threat of "thirds" is of vital importance. Mutual confirmation in the initial phase of treatment implies exploring "what happened" and "what might happen now and in the future," inside and outside the therapy sessions. Staying together is the result, not the previous requirement, in the form of commitment. Yet, most of all, the therapeutic effort consists of putting the stable romantic relationship first, with all the characteristics we mentioned before. This also means removing the ER from the limelight as soon as possible. Completely stopping the ER and forgiveness are part of the process of mutual bio-psycho-social confirmation in the couple.

In some cases, individual therapy and couple sessions can be combined. There are different kinds of rituals and active techniques like temporary separation, dating the partner again, and packages of behavioral interventions that have proven to help rebuild positive regard and conflict resolution. But one thing should be made clear: none of these techniques alone will promote tangible changes in the relationship unless there is a real improvement in the quality and quantity of intimacy and a decrease of resentment and hurt.

Conclusions

Working with infidelity is the most difficult area of therapy and is the most complex for the therapist, with the exception of degenerative and/or terminal illnesses in a partner (Weiner Davis, 2017). The therapist needs special skills to manage uncertainty and the high dosage of emotions that can and have to be part of the sessions. Probably, here more than in any other situation, the professional's own capacity to self regulate and stay in his or her own window of tolerance is crucial. A therapist who is afraid cannot help because his/her own brain will not be capable of using language, good communication tools, and appropriate decision-making to choose the right interventions at any specific point in time. "Couples therapists are like midwives: the result of an intervention may be the death or the (re)birth of the couple relationship. There may be no other decision as important as the decision to separate. There are always reasons to separate. The question is if we can find and co-create the conditions that make staying in the relationship worthwhile." (Doherty, 2011)

References

Bauman, Z. (2005). *Amor líquido: Acerca de la fragilidad de los vínculos humanos*. Buenos Aires: Fondo de Cultura Económica.

Doherty, W. (2011). *In or out? Treating the mixed-agenda couple*. Psychotherapy Networker. Recuperado de https://www.psychotherapynetworker.org/magazine/article/315/in-or-out.

Gottman, J. M. (2015). *10 principles for doing effective couples therapy*. New York: Norton.

Kreuz, A., & Gammer, C. (1989). *La Terapia Familiar Fásica: Un modelo flexible de intervención*. Informació Psicológica, Collegio Oficial de Psicólogos de País Valenciá. No. 40. pp. 54–60.

Manrique, R. (1996). *Sexo, erotismo y amor*. Madrid: Ed. Libertarias.

Moultrup, D. J. (2005). *Husbands, wives and lovers: The emotional system of the extramarital affair*. Nueva York: Guilford Press.

Perel, E. (2017). *The state of affairs: Rethinking infidelity*. New York: Harper Collins.

Pinsof, W. M. (2002). The death of "till death do us part": The transformation of pair-bonding in the 20th century. *Family Process, 41*, 35–157.

Pittman, F. (2003). *Mentiras privadas*. Bacelona: Amorrortu.

Scheinkman, M. (2005). Beyond the trauma of betrayal: Reconsidering affairs in couples therapy. *Family Process, 44*(2), 227–244.

Tatkin, S. (2011). *Love and war in intimate relationships: Connection, disconnection, and mutual regulation in couple therapy*. Nueva York: Norton.
Tatkin, S. (2013). *Wired for love. How understanding your partner's brain and attachment style can help you defuse conflict and build a secure relationship*. Oakland: New Harbinger.
Tatkin, S., Adurman, E., & Kreuz, A. (2014). *Clinical application of attachment theory in PACT couple therapy*. Mesa redonda en el XXI IFTA Congress. Panamá.
Weiner Davis, M. (2017). *Affair repair*. Psychotherapy Networker. Recuperado de https://www.psychotherapynetworker.org/magazine/article/1078/affair-repair.

Additional Bibliography

Allen, E. S., & Baucom, D. H. (2004). Adult attachment and patterns of extradyadic involvement. *Family Process, 43*(4), 467–488.
Baucom, D. H., Whisman, M. A., & Paprocki, C. (2012). Couple-based interventions for psychopathology. *Journal of Family Therapy, 34*, 250–270.
Brown, E. M. (1991). *Patterns of infidelity and their treatment*. Nueva York: Brunner & Mazel.
Burbach, F., & Reibstein, J. (2012). Focusing on couple therapy: Going forward. *Journal of Family Therapy, 34*(3), 225–228.
Special issue: Couple therapy. (2013). *Family Process 52*(1): 1–153.
Kipnis, L. (2003). *Against love: A polemic*. Nueva York: Pantheon Books.
Kreuz, A. (2006). La infidelidad en la pareja. En J. Navarro y J. Pereira (Comp.) *Parejas en situaciones especiales*. Barcelona: Paidós (edición revisada).
Kreuz, A. (en Prensa). *Mal de amores. Duelo y transiciones vitales*. IV Simposium del Observatorio del Duelo, Asociación Victor Frankl, Valencia, Noviembre, 2016.
Kreuz, A. (2018). Cap. 6: Terapia Sistémica con Parejas. En Moreno, F. A. (Comp.) *Manual de Terapia familiar (Vol. 2)*. Bilbao: Desclee de Brouwer.
Linares, J. L. (2010). Paseo del amor y el odio: La conyugalidad desde la perspectiva evolutiva. *Redes, 23*, 11–22.
Manrique, R. (2011). *Conyugal y extraconyugal: nuevas geografías amorosas*. Madrid: Fundamentos.
Marrone, M. (2016). *Sexualidad. La tuya, la mía y la de los demás*. Madrid: Psimática.
Nelson, T. (2013). *Case study, women who cheat: Understanding the message of the affair*. Psychotherapy Networker. Recuperado de https://www.psychotherapynetworker.org/magazine/article/183/case-study.
Pereira, R. (2014). Aida o las parejas en conflicto crónico. En: J. L. Linares & P. G. Semboloni (Eds.), *La familia en la ópera: Metáforas liricas para problemas relacionales*. Barcelona: Gedisa.
Pinto, B. (2005). *Colisión, Colusión, Complementariedad en las relaciones conyugales*. Universidad Católica Boliviana.
Sánchez-Benitez, J. C. (2008). Aplicaciones de la teoría del apego a la terapia sistémica de pareja. *Redes, 20*, 111–121.
Sandberg, J. G., Busby, D. M., Johnson, S. M., & Yoshida, K. (2012). The brief accessibility, responsiveness, and engagement (BARE) scale: A tool for measuring attachment behavior in couple relationships. *Family Process, 51*(4), 512–526.
Willi, J. (2008). *Psicología del amor. El crecimiento personal en la pareja*. Barcelona: Herder.

Love, Sexuality, and Aging: Reflections from Couple Therapy

Ana Maria Gomes

The Time to Be

Concepts on Aging

> *There is no better age to experience joy and happiness, good humour and love, to do the things we want to do and to start all over again…*
>
> *The best solution I can find is to call older age the best age… thanks to its grown ideas, perspectives, experiences, and outlooks on life…*
>
> *I do not accept age as an excuse, for I believe no age is better than our actual age.*

Within the lost balance between those who are born, those who die, and those who grow old, there is a tripartite triangle of factors almost all over the world, where both births and child mortality have decreased, whereas the average lifespan has increased alongside a better quality of life during the aging process.

Our duty is to **(re)write the history of the Human Life Cycle**, adding value which was lost to its last stage, which will then originate deep mind-set, relationship, and institutional changes. There is a crucial need to promote a holistic/systemic vision of the aging process and conclude that this phenomenon affects everyone and every aspect of the social life.

The aging period should guide us not only towards the inclusive right, which rejects segregation due to age, gender, abilities, and disabilities, but also towards the right of knowledge and personal recognition, regarding the uniqueness of each person's journey, history, and project. Every person ages differently. The aging process is highly customised, and thus presents significant differences in the way people grow old and their resulting personal performance in both physical and mental activities. It is also known that older age is not necessarily followed by dependence

A. M. Gomes (✉)
Sociedad Portuguesa de Terapia Familiar, Lisbon, Portugal

R. Pereira, J. L. Linares (eds.), *Clinical Interventions in Systemic Couple and Family Therapy*, European Family Therapy Association Series,
https://doi.org/10.1007/978-3-319-78521-9_8

and illnesses since a lot of people in their 70s, 80s, or older can still be more active and display a better performance than those in their 40s, 50s, or 60s.

If none of us grows old in the same way, we must acknowledge that besides physical and genetic personal characteristics, it is necessary to take background matters into account—where, with whom, when, and what we have lived. A wide variety of individualities and life paths arises from this process. There is a fine line between generalisation and discrimination.

No Stage of the Life Cycle Is a Paradise, and Old Age Is Not a Living Hell

In fact, there still is a negative social image of old age associated with negative stereotypes, connecting it to sickness, immobility, dependency, and disability. Popular consciousness is built around the young-elderly polarity, where youngsters are associated with positive concepts, and the elderly with negative concepts. We must go beyond these stereotypes and rethink the image of senior citizens.

Once the aging process is accepted as a heterogeneous, natural process and event, it becomes effortless to seek the skills, experiences, and human resources provided by elderly groups. In order for that to become a reality, it is still necessary to change the current mind-sets. There are two main concepts to keep in mind:

- **The heterogeneity of aging**
- Psychological aging does not display the same patterns as biological aging. Indeed, the differences between individuals are tremendous, for some life paths are more damaging to autonomy and independence than others.
- **The ability to deal with the aging process**.
- Having a sense of life, strong bonds with other people, a positive self-concept, and an active participation in the achievement of goals.

Regardless of the chosen therapeutic or educational intervention, it must be perceived as a tool that fosters a true and complete assessment of the person's condition, a co-construction of positive emotionally and relationally focused strategies that promote a friendship- and intimacy-oriented culture in close social spheres, as well as inclusion and social participation as a fundamental act of citizenship and healthy lifestyles.

One of the goals is to emphasise the importance of qualifying and empowering people so that they become able to make decisions on their own life and the life of the community, and therefore go from simple recipients of these politics to active participants in their definition, development, and assessment. It should also be emphasised that performing a large number of social or interpersonal roles is significantly correlated with the high level of adaptation and life fulfilment that the old person experiences. The preservation or discovery of new kinds of relationships within family, work, and social roles increases life fulfilment.

We know that elderly people are becoming healthier, older, more educated, certainly more participative in all domains of society—including broader politics—and of course, more demanding. Old age will increasingly represent a time of development of both individual and group projects.

> *... a reporter interviewed a 100 year-old woman and asked her what she had done with her life in general. The lady immediately replied: "I cannot tell you yet, since I am still building my life!"*

The image that elderly people portray depends on the ideas and actions that society has of them. Everyone should be involved in bringing down current prejudices and discriminative behaviour, while valuing, promoting, and dignifying this time in life. We must be concerned with finding more about the impact of aging in different social structures, without forgetting the strong discontinuities and inequalities, which should stop us from generalising and defining false classifications, while also establishing endless respect for the singularity of the different personal and family backgrounds.

> *"Old age is like climbing a mountain. You climb from ledge to ledge. The higher you get, the more tired and breathless you become, but your views become more extensive".* (Ingmar Bergman)

Changes Within Family Context

> *"We make a living by what we get. We make a life by what we give".* (Duane Hulse)

In a brief glance on the evolution of family throughout history, we realise its numerous changes. It is not only the family structure that presents new facets and raises new questions, but also the functional and communication aspects. We are before a new resizing of the relationships and expectations regarding the roles of each element, their place in the relationships and in the family itself within society in general. Longevity is one of the factors that significantly influence changes in family organisation and dynamics.

Time in life is changing. Having more time brings another sense to the life journey of people and their families.

At the beginning of the last century, when the average life expectancy was 45 years, a child would lose their father or mother at the average age of 14. Families with three generations were rare. Certainly, old and very old people have always existed, but they were a minority. We move from a "horizontal family" with successive generations, to a "vertical family" where generations coexist. Nowadays, we may even encounter families with five generations. Hence, a variety of family scenarios and interactions arises, which makes the reading and comprehension of the Family Life Cycle more complex and enriching. As basis, I am using some examples of family realities which are becoming increasingly present in our daily life.

> "Active parents in their jobs, which demand a growing efficiency and updated participation, feel the responsibility of helping their children during the increasing number of school years, in the lack of jobs available, throughout the never-ending relationships. On the other hand they take care of their own parents and grandparents who are often in a sickness and/or dependency condition".

> "Grandparents, who are often retired, provide support to the entire family, helping on the one hand their children who have reached the age of 40 and face difficulties, namely unemployment, as well as providing support to their grandchildren, whether they are children or teenagers…"

There was a significant increase in the number of parents/grandparents living in their adult children's home, as well as the number of adult children who are returning with their families to their parents/grandparents' home.

Of course, the reality of the economic and social crisis also leaves its mark. The high cost of houses, the low incomes, the precarious jobs, the unemployment, and the emigration are social forces behind this trend. Likewise, the increase in the number of divorces leads to a greater recourse to families of origin, as a support in times of crisis and in periods of emotional relationship rearrangements of younger generations. These circumstances are more common within urban and suburban context, but it should be highlighted the very significant number of older people living in complete loneliness and isolation in rural areas of the province, where support resources for this stage of life are more limited.

This leads to a scenario where the generation in their mid-60s is requested to become a family support for younger generations and to respond to the need for care of the elderly in the family. If in the recent past, a person would live an average of 10 years after leaving the labour market, nowadays, we live, in general, 20 or 30 more years in good physical and psychological conditions.

Enough Time to Live a New Life

These families who are now experiencing this "new" extension of their Life Cycle, which was something rare and unpredictable up until now, are sharing concerns leading us to new approaches. How can we ensure a dynamic, healthy, comfortable, and respectful environment between generations who will inevitably coexist, with their relationship, cultural and social specificities, without neglecting the particularities, differences, autonomy, and privacy of each person and each subsystem?

The synchronic diversity of roles and status is a great challenge faced by current and future families, wherefore they carry once again, the reciprocity of the relation. Older persons of the modern world are the first generation experiencing an extended life, defined by the coexistence of numerous identities, who can simultaneously be son, grandson, father, grandfather, providing help/support to others and also be helped/supported by others.

The circumstances of taking care/being taken care of have positive aspects, such as the feeling of reciprocity, accomplishment, and of personal growth, but they also have negative aspects related to living with the burden since taking care of others may become exhausting. In a systemic point of view, any intervention must consider this multitude of factors, and, for that reason, a realistic vision of the current social context is inevitable.

Love After Youth

Some say that love in old age is "Silver Love" and that sexuality is an exceptional experience for the more daring ones. Such beliefs are a thing of the past, when this stage of the life cycle was considered to be short in time and was mainly characterised by the preparation to leave this world.

Which is not surprising, since these persons initiated their sexual socialisation 40 or 50 decades ago, in times of great sexual repression. But the changes appear to be irreversible. Today, we live more years, but many concepts supporting the understanding of those times, have not evolved.

We are, therefore, before more or less extreme versions, with a shared idea that it is not possible to return to the Golden Age. Some believe that love in old age is full of advantages because the ultimately wise souls know what they want and what they have to offer. Others keep the idea that nothing new can happen and that stability in the interaction of the couple is the possible or more evident indicator, as all that remains for old people is dedicating themselves to take care of their children and grandchildren.

The more intellectual conversations or approaches on these subjects always seem to bear some surprise! As if it was a new, unknown territory, where there are doubts regarding the value of the land, its extension and the possibilities and potential of its inhabitants, leaving questions as to whether or not to explore and invest!!

Even young people remain puzzled and clumsy when the subject is the love and sexuality of old people. It almost seems as though it is not supposed to happen. This epidemic idea remains as a reference in many social contexts, such as in retirement homes where the members of the couple are separated and live apart and where love experiences amongst residents is forbidden.

Negative social beliefs and attitudes prevail in the social culture and standards of the twenty-first century. We may underline that the social vision is one of the main obstacles to romance between the elderly. The great monster of social vision persists, i.e. what other people say, what other people think, and this fear of social scrutiny inhibits, prevents, imprisons, and deprives older people from taking steps towards freely living the sexuality and love to which they are entitled.

The main talks of our society on aging are negative and stigmatising. Some examples of such negative talks are on aging as a series of losses, as an experience of suffering to be avoided, as a social or economic problem. Being a therapist is to be committed to breaking outdated paradigms, to go beyond this common sense but without neglecting it, and to question the strengthening of new myths standing out from old myths, all of them feeding on the stereotype of nice and wise old people, or old people who have no use, do not produce and have no place in society. I must stress what I have learned deconstructing preconceived ideas, in the experience of therapeutic relationships with couples in their mid-60s and older.

They also carry a world of uncertainty and hesitation. Is it too late, does it still make sense or is it appropriate, won't it look ridiculous…they identify themselves in a mixture of shame, fear, and courage, which they consider to be necessary in order to decide to share their feelings and their intimacy. And, with the increasing age, the idea that it is not the time of their "rights" becomes more and more present.

Love in old age goes beyond the body and biological age, becoming a story that gathers culture and history, and integrating, above all, a new family. Common sense tells us that young people should take the time to meet new people, to date, while older people should take care of their grandchildren and dedicate themselves to their children, to knit or watch television…

Back in the days of our grandparents, falling in love after the age of 50 was uncommon. We know that late love can be beneficial and can even cause as much stir as in teenage years. Although it carries the background of a lifetime, be it romance or life experiences, love in **old age** can have as much ups and downs as in other stages of life.

Old people have more time to love. They are more experienced in many matters and have learned a lot about the body and emotions of their partners. The success of couples in old age is related to intimacy, companionship, and the ability to express true feelings to their partners, in a safe and reciprocal atmosphere. Maintaining the sexual activity in old age is related to intimacy, and it is very unlikely to have one without the other. Perhaps, rediscovering the first forms of love of the human being, where tenderness, physical contact, corporal expression and using the senses reach their deepest growth, comes with age when the personality attains its last development stages.

In general, relationships between older persons provide a kind of encounter with one's inner self, both emotionally and bodily, bringing a new sense to life. The most curious thing about love in old age is that it comes without warning. Many life stories are marked by emotional failures, resulting in the conformism that loving is pain… the extent of risk increased inhibition and disbelief.

Clinical practice shows us that there is a growing number of persons who take commitments, take risks and desire to date, to find an old or a new love, to remarry, to make new friendships, and to have a vibrant social life. Love at first sight, sexual discoveries, and revival of love connections are common situations amongst old people who increasingly chose not to be alone.

Nowadays, relationships between older people and younger people are common. The idea that older people can have sexual intercourse with younger people is not very culturally accepted, and it is preferred to ignore and vanish the sexuality of the older person from the collective imagination.

It is considered more normal when older men have relationships with much younger women, but now we often see affective or sexual relationships between older women and much younger men. We can say as conclusion that the intensity of love and sexuality of older people is not different from that of younger people. Despite the prejudice and taboos, it is necessary to face these challenges with the maturity that comes with age.

Actually, love in old age is the same and as intense as love in young age, but is just lived with more experience. Youth is in the mind, in the will to live, in the intensity and authenticity of feelings and desires.

"It is life, more than death, that has no limits".
Gabriel Garcia Marquez "Love in the Time of Cholera"

Erotic Limitations

"Old age… man and woman, whose love, just like wine, has gained quality over the years, have also received from life what it has to offer in all its intensity, delightfulness, and intoxication". (Auclair)

There are no time limits for the ability to love and enjoy sexual life, for it does not depend on the biological age and represents an important part of the human existence in every life stage.

Old age is hardly ever associated with any form of eroticism, due to the contrast with the current aesthetic model associated with youth. The media, advertisement, and beauty standards depict society and overvalue youth, perfect bodies, and physical attraction as essential requirements for happiness. Either elderly people submit themselves to artificial treatments in order to dimly recover their youth, engaging almost exclusively in the search for a utopic fountain of youth, or when this does not happen, they feel exposed, unhappy, and flawed. They assume that they are not physically attractive, lose all interest in the possibility of wooing or being wooed, and are incapable of having any sexual stimulation. These stereotypes persist and are widely spread.

However, if society's prejudiced behaviours depict any area of the life of elderly people, the most evident one is definitely sexuality. Old people are seen as asexual or incapacitated for sex, while anyone who displays any kind of erotic interest might be considered perverted.

Sexual behaviour is determined by beliefs and morals regarding education, culture, and religion, that deeply influence the way a person lives and deals with their sexuality during their whole life. The current older generation is the result of a very strict and repressive education. Indeed, their parents also mirrored this culture which favoured an impoverished sexual life due to strict morals and excessive prejudices, inherited from another generation even more repressive that considered the practice of one's sexuality as something dangerous, filthy, and sinful.

The real limitation of eroticism and sexuality in old age is in the psychological field, in prejudice, and in social intolerance. Placing respectfulness as a moral obligation requires seniors to have less opportunities of enjoyment, since it is expected that they will control their urges even more than other age groups.

We know that aging often decreases vitality, strength, exuberance of the body, and reflexes, but not enough to silence and leave out sexual desires. These desires change, but do not disappear. Like most things in life, older age comes with further experience and wisdom, and there is no reason why older people cannot have a fulfilling love and pleasurable life.

The elder person will start to believe they are unable to love and will behave according to expectations, for they fear that they will be considered degenerated, libidinous, or indecent if they act otherwise. And if this is true for elders of the male gender, it is even more so for elderly women. This situation may influence the person's behaviour, resulting in disinterest and decrease of sexual activity and, consequently, in sexual frustration.

Thus, the stereotyped image of aging without sex, sensation, or desire is also the narrative learned and supported by many old people as well. It is our duty to change the idea that turning 60 something years-old is a big deal and take down the myth of asexual aging. Contrary to popular belief, old age can also bring freedom and great joy, as long as the body is cared for.

The possibility of sexual pleasure does not end with age. Relationships between persons of older age usually fosters a type of self-discovery, both emotionally and physically. Love and erotic practices in old age represent a positive attitude associated with a feeling of engagement with life. It is worth highlighting that the continuity of sexual activity in old age is closely linked with intimacy, and it is unlikely that one will happen without the other.

Health problems may be an obstacle to a complete sexual experience, but they do not stop nor prevent anyone from searching for alternative ways of showing affection and living each person's sexual intimacy. Body control faced with diseases and aligned with the perception of this body as pathological results without a doubt in a loss of eroticism. It is fair to say that sexuality has also varied due to the lifespan. The elderly had to adapt their sexuality, renouncing disappointing and discouraging Victorian taboos, taking care of their bodies in order to be more seductive and worrying more about being attractive in the sensual world. They learn to be creative in their social attempts to beat boredom and, above all, they try to establish respect for individuality moments. These are the couples that put all these playful patterns in sexuality, overcoming the obstacles that biology establishes. In the end, the sexuality domain incorporates many of the dynamics developed in daily relationship games.

I believe one of the biggest challenges may be the erotic investment in the relation. Taking care of the couple's eroticism greatly depends on how this eroticism was carried out throughout their life. It is an act of will, an investment of intelligence and desire. It involves knowing the other person, and meeting their needs, relying on a series of elements and components such as surprise, innovation, imagination, fantasy, expression, playfulness, amongst other aspects. Opening up the erotic treasure chest and putting everything that it gives you to use. Share with one another, create and recreate.

The loss concerning sexual performance requires the reinvention of eroticism, which is what fuels the desire, in a search for new pleasurable practices. That is the erotic intimacy associated with maturity and the advantages of experience. The regularity of the sexual activity will lead to better quality and to exploring new ways of contact, including petting, to touch and be touched, intimacy, a sense of cosiness, affection, and love. The notion of quantity must and should be replaced with a notion of "quality".

Besides physical fulfilment, sex in old age can also play a role in reaffirming the identity of each partner, showing that each person can be valuable to another. My experience indicates that a faulty understanding of sexuality in old age can lead to unnecessary difficulties in overcoming doubts or problems that may arise, and that clarifying this widely spread distorted information regarding sexuality may contribute to the decrease of beliefs and taboos in this prejudiced topic. The majority of the times, sexual dysfunction or sex avoidance derives from pessimism and anxiety arising from such faulty information.

We must question these distorted beliefs and even taboos regarding sexual practice, replacing them with realistic and unprejudiced information. It is exactly in the mature age that we can reassess our own concepts and values, taking on new paths. Beyond the relationship play that is developed by old couples within their different alternatives, it is even more important **to keep the affectionate engine going**. Love is perceived in very distinct ways throughout the different evolutionary cycles of each human being. Youth, adulthood, old age, and very old age groups encounter a love that is transformed according to each person's relationships, interests, development, and backgrounds although this love is what propels progress and will to live.

Longer lifespans have resulted in longer marriages which is a fairly new phenomenon. Of course, we must take into account the routine and monotony that arise over time in the couple's relationship, and that may interfere negatively with the way couples express their love and sexuality. However, most couples who are still together in old age usually consider their marriage to be more fulfilling than those of intermediate adulthood. The large majority states that their marriage has improved overtime: companionship, affection, love, and devotion are usually what these couples value most, but sexuality does not disappear. It is assumed that this is due to the difficulties that they have overcome together which has made them learn to look past each other's differences and reach a mutually fulfilling relationship.

Loving is good. People who are willing to maintain a loving and sexually active life end up leading a longer and better life. Love has been known to be an excellent healer for loneliness, abandonment, and depression, which are the most serious issues that older people face. Having mental, physical, and sexual activities is the best way to stay healthy at any age.

Returning to the initial question, which are the best years of our lives?

Probably all of them, as long as they are fully lived. We should not forget the advantages of being older. Indeed, there is no way of avoiding it: we lose eyesight, hearing, muscle strength.... But if we learn how to live with that, it is possible to enjoy the chance to do new things in different ways. This is the right moment to soften our approach on life.

"Age does not depend upon years, but upon temperament and health. Some men are born old, and some never grow so". (Tyron Edwards)

Therapeutic Intervention

The different systemic therapy concepts rely on three intervention pillars:

- Promoting active aging
- Empowering encouragement regarding autonomy and independence, well-being, happiness, and defence of dignity and rights
- Attention to the specific needs and expectations, which require more or less integrated customised solutions, as Family or Couple's Therapy for instance

If aging is a general demographic trend, old age, i.e. the different ways of living longer lives are numerous and require customised interventions and initiatives, compliant with the needs and abilities of personal fulfilment, autonomy, and participation. In the end, growing old and being old are symbolic constructions.

Think about aging as someone who has gone through a series of changes over time, and where identity is an always-updated summary of those various stages of their life, as well as the perspective of what they will become in the future. Time is, in this case, where various facts and events take place that influence, strain, and question the subject's identity.

The level of influence on the subject's identity may be determined, as part of an age policy used in each society, when it controls the development of individuals, imposing rules regarding what it means to be a certain age. The aging process is a different way of envisioning oneself in all the possible temporal dimensions: past, present, and future.

This perspective regulates a field of subjective transformations and diverse identities, which translates into specific ways of responding to the changes that aging brings, always taking multiple and ever-changing social contexts into consideration, which then provide meaning, roles, and judgement. Aging requires the combination of continuity and mutability over time.

Therapeutic intervention reveals the role that narrative plays as a means to connect and give meaning to the changing circumstances of life. The subject "writes" and describes their own story all the while being its reader and subject to assessments although also representing an agent of change.

Refiguration is the process through which a subject alters their reading of themselves due to an event or life experience that may be significant to them, making new positions a possibility. Configuration involves the task of grasping a set of discontinued and incoherent circumstances as a whole, giving them a meaning through which they may follow and understand their personal story.

The narrative function will have a representation of the person throughout their life as its cohesive goal, by making intelligible what once was unintelligible and giving continuity to what once was discontinuous. There are two main purposes:

- Give life's time dimension a narrative discontinuity
- Link discontinued stories of life that would otherwise interfere with the sense of self which would then lead to a greater understanding of oneself and thereby re-establish a subjective and relational well-being

Aging encompasses concepts related to finitude, the loss of roles, social prejudices, body and social image changes, which will test narrative bonds and may require significant effort on both personal and family system levels. The weight of family and community should also be emphasised as the two most important environments where we are able to create and change meanings.

On the other hand, the social dimension of the aging and old age concepts requires that we take into account, without forgetting its existing direct relation with the bio-sociological changes that occur throughout time, the fact that such changes are interpreted in the light of a culture that gives them a meaning within a specific and ever-changing context.

Three Couples in Couples Therapy. "The Time Lost or the Time Regained"

First: A Maze of Sorrow

72-year-old Maria and 73-year-old Manuel married 45 years ago and have been "sleeping in separate beds" for the past 16. They have two adult sons who live in their own houses.

Maria tells the story of her marital life as a sad story, a story of misery and some violence, where she felt neglected and where sex was an "obligation". She remained living with her husband but, for a decade and up until 5 years ago, she had a lover with whom she felt happy and in love. They talked a lot, danced on weekends, and had an intense sexual life.

On the other hand, Manuel tells a different story, where he points out the disease that has been affecting him for many years and complains about his wife who always rejected him sexually, who forsake affection and cheated on him.

The constant fighting in the past years contrasted with the silence in the first years and disrupted all family meetings. For this reason, one of the sons gave them an ultimatum: either they attended therapy, or he would keep a distance and deprive them from being with their grandchildren.

The therapeutic process of this couple was a joint journey, and everybody gladly participated. The initial resistance was followed by the desire to stay and repair.

Maria built new stories where she was able to include her courage to surrender to passion, and to desire and demand the sexual pleasure she was entitled to. She keeps that good memory, but recognises that her husband is the love of her life.

Manuel accepted his struggle dealing with emotions and affection, taking us back to his childhood memories, where he learned to "forsake" in order to overcome loneliness and how he was a victim of abandonment. Also, how his disease weakened him and exposed his increasing intolerance as well as his impotence.

For 1 year, in fortnightly appointments, I participated in the construction of a new romance. **We entered mazes of sorrow and found possible ways out**. Little by little, the stories swept away the pain from the distancing, the rejection, the countless bitterness and resentment, thus highlighting the good things bringing them together and the unveiling of new love equations nourishing them both. In an environment of growing trust, I witnessed an increasing sexual desire. They decided for a new marriage. And after all, everything was transformed!

Second: Never Again Me Without You. Always With You!

68-year-old João and 73-year-old Ana, met in a Retirement Home and fell in love. At first, they had to live a secret love, which soon became a nightmare. During one of my visits to the retirement home, Ana asked me to help them. She confessed that they were thinking about running away… because they couldn't bear the contempt of João's son, nor the constant laughing and criticism of the staff in the retirement home, when finding out about their love. Therapy started and during those 6 months of collaboration between the three of us, we decided to start a revolution.

João was an emigrant for 40 years and returned to Portugal when he reached retirement age. His wife passed away a few months later and, along with his family, he decided to go to the retirement home to be taken care of.

Ana, single, lived with her parents, who she looked after until they passed away. Ana also took care of two brothers, nephews, great-nephews, but she had to go to the retirement home in order to be taken care of, after falling and due to her fragile health condition.

João has many assets and earns a good pension. He recalls how sad, tired, hopeless a man he was, without any more dreams or projects… until he met Ana.

Ana has financial difficulties, even with the payment of the retirement home. She has always been a fighter, just like "Cinderella" but without the Fairy Godmother. Ana never stopped believing that she would be happy, even if just for one day.

The sons of João were surprised and terrified when they found out that their father had fallen in love, stating that he was being deceived and manipulated.

Therapy sessions were held with the couple. The main concern was the sexual maladjustment, loaded with fear, impatience, prejudice, resulting in a clear inhibition. The positive and paradoxical connotation of such inhibition gave rise to the deconstruction of their fantasies where everything had to be perfect, just like the feeling bonding them.

When I mentioned that I called sexual intercourse as "the poor sex", they unexpectedly took this as a pillar and, thereafter, they allowed themselves to do and accept what is new and different, to explore and enjoy an ocean of affection, caress, touch, and exchange of pleasure which has been delayed up until then. They found out that the most important thing in love and sexual life laid within these caring and delicate "little things".

Therapy sessions with João, his son, and daughter-in-law were held. It was clear that the concern was not focused on the love life of the old couple, but in the risks threating financial interests. When João told them that he would like to remarry, they blamed Ana and his absurd madness.

They asked them about the inheritance and the future of joint investments. The therapeutic process evolved, when it became possible to focus on the emotional relationship, on retelling the family history through a detailed genogram. Father and son solved past misunderstandings, conflicts, and crisis, which were mostly experienced in a silence greater that the physical distance between them. João regained his freedom and authority as a father, confirming his presence, although somewhat unclear. The respect and love between father and son prevailed. Ana never wanted to attend these sessions, but the son started greeting her. This young man soon understood that his marriage would pay a price due to the lack of condescendence of his wife towards the positive evolution of the father–son approach.

An intervention work took place within the retirement home, which included meetings with the administration, the technical team, and all remaining personnel on the meaning of love and sexuality in this stage of life and on the impact in the institution. An afternoon celebration of Love took place in the retirement home with the participation, sharing, and celebration of all residents.

Ana and João were role model heroes of discretion and courage.

> Both told me "*...it was necessary to have such a long path in order for what seemed impossible to happen... our love is so big, that seems never ending, just like the universe...*"

Third: When Love Ends... If It Is Love, It Does Not End!

The first marriage of 71-year-old António was with Sara and it lasted for 30 years. They had 3 children, aged 29, 27, and 25, all of them living and working abroad, very close to each other and in the company of their mother. After his father passed away, António formalised the divorce and lived alone for 5 years. The second marriage with 57-year-old Eva lasted 5 years and they had no children.

António is a renowned and successful lawyer, just like his father and grandfather. The family of António is very conservative, where the unlimited authoritarianism of his father and the unconditional submission of his mother were always known. As the older son of a family with three children, he had the responsibility to carry on the ancient family values. The middle brother committed suicide after a deep depression and the youngest sister initiated problematic behaviour from a young age, which took up all of the mother's attention and increased the distance of the father.

Eva is a painter and has many hobbies related to nature. Considered the "black sheep" of the family, Eva overcome many obstacles from her family, which, just like the family of António, is very conservative. She chose to live a life based on aesthetics, pleasure, and enjoying each and every moment. She had many occasional love affairs but without any strings attached. At the age of 51, Eva is allured by the vast culture of António and, in his turn, he is enamoured by her unique beauty.

They were both in need of affection and fell deeply in love. António, at the age of 65, allows himself to experience a lifestyle which was unknown to him up until that day, and a complete opposite to his own experience. He is living in a cluttered house, has no schedules for meals, takes care of several animals living at home, goes on vacations without destination… and he discovers, for the first time, his qualities as a passionate lover. After 4 years living with Eva, António suffers a minor stroke related to overwork. From that day on, the couple's life began to suffer a snowballing change. António has frequent headaches and other somatic complaints, and turns inwards, declining social interaction and trying to bring his rules from the past to his everyday life. The desire starts fading and he avoids physical contact. The adaptation of Eva is sympathetic at first, but she starts showing an increasing disenchantment and intolerance.

When the therapeutic process started, the couple was living a breaking period. Building systemic stories, using sculpture, pursuing the settlement of myths and beliefs, understanding the stories… nothing worked in the couple's reconciliation. They decided to proceed with the divorce and, together, we aligned different life paths for each one, where the beautiful story of their encounter could be kept. Unexpectedly, Eva leaves home and immediately starts dating António's best friend.

António returns all by himself to the appointment and asks me for help discovering his true identity and restore his relational life. We are still in this discovery process. He still likes to recall how much he loved Eva. But he conquered the freedom to love again.

As Conclusion. What I Would Like to Highlight

In clinical practice, I learned with many couples that love in old age is the same as any other. It does not have to be more peaceful nor wiser, or mature. It encompasses the abundance of experiences lived, but it can happen as spontaneously and naïvely as the first love, it may open space for new desires and achieve challenges related to changes, or it may just reproduce well-known standards.

Love has no age to begin, to end, to be lived in a rewarding or cruel way. Experiencing sexuality, with or without love, has no age. Throughout life, the freedom of choice and decision should remain. The desire and need of affection remain and old couples may have the same problems that cover all age ranges.

The dichotomy that we are no longer 20 years old, and that when we're 20 we do not have the personal background with that many relationships and experiences, is inevitable. Nowadays, love keeps the quality of past love at any age, but, likewise, each individual may strengthen the magic of no longer being slave of such feeling and be entitled and willing to start again and further experiencing.

Memory does not forget, but it transforms and includes!

Consultation Bibliography

Andolfi, M., Angelo, C., & Saccu, C. (1995). *Casal Em Crise*. São Paulo: Summus.

Campo, C., & Linares, J. L. (2002). *Sobrevivir a la pareja*. Barcelona: Planeta.

Elkaim, M. (2007). *Como Sobreviver à Própria Família*. Lisboa: Sinais de Fogo.

Gaillard, J.-P. (1999). Le couple contemporain: entre institution et connexion. In "Crises de Couple. Perspectives Therapeutiques", Cahiers Critiques de Thérapie Familiale et de Pratiques de Réseaux, 23, Bruxelles.

Gimeno, A. (2001). *A Família. O desafio da Diversidade*. Lisboa: Instituto Piaget.

Minuchin, S., & Nichols, M. (1995). *A Cura da Família*. Porto Alegre: Artes Médicas.

Narciso, I., & Ribeiro, M. T. (2009). *Olhares sobre a Conjugalidade*. Lisboa: Coisas de Ler.

Neuburger, R. (1999). De la passion, de la folie et des rêve. In "Crises de Couple. Perspectives Therapeutiques", Cahiers Critiques de Thérapie Familiale et de Pratiques de Réseaux, 23, Bruxelles.

Neuburger, R. (2009). Quelques techniques utiles en thérapie de couple. In "Le couple dans tous ses états", Cahiers Critiques de Thérapie Familiale et de Pratiques de Réseaux, 42, Bruxelles.

Relvas, A. P., & Alarcão, M. (2002). *Novas Formas de Família*. Coimbra: Quarteto.

Satir, V. (2002). *Nuevas relaciones Humans en el Nucleo Familiar*. Ciudad de México: Editorial Pax México.

Zeldin, T. (2017). *História Intima da Humanidade*. Alfragide: Texto Editores, Grupo Leya.

Psychotherapy and Technology: Relational Strategies and Techniques for Online Therapeutic Activity

Gianmarco Manfrida, Valentina Albertini, and Erica Eisenberg

Introduction

The issue of remote communication via technological means between therapists and clients is not a new topic: already in 1951, the psychoanalyst Saul (1951) began exploring the use of technology in psychoanalytic treatment, arguing that the telephone was a tool that could help the patient overcome resistances related to transference reactions.

In the history of the systemic approach, Selvini Palazzoli, Boscolo, Cecchin, & Prata (1978) created a structured telephone data sheet in order to collect data from the very first contact with the patient, making that data immediately usable by the team.

L'Abate (2004) has developed a distance-intervention model based on the use of psychotherapeutic workbooks containing a series of tasks and assignments aimed at developing an interactive practice, useful for educational, preventive, and therapeutic purposes. The exercises can be completed in session or returned via e-mail, fax, or other distance data transmission modes. Help via workbook is aimed at a very diversified target of users, including but not limited to people suffering from dementia or depression, battered women, gambling addicts, prison inmates, couples preparing for marriage, children with school refusal.

More recently, the increased social use of text-messaging (and chat or instant messaging applications such as "WhatsApp" or "Hangout") has created a new area of concern for psychotherapists; the management of communication between one session and another.

In particular, Manfrida and Eisenberg (2007), Manfrida (2009) and Manfrida, Albertini & Eisenberg (2017) have proposed that text of instant messaging can be used to support the psychotherapy process, examining the communicative

G. Manfrida (✉) · V. Albertini · E. Eisenberg
Centro Studi e Applicazione della Psicologia Relazionale (CSAPR), Prato, Italy

R. Pereira, J. L. Linares (eds.), *Clinical Interventions in Systemic Couple and Family Therapy*, European Family Therapy Association Series,
https://doi.org/10.1007/978-3-319-78521-9_9

characteristics of both the information contained in the message, and of the emotions expressed therein. Messages sent via mobile phones can be a resource; by ensuring the therapist's availability they can provide support during critical situations; they can extend the impact of the therapeutic relationship by prolonging the intervention beyond the time limit of the session; they can lead to reducing the frequency of the sessions themselves. A quantitative analysis of messages confirms the hypothesis that an intentional psychotherapeutic use of text and/or instant messages within therapy can be useful, especially underscoring the flexibility of this tool which seems to lend itself equally to the purpose of conveying practical information; supportive communications; and, from time to time, concise and effective therapeutic interventions. Grammar, syntax, emoticons ("smileys" and pictures) which make up the messages can be used during the interval between sessions to extrapolate diagnostic information and support therapeutic interventions.

Other authors (Vallario, 2012) warn of the danger of the non-prearranged use of messages between therapist and patient, warning against potential risks such as the patient's resistance; the weakening of the therapist's image; of symmetry within the therapeutic relationship; the distortion of the setting itself; and the transformation of a professional relationship into an intimate one.

In addition to text and instant messaging, e-mail can be a valid support to therapy: as part of training courses at the Centro Studi e Applicazione della Psicologia Relazionale of Prato, a copy of the concluding feedback shared at the end of each therapy sessions is e-mailed to family members to facilitate in-between session reflection on what occurred during the therapy session. More recently, the widespread use of smartphones has highlighted the possibility of integrating psychotherapy sessions with video sessions using applications like "Skype" or "FaceTime."

These experiences illustrate that therapists are "children of their time," confronting themselves with social and technological developments: if, however, there is no "bad" technology, there are good (and bad) ways to use it. Technology can become our ally inside and outside the therapy room: demonizing modernity can be an antihistorical attitude, exalting it could lead to severe human and medical errors.

How Consistent Is the Online Therapy Setting with a Relational Approach?

The issue of use of new communication technologies in psychotherapy does not end with the phone call, text messages, e-mails, and video calls. For years, the debate has moved on to a much more critical, albeit fashionable, ground: the creation of an online setting and the evolution of an online therapy process. Given that technology is a tool that can definitely help, can it replace the therapeutic setting, or the therapist himself? The *Internet* provides a myriad of online (and low-cost) therapeutic solutions ranging from consultations provided via chat or Skype to software programs meant to provide free and immediate psychological support.

Despite believing that the outright demonization of technology is an improper and defensive attitude, we also believe that there are areas of people's lives which cannot, and should not, be reduced to the binary system. Psychotherapy is, in our opinion, one of those.

The issue of online psychotherapy is of great clinical and scientific interest. Risks and possibilities have been extensively debated (Fenichel, 2014): starting from ethical and legal risks (which the American Psychological Association is currently tackling); pragmatic issues such as the inability to access non-verbal content are discussed; there are also open considerations regarding the fact that online users tend to be less inhibited (Fenichel, 2000). Furthermore, relational difficulties which should be worked on in treatment can be rigidly reinforced via online therapy: it is no coincidence that—as some researchers discovered—patients with social phobia adhere better to online treatments than to those administered in presence (Titov et al., 2009). (Is it surprising? We could also ask Internet addicts which type of treatment they would prefer).

Many authors have questioned the efficacy of online psychotherapeutic treatments. Most of the studies focus on the application of cognitive-behavioral protocols, or on the assessment of online self-help groups.

A group of researchers from the universities of Linköping and Stockholm showed that in treatments for depression online support from self-help groups has the same effect as face-to-face groups (Andersson et al., 2005). The same results were achieved by studying the effectiveness of online self-help groups for the treatment of states of anxiety and stress (Van Straten, Cuijpers, & Smits, 2008).

Other studies have compared the outcomes of two different cognitive-behavioral techniques (BA Behavioral Activation, and Mindfulness) in self-help treatments delivered through smartphone applications: in conclusion no significant differences were observed (Ly et al., 2014).

For systemic-relational therapists, the delicate issue of therapeutic alliance remains open: we know that, regardless of the theoretical approach adopted by the professional, the relationship with the patients is, in itself, the most important instrument (Horvath & Symonds, 1991). There can be no relationship if there is no alliance; is it possible to build an adequate online alliance, without seeing, hearing, meeting the patient in person? Some researchers (Cook & Doyle, 2002) compared two groups of patients (one in a traditional therapy setting, the other online) administering the WAI (Working Alliance Inventory) to assess whether there were any differences between the two treatments. The results, despite the small sample and not taking into account the outcomes of the individual therapies, did not show a significant difference in the therapeutic alliance measurement. Patients in the online group pointed out how online therapy was disinhibiting, easy (in travel terms), flexible, handy, and convenient. In other words, anxiety medication in the form of an App, which is the exact opposite of what we advocate: the need for commitment by both therapist and patient to build a caring relationship that is serious, profound, responsible, and that encourages a process of freedom, growth, and independence.

According to Stern (2004), change within the therapeutic relationship is based on the experience of the "present moment," the moment of implicit communication:

the short interval of time during which psychological processes gather perceptual units which acquire sense and meaning in a relational context. There has to be a real experience, a subjectively experienced event, with real-time feelings and actions, with real people, in a shared moment experienced as the present. How to reconcile this relational approach to psychotherapy theory via workbooks and with the possibility of a completely web-based treatment?

Even a neuroscientific model, consistent with Stern, cannot be integrated to such an approach; according to Gallese (2003) the same neural circuits which are activated in the subject (patient) who performs actions, expresses emotions, and experiences feeling, are automatically activated in the subject (therapist) as he or she observes these actions, emotions, and sensations. How much will be lost in an exchange that forsakes face-to-face meetings? We are able to be in contact with each other thanks to mirror neurons and learning occurs within an integrated relational process at the neural level; can this function be conveyed through the video and telecommunication channel without there being a direct proximity which enables one to participate even in the smallest communicative exchange?

Online therapy can seem attractive for a number of reasons, starting from the illusion of cost limitation and therefore the spread and expansion of access to the service. Research that supports this argument claims that for every individual who accesses psychotherapy, there are at least five others who would need professional help, but do not receive it (Pinsof & Wynne, 1995).

In fact, the very idea that access to the Internet per sé will warrant equal access to services is wrong: it is sufficient to consider the difference that factors such as age or social class have on Internet usage. To totally adhere to the myth of a virtual non-place as an area for the creation of equality is likely to deceive because, as noted by Bauman (2000) "rather than homogenizing the human condition, the technological annulment of temporal/spatial distances tends to polarize it." The many research studies asserting the equivalence of online therapy and face-to-face therapy make us question not so much the quality of the online therapies as much as that of the therapies conducted in presence! Among others, a risk presented by web-based therapy is to further fortify that fear of relationships which is a great danger in our profession: if being with patients were easy, looking them in the eyes, observing the slightest movement or feeling, attending to their emotions… if all that were easy there would be no need to work so much on transference, countertransference, and healing relationships. For those who adopt a systemic-relational approach, the issue becomes even more complex: online therapy does not allow for the possibility of working on multiple requests, a possibility which is often necessary for the success of an intervention within this approach. Imagine an online couples' therapy: how would it be possible to use sculptures or to share tasks and exercises during a session?

In the narrative intervention style based on the Shared reality model (Manfrida, 2011, 2014), the observation of all that is discordant from the story of the ordinary and dominant daily reality brought by patients becomes the key point around which to develop intervention hypotheses and system change. There can be many discrepancies during a session, to capture these the therapist must alert all senses: can this be done, and to what extent, from behind a screen? How can we use—for example—the information provided by the strident contrast of a man who comes to a session wearing suit, tie, and tennis shoes, if we cannot see his feet? Or that of a woman who comes to therapy elegantly and carefully dressed while reeking of alcohol? Without the lapses, the pauses in the speech, the shifting looks, would we still be able to grasp what the patient wants to express without consciously knowing how to (or if to) say it?

We claim that technology (telephone, e-mail, text-messaging) is a valuable—extremely valuable—support for therapy, but it can never replace a live, face-to-face therapeutic relationship. Sitting behind a computer display carrying on an online therapy seems a very useful avant-garde form of armor, a way to avoid putting one's courage to the test—a quality which we believe is essential to the therapist (Manfrida & Albertini, 2014, 2015).

Diagnostic Reading and Therapeutic Use of Text and Instant Messaging

What is the difference between a text message (an SMS), an MMS, an iMessage, or a WhatsApp message?

SMS/MMS messaging enables one to send text messages and media to other devices using phone credit; iMessages allow one to send text messages and media to other iOS devices via Wi-Fi without charge; the same goes for WhatsApp and similar messaging apps, with the added difference that these apps are available for iOS and other operating systems such as Android, Windows Phone, and BlackBerry.

According to data published by AGCOM (National Agency for the Regulation of Communications, Italy), on the use of communication tools in Italy, WhatsApp has overthrown old text messages, leading to an incredible drop in the use of the latter: sending standard text messages via phone has now been supplanted by online messaging and text message use is mostly limited to businesses or for exchanges which require some level of formality. iMessages, WhatsApp messages, and the likes are used instead for personal and informal communication with acquaintances. Given that they do not rely on the availability of a Wi-Fi network, traditional text messages actually have a greater guarantee of delivery; usually contact with a professional is initiated via text message: once therapy has begun, the use of text messages is often replaced by WhatsApp messaging. On the other hand, traditional text messages protect the therapist from the embarrassing problem created by WhatsApp sharing information about the user such as "last seen at ..." or "message read at ...". In fact, once the WhatsApp message has been opened this is signaled to the sender (unless the user disables this function), therefore the time passing between the therapist reading the message and a reply being sent will be interpreted in a relational sense as an immediate guaranteed availability or lack of substantial interest which may affect the therapeutic relationship. Choices such as disabling the message receipt notification, when to open a message, when to read it, and when to reply to it, acquire therapeutic value and imply an acceptance of responsibility on behalf of the therapist which should be managed within the relational context, consistently with the therapy goals. Should we exclude our clients from the reassuring possibility of seeing that we have indeed received their message or will this entail a constant commitment throughout our day? Sooner or later, however, we will have to reply to these messages and give them our full therapeutic attention.

On WhatsApp, it is possible to add a profile picture; while these images and pictures can give us some information regarding our patients, they can also—inversely—provide our contacts with information about us; therefore, therapists should be extremely careful when choosing a profile image. For example, using a picture of one's happy family can have an impact on the relationship with less fortunate patients; pictures of ones' children can create problems for patients who might be trying to have some; using funny images can expose one to the risk of ridicule during moments of conflict which may occur during therapy. Using pictures of other people or pets can open the therapist's life to potentially embarrassing and uncomfortable violations of privacy.

Recently, use of WhatsApp voice messages is becoming more popular: a therapist should never agree to reply to this kind of messages, unless the senders have serious reasons for not using their hands. In fact, a voice message is imposed on the receiver in an intrusive way, it forces the receiver to listen completely without the opportunity of replying, it does not allow the sender to reflect on what he or she is writing, there is no objectification of anxiety, of the concerns, or thoughts which push one to communicate. The therapist is forced to seek temporary isolation in order to listen to his client's voice in privacy, in an extorted and not agreed upon alliance.

The way in which WhatsApp, text, and e-mail messages are written should never be considered lightly, this concerns both messages being received or sent by the therapist. A text written in all caps or one that is interrupted by an excess of ellipsis seems to suggest a diagnosis of histrionic personality, if only for the choice of characters: thus a message may already contain a diagnostic suggestion. An unsigned message suggests that the patient expects to be immediately recognized or that he/she is unique for the therapist; if so, responding with a message that underlines that lack of a signature, immediately restores the reality principle to the therapeutic relationship, additionally sparing the therapist the task of cross checking his or her phonebook to identify the sender. The fact that the sender's name can be often identified by the phone should not detract from the significance of this observation because patients should not assume that they are recorded in the therapist's phone directory and, in any case, it is good practice in a professional context to sign one's messages.

Sometimes messages contain inconsistencies and contradictions which can be reported immediately and examined later in therapy by the therapist, both to activate the patient's curiosity and to train him or her in the skill of psychological investigation.

The "expressive" use, if not consciously rhetorical, of messages is also indicated by the use of punctuation, capitals, and emojis as in the following example, in which it is clear that the patient wants to communicate her "sensational" news:

- Doctor! This is Verushka.😃 This morning I received the notification for a new job!!! 😃🎉It should start (if all goes well) on July 3 🎉🎉LET's HOPE! 😃😃🎉🎉

Much attention should be given to the time at which a message was sent: a series of WhatsApp messages sent in the middle of the night may suggest a situation of alarming solitude. The following messages were sent from a 60-year-old man who was having a very painful affair with a 30-year-old woman; she is threatening to break up with him if he does not leave his family; a situation—per sé—not very disturbing—if it were not for the content and timing of the messages.

7:53 PM, patient: Doctor, I can't take it anymore, I have to leave her, it's a constant argument with her, she wants me to go on holiday with her, wants me to skip my grandsons' baptism I am tired of her, is it worth it just for sex and to be seen around with such a young and beautiful woman?

7:58 PM T: (skeptical, having heard these considerations before): Wise words

10:17 PM Pt: Wise words but when I do not hear from her I miss her, and now she is not answering!

Pt.: I miss her, doctor, I miss her and I'm not happy, it's one big argument.

01:49 AM Pt.: Doctor, I can't sleep, I always think of her, I do not want to lose her.

02:03 AM Pt.: I cannot go away with her but also staying in the family is no great solution, there is no sleeping tonight.

05:02 AM Pt.: Doctor, she told me that in a fortnight she is going to Ibiza with friends I cannot continue like this. I'm sick. This relationship is making me ill.

08:25 AM T.: Come see me today, Robert, maybe it's better if—aside from being close to you at this time—I also prescribe some medication.

Using a patient's name may convey a more "personalized" message, giving more warmth to written words. The placement of the name in the sentence can also express different shades of meaning, e.g., "John, you did something stupid" is more friendly and less accusatory than "You did something stupid, John!", where the proximity to the end of the sentence, especially if there is an exclamation point, seems to imply a scolding rather than consoling solidarity. Solidarity can also be enhanced by the use of punctuation: "John, you did something stupid."

It can be stated that sentence structure, word distribution, punctuation, the way in which sound resonates within the reader, and other resources give written messages those connotative aspects of meaning which are ascribed to the analogical component of language (Watzlawick, Beavin, & Jackson, 1967).

Therapists should always sign their messages, in full or with their initials; this is not a simple matter of form or good manners. Closing a message with "Dr. A. (initial) B. (full surname)" or "GA (abbreviation)" represent context markers, indicating

Table 1 Using smileys (emoji)

To send this:	Type this:	To send this:	Type this:
Smile	:-) or :)	Open-mouthed	:-D or :d
Surprised	:-O or :o	Tongue out	:-P or :p
Wink	;-) or ;)	Sad	:-(or :(
Confused	:-S or :s	Disappointed	:-| or :|
Crying	:'(	Embarrassed	:-$ or :$
Hot	(H) or (h)	Angry	:-@ or :@
Angel	(A) or (a)	Devil	(6)
Don't tell anyone	:-#	Baring teeth	8o|
Nerd	8-|	Sarcastic	^o)
Secret telling	:-*	Sick	+o(
I don't know	:^)	Thinking	*-)
Party	<:o)	Eye-rolling	8-)

Source: http://graphicsheat.com/emoticons/#sthash.SbzQvk3i.dpbs

that it is a message within the context of a professional relationship, reducing the risk of excessive familiarity.

If therapists feel that they are receiving too many messages, or should they wish to emphasize the unequal balance of the relationship for therapeutic purposes, they can use messages in several ways: it is possible to answer with a message that underscores the excess of incoming messages; choose not to reply; choose to reply only after a length of time that would suggest to the patient that he or she overdid it; or save the messages and work on them during the next session. The therapist's choice of the appropriate words to generate the desired psychological effect in the patient also requires a significant degree of commitment: a simple encouragement can be very different if expressed with a "Bravo!" or a "See you soon." A joke or a witty comment can confirm mutual understanding in a specific situation, e.g., "Congratulations, a prestigious result that will give you credit and customers!". In other circumstances, it is appropriate to use more generalized expressions, e.g., "I'm glad you have had such a good result."

Messages can be enriched by the use of emoticons or emojis; these more or less cheerful icons are part of a shared code of communication of emotions and moods. Emojis are usually added to messages to specify the emotional status of the sender in order to avoid the risk of a misunderstanding. The words "I hate you!" take on a different meaning when they are followed by a smiley face ☺ (Table 1).

When texting it can sometimes be difficult to convey feelings and emojis can help solve the problem. Some people prefer to use characters (shown on the right hand column in the table) to create expressive images, like :-) or :-(. "You can be a real nuisance! :-)" is more reassuring than "You can be a real nuisance! :-(:-(:-(8-[". The creative ways in which emojis and characters are used underscore the importance that humans attach to the relational aspect of communication, which is assimilated from early childhood in the social process of building a shared reality where analogical aspects give significance to digital information.

Therapeutic Exchanges via WhatsApp

1. Building a therapeutic alliance before the first session with a 30-year-old very manipulative, severely depressed woman with psychotic experiences:

   17/05, 17:45 Nadia: Hello doctor, I am the friend that Dr. Scott wrote to you about today. I would like to make an appointment with you. I am waiting for your reply. Thanks a lot.

   17/05, 17:46 T.: Call me now. Dr. E.

   18/05, 13:32 Nadia: Dr. Good morning! Sorry to bother you but I am having a panic attack after the other.

   18/05, 13:33 And I do not know how to handle them.

   18/05, 17:18 T.: Call me! Dr.E. (Nadia does not call)

   18/05, 17:36 T.: Nadia, I'm free for another 10 minutes and then I have to return to therapy and I have to turn off my phone. If you do not call me now send me a message to tell me how you are. Dr.E.

   (Nadia calls and is referred to a psychiatrist for medication)

   19/05, 07:56 Nadia: Good morning Dr., I sent a message to the psychiatrist you referred me to, I hope he calls as soon as possible because I don't know what to do. Thank you.

   19/05, 08:14 T.: Nadia, I spoke to him yesterday evening and he told me he is available to see you. Greetings. Dr.E.

   19/05, 08:17 Nadia: Thank you very much!

   19/05, 16:44 I've just been to the psychiatrist! Wonderful person! He told me to come see you anyway if you can manage to move up my appointment I would be grateful.

   19/05, 17:05 T.: I am very happy to know that you have already been to the psychiatrist. If a space frees up before I will definitely let you you know. Dr.E.

   20/05, 12:15 Nadia: Dr. I'm sorry to bother you.

   20/05, 12:16 I need to ask you something.

   20/05, 12:16 If you can tell me when I can call.

   20/05 12:30 T.: Nadia, I am at a conference, but please write what you want to ask me and I will reply. Dr.E.

   20/05, 12:33 Nadia: Everything is becoming all the more difficult.

   20/05, 12:33 I just want to throw myself off a balcony.

   20/05, 12:34 I want to know how I can help myself.

   20/05, 12:34 If I can read a book.

   20/05, 12:34 Do something.

   20/05 12:41 T.: Nadia, I understand that you are not well, that is why I asked the psychiatrist to see you right away and he did see you immediately. Dr. Scott has referred you to me for help, so we're all working together to help you. Rather than read a book in which you will not find the magic trick that will solve your pain immediately I ask you to hang in there a little longer, giving the medication time to work and to us all the time to move forward to work together. Dr.E.

20/05, 12:49 Nadia: Ok. Thanks. I'll try

20/05, 12:53 T.: Nadia, I do understand very well how you are feeling, and my actions already have shown that I am honestly concerned for you, but this means that we have to work together, so it is good that you try to hang in there a bit longer and even succeed. Dr.E.

20/05, 12:53 Nadia: Thank you so much.

20/05, 12:54 I hope I can start eating again.

20/05, 12:54 T.: Psychological distress does not magically go away, but it does by starting to do the right things. I asked myself to be ready to help you; I asked the psychiatrist to see you right away; I am asking you to begin to swing less between: "Dr. save me!" and "Ah, no Dr., this is not working and I'm getting worse," but hold on a little more, and then you will have a chance to get to feel good. Dr.E.

20/05, 13:00 Nadia: You're right.

20/05, 13:00 I have to be strong! strong! strong!

20/05, 13:05 T.: More than being strong! strong! strong! you should spend less time oscillating between these characteristics, you devote your time swinging from one to the other, and you are not gaining anything for yourself, start investing your time in doing something good for you. Dr.E.

20/05, 13:35 Nadia: I'll try to follow your advice as best I can

20/05, 13:35 Thank you so much Dr.

20/05, 14:20 T.: I hope so because it would mean doing something for yourself. Dr.E.

2. Use of WhatsApp to involve Franco, the father of a teenager suffering from paranoid ideas and hallucinations, in family therapy in order to begin restructuring the family.

Franco, father of Pietro, an adolescent suffering from delusional ideas of persecution in family treatment: Dott. Elena good morning, I am Pietro's father, today I will not be able to join you, my wife and my children or maybe just Pietro will attend, I will let you know, thanks for now… talk soon.

T.: Dear Franco, it would be much better if you came, because Pietro needs you too and it would be good for you to explain in session why you do not want to come. I will be waiting for the four of you. Dr. E.

Franco: Again, I will not come to be insulted by my wife, my family will come this time, I will come the next. Good day.

T.: Dear Franco, you react to your wife's insults by shutting down, being evasive, or putting your foot down by saying you are not coming, but the one who is damaged by this is Pietro. I believe you have every reason in the world to use the session to tell your wife what you think with calmness and determination, as should a man, this is an act of dignity that you owe yourself and it will provide a healthy male role model for your children. Please don't stomp your feet or avoid the issue with me too, come, be responsible, and we'll talk about this together as adults. Dr.E.

Franco, as requested, participated in the family session.

Therapist Groups on WhatsApp and via e-mail

WhatsApp allows users to create group chats; this can be a useful tool to communicate instantly with a number of people, thus coordinating therapy interventions among different therapists working individually with members of the same family or anyway relationally connected. This way different therapists can stay in touch and help each other during critical moments. Furthermore, group chats enable participants to share information which can be priceless when patients are reticent: even if the data obtained from colleagues cannot be used within the sessions, such information can be helpful in leading the discussion towards potentially unwanted topics. Finally, groups can represent a resource by providing emotional support for those therapists who—at times—may feel uncertain or may be facing an especially difficult moment, they can be reassured by their colleagues' participation in the process. The sine qua non condition that must be enforced is the utmost respect of patient confidentiality, limiting participation to the group discussion only to those therapists who are directly involved in the case work. The consent form, which therapists ask their clients to read and sign at the beginning of a therapy, includes the request for permission to contact and exchange information with other therapists and supervisors: no special reference is made to how the contact is established (telephone, e-mail, messages, meetings). When joining a group chat, each participating therapist should have the patient's consent to share sensitive information.

Use of e-mail to Send Families the Concluding Interventions of Their Therapy Sessions

At the Center for Family and Couples Therapy, in Prato (Centro Studi e Applicazione della Psicologia Relazionale), where sessions are conducted with the aid of the one-way mirror and videorecordings, it has become our standard practice to send each participant over the age of 12, the conclusive feedback at the end of each session. As sessions usually occur on a monthly basis, sending the patients an e-mail with the summary of what took place during the session is also a way of keeping them involved in the process during the interval. It is also possible to share the session feedback with therapists who are individually seeing family or couples members, in order to coordinate contents and timing of therapeutic interventions, both on the individual members and on the couples or family systems.

Concluding Intervention of the First Session with the Family of Evelina, a 14-Year-Old Girl Who Has Not Attended School for 3 Years and Suffers from Social Phobias and Obsessive Symptoms

Yours is a strange family indeed, you can get lost on your way here, and you will not call us to ask for directions, but you are also capable of not giving up hope after years of disappointment and immobility.

Evelina has many voices, some are childlike, with others she is not afraid of confronting the famous professor M.!!

She has not been going to school but she speaks like a book; and she is well aware of having a brain whose autonomy she prizes most of all. For reasons we will only be able to understand with everyone's help, she is afraid of doing things. She is proud of the autonomy of her thoughts and of her capacity of getting others to give her what she wants, but it does seem that she is lacking the personal commitment, the effort which is necessary to achieve practical results.

Standing next to her, not above her, are mother and father, who look upon her with both admiration and fear, constantly asking themselves: How do we manage her?

If the challenge does not scare Evelina and if her parents think they can manage it, we are available to work with all three, perhaps even with her older sister if she wishes to participate, and to schedule those sessions which will be necessary to give substance and significance to a life which will otherwise continue to be more fantasy than reality.

We would like to see you next on September 4 at 5:30 p.m. This is our phone number. Please Evelina call us the week before the appointment. Dr. R. and Dr. M.

Supervisions by e-mail

When there is no possibility of meeting face to face, it is possible to use e-mail to provide supervision for therapists when they feel unsure regarding interventions with their patients.

Following are an e-mail with the Supervisor's advice for Lucia, a young therapist, and the intervention she prepared for her next session with her patient, based on that same advice.

Supervisor's Advice

Dear Lucia,

It seems to me that the intervention you prepared is fine; you insist, in a sufficiently challenging way, on the patient's inconclusiveness and so you should. I would recommend you do two things:

1) I would write something with regard to the fact that perhaps you are not the best fit of therapist for him because you plan to work hard and not waste time the way he is accustomed to do: you expect him to remember what is said. I would add that perhaps you might scare him and he will run away, and that if he wants to waste time and procrastinate, there are plenty of other people out there who can help him do that.
2) I find it is inconsistent to give him the assignment of sending you two text messages during the holidays, aren't you telling him that he should decide what to do with his life? There are no symptomatic emergencies that need to be monitored, only chronic obsessive issues. It would be enough for you to tell him that, if he wants to, he can reach you even during the holidays by sending you a message... unless of course he loses your number or forgets your name!

I have corrected some of the terminology you used and removed some repetitions. Michele is capable of spending the session correcting the grammar to avoid looking at the content! That aside, it's fine. M.

Therapist's intervention

Dear Michele, thank you for the story you shared during our last session. I have worked on it and here I am, with a consideration. You are really special, and it is a pleasure to listen to your dissertations, which I find intelligent, funny, scholarly, insightful... really pleasant.

These dissertations are a symptom... so I cannot but point out to you how much you are settling for. It is true, you clearly show that you are an intelligent and educated person, but what use do you have for that same intelligence and culture? If you were enjoying yourself, even in the face of your family who has—for years—handed out money to you; or if you collected your successes and were content with that, I could shut up about this. The point is, you are not happy with yourself, there are no areas of your life in which you have made any progress or in which you feel certain of what you want to do. You have transformed dissertation into an art form, a socially accepted way of wasting time.

It seems to me that your life is marked; you are a slave to fear… Fear of not being up to the job? Fear of making mistakes? Of disappointing? So you seek refuge in reading philosophy which should help you justify how hard it is to get on with life. This is true only on a philosophical and sociological level because you do everything and anything in order to avoid yourself and continue to achieve nothing in your life.

Your progress is exasperatingly slow, which per sé—with time—becomes a source of anxiety. How to be content with oneself? Where to find the reasons to trust?

It is truly a pity, Michele, because you lack nothing, other than faith in yourself and courage!

Maybe family expectations weighed you down? The ones that wanted you to become professor? Maybe you did not have the courage to say that that was not what you wanted to be? Perhaps you would have preferred to become a craftsman? Or an engineer? I can understand you, but you are on the verge of turning 40, you got your Ph.D. 5 years ago, some substitute job here and there, still trying to see if someone will publish your thesis paper, and you haven't written anything else since.

You are in the academic world but you still don't know why; you've had a girlfriend for 10 years but you don't know where that is going…

Michele, the first time we met was just before the summer holidays, you were doubtful and said "Maybe my problems aren't therapy material"!

I am not sure that you can carry on a therapy; you definitely have the capacities, no doubt there! But the fear… I do believe you need therapy, urgently too, if you still want to try to pull yourself together and work towards something that has meaning for you. Otherwise, you are looking forward to a life of dissatisfaction and unhappiness. If you are too scared to start living that is fine, it is your life, but at least try to understand why. You do love knowledge so much, so have the courage to look into the book that is your life rather than other people's. You can always choose to stay exactly the way you are, but you will be more aware and possibly more alive.

I am really sorry, but I know you do not feel the same way, so I am going on holiday without feeling too guilty. I will see you again at the end of August. You will have had time to think (I said think, not ruminate!!) about what I have said and when I come back you can tell me what you want to do.

Sessions via Skype, FaceTime, and Video Calls in General

Unless there are severe impediments, such as the patient being housebound due to illness, we discourage from a therapy plan which does not include regular meetings in person. We are well aware of how difficult treatment can be, so it is important to note that a patient's request for a long-distance treatment may conceal an attempt to remain distant, without ever entering the therapist's office be it virtual or physical. The same concern applies to the therapist who can, subconsciously, search for a long-distance relationship as a protection from involvement.

Even therapies with protocols that do not rely heavily on emotional and improvisational aspects still need a basic emotional involvement in order to be productive:

simply seeing or listening to the therapist cannot replace that physical proximity which, itself, helps generate trust. In order to decide whether the therapist is trustworthy, whether the session is just a lesson in theory or whether it can be a life-changing opportunity, it is necessary to hear the tone of voice, see expressions up close, and perceive the full size of the therapist, not just that conveyed by a 4 or 7 inches display.

The physical presence is even more significant when treatment is aimed not only at reducing symptoms, but to the underlying personality disorder, in this case the therapeutic alliance is, per se, the most powerful therapeutic tool (Cancrini, 2006; Smith Benjamin, 2003).

Due to chance (emergencies, temporary unavailability of the clinical setting, etc.) or to specific life events (patient or therapist relocating, illness of either party, long breaks due to holidays, etc.) it may be necessary at times to hold long-distance sessions.

In these circumstances, video conference tools might be a valid way of preventing the interruption of therapeutic work, and to warrant some kind of continuity in a way that is most similar to the usual one, avoiding the sequentiality of written messages and maintaining the feeling (illusion?) of a direct interview. Despite the undeniable convenience of these means, management of the online setting becomes an important issue. Online sessions are not a simple technical transposition of a face-to-face session (Mingione, Moscarella, & Scappaticci, 2016) since they acquire new communicative dimensions.

First and foremost, the scenario may be different from the setting which both patient and therapist are accustomed to; within the practitioner's office, every element is framed in a professional context. In a video conference, one or both parties will surely be in a different context: there will be many elements which may require special attention, such as pictures hanging on the wall (regarding the patient, these may provide a topic for the session; for the therapists, they may reveal aspects of their private lives which they would prefer not to share). Lighting, images, photos of friends or relatives... not to mention household pets.

The therapist can access the patient's world in a more direct way than what is possible during a live session, and this element too requires careful consideration, and might need to be addressed.

It is essential that patient and therapist be alone, in a room which should warrant privacy for the duration of the interview, without the possibility of a bystander accidentally overhearing or—worse—actually walking into the session. It might take longer to initiate as both parties will have to adjust to the new setting, after a few minutes though, the discrepancy with the original session will weaken and possibly disappear entirely if the parties have already established a solid working alliance.

Just as is customary for normal sessions, appointments for the next online session must be decided at the end of the previous one; some aspects that must be taken into account for long-distance sessions are time differences, and the necessary conditions of privacy for both patient and therapist.

Given that today's technology allows one to host a videochat not only from a desktop computer but also through the use of smartphones or tablets, it is important that the therapist does not improvise the location of the session, for example, using FaceTime to have a session from the beach. Even if the therapist is fully clothed, it is very difficult for the patient not to feel that he/she is being thrown a scrap of free time of an otherwise very busy life. Some forms and formalities must be respected in order to replace the privacy, continuity, and confidentiality usually provided by the therapist's office.

Therapy via Skype

Francesco, a 38-year-old man, asks for an appointment to get help during a critical moment after his recent separation from his wife. During the phone call information is gathered both concerning the patient request and the family situation, but it is only during the first interview that Francesco mentions something that is so ordinary for him that it didn't strike him as important to say during the telephone conversation; Francesco lives in Africa for 8 months a year, both he and his wife work for a non-profit relief organization. Francesco is so accustomed to handling all his professional, personal, and family relations via telephone or online that he did not think this part was worth mentioning: "I took it for granted that we could meet via Skype," he replies when asked why he had not described this peculiar life arrangement during the first telephone contact.

His initial request took place almost 5 years ago. It was accepted by the therapist as an interesting challenge, a chance to experiment with a blended setting, with some face-to-face sessions and some online.

The first sessions take place during Francesco's 2-month stay in Italy, this allows patient and therapist to establish a good working alliance. In Francesco's family history, the figures of both grandfathers have a prominent role: the maternal grandfather emigrated from southern Italy towards Tuscany in search of fortune, the paternal grandfather moved to Egypt in the 60s to work on oil wells. Both men represented important figures for his development and education, he always perceived them as brave and adventurous men—traits which he feels are entirely lacking in his parents. Mother is a housewife, father—instead of taking advantage of his university degree—settled for a clerical work in public administration, and married his next-door neighbor, whom he had known since childhood.

For Francesco, it becomes vital to reclaim that adventurous side of life: 10 years prior to our meeting he had immediately employed his degree in Political Science to begin a career within an international organization, in which he met his wife, far more adventurous than he, who also revealed herself to be a very unstable personality-wise.

The first months of therapy proceeded quite easily, but everything changed once Francesco returned to Africa. The first setting dissonance concerns seasons; Francesco returned to Africa in February, moving from full blown Italian winter to African summer. The first sessions show a therapist heavily clad in winter clothing vis-**à**-vis a tanned, T-shirt wearing patient who is enjoying summer in the boreal hemisphere. The feeling of not being "in the same time" is analyzed during their first Skype session.

The second change concerns the setting itself which the therapist can observe through the PC screen; a drab and scanty office if the appointments are scheduled in the morning, a lonely house if the appointments take place in the evening. Francesco's life in Africa is represented by these images: lonely and unsatisfying.

The fact that the therapist could directly "access" these images enabled therapy to tap into a very important albeit yet untouched issue for Francesco: being tired of that very adventurous but also very sad life he had been leading for years. Separation from his wife increased his weariness, and the presence of their child is the only thing keeping him below the equator line.

During the online therapy, it was possible to access that part of Francesco which he had walled off and kept at a distance, the part of him remembering his father, quiet and peaceful, who dreamt of a secure job, close to home, and a gentle—if potentially "boring"—wife. At that time, there were two Francescos in treatment: the adventurous and reckless one who showed up for the face-to-face sessions and the home-loving, predictable one online.

This division was the topic of many sessions, and it was exactly this discrepancy between the two settings that helped Francesco to piece this together.

When his ex-wife informed him of her decision to move to South America with her new husband, Francesco decided to leave Africa and move back to Florence.

Today, Francesco works in the Florentine branch of a non-profit association. He has a good rapport with his ex-wife, and he often visits his son in South America, on top of the scheduled winter and summer holidays with him.

He seems to have adapted to a quieter life, even though his adventurous side has emerged in a new relationship; he has chosen a beautiful and interesting woman who is also deeply histrionic and creates lots of excitement in his life.

Conclusions

We have attempted to present this brief—certainly not exhaustive—excursus on the use of communication technology in a clinical setting. We believe that our profession should be concerned with what occurs in the contemporary world, and this cannot happen by ignoring the tools which are being used by everybody in the world; a good therapist should regularly install updates.

Naturally, ideological drifts hide behind every corner, in one way or another, and while anachronistic prejudices which refute the use of any form of technology are becoming more and more rare, there is the opposing risk of excessive reliance on technology itself.

As always, the golden mean is the wisest and most effective path to follow in order to avoid rejecting all that is modern and contemporary, while at the same time preserving the deeply interactive, relational, and human quality of our profession.

References

Andersson, G., Bergström, J. F., Holländare, F., Carlbring, P., Kaldo, V., & Ekselius, L. (2005). Internet-based self-help for depression: Randomised controlled trial. *British Journal of Psychiatry, 187*, 457–461. https://doi.org/10.1192/bjp.187.5.456

Bauman, Z. (2000). *Globalization. The human consequences*. New York: Columbia University Press.

Cancrini L. (2006). *L'oceano borderline*. Milano: Raffaello Cortina. [Spanish Ed. (2007): *Océano borderline: viajes por una patologia inexplorada*. Barcelona: Paidòs]

Cook, J., & Doyle, C. (2002). Working alliance in online therapy as compared to face-to-face therapy: Preliminary results. *Cyber Psychology and Behaviour, 5*(2), 95–105. https://doi.org/10.1089/109493102753770480

Fenichel, M. (2000). *APA Town Hall Meeting – August 5. Humanity at a digital crossroads: Psychology's role in a converging internet culture*. Accessed June 6, 2014, from http://www.fenichel.com/TownHall.shtml.

Fenichel, M. (2014). *Online psychotherapy: Technical difficulties, formulations and processes*. Accessed June 6, 2014, from http://www.fenichel.com/technical.Shtml.

Gallese V. (2003). La molteplice natura delle relazioni interpersonali: la ricerca di un comune meccanismo neurofisiologico. *Rivista Networks*. Accessed July 20, 2014, from http://lgxserve.ciseca.uniba.it/lei/ai/networks/03-1/gallese.pdf.

Horvath, A. O., & Symonds, B. D. (1991). Relation between working alliance and outcome in psychotherapy: A meta-analysis. *Journal of Counseling Psychology, 38*, 139–149. https://doi.org/10.1037/0022-0167.38.2.139

L'Abate, L. (2004). Using workbooks in mental health. In *Resources in prevention, psychotherapy and rehabilitation for clinicians and researchers*. Binghamton, NY: Haworth Press.

Ly, K. H., Truschel, A., Jarl, L., Magnusson, S., Windhal, T., Johansson, R., et al. (2014). Behavioural activation versus mindfulness-based guided self-help treatment administered through a smartphone application: A randomised controlled trial. *BMJ Open, 4*(1). https://doi.org/10.1136/bmjopen-2013-003440

Manfrida, G. (2009). *Gli SMS in psicoterapia*. Torino: Antigone.

Manfrida, G. (2011). Plausible, convincing and appealing. Characteristics and development of therapeutic stories in a shared reality approach. *Journal of Systemic Therapies, 30*(2), 22–41. https://doi.org/10.1521/jsyt.2011.30.2.22

Manfrida, G. (2014). *La narrazione psicoterapeutica. Invenzione, persuasione e tecniche retoriche in terapia relazionale*. Milano: FrancoAngeli.

Manfrida G., & Albertini V. (2014). Courage and psychotherapy: Some results from a qualitative investigation. *EFTA Newsletter 14*. Accessed July 2, 2017, from http://us7.campaignarchive1.com/?u=c75f1cbece98fa4abdfe2ba56&id=aa83422b60&e=UNIQID.

Manfrida, G., & Albertini, V. (2015). Il coraggio uno non se lo può dare…oppure sì? Indagine sul coraggio nella pratica psicoterapeutica. *Terapia Familiare, 107*, 39–57. https://doi.org/10.3280/TF2015-107003

Manfrida, G., & Eisenberg, E. (2007). Scripta Volant! Uso e utilità dei messaggi SMS in psicoterapia. *Terapia Familiare, 85*, 59–82. https://doi.org/10.1400/94241

Manfrida, G., Albertini, V., Eisenberg, E. (2017) Connected: Recommendations and Techniques in Order to Employ Internet Tools for the Enhancement of Online Therapeutic Relationships. Experiences from Italy. *Contemporary Family Therapy 39*(4):314–328

Mingione E., Moscarella A., & Scappaticci M. (2016). *Whatsappo quindi sono. Il setting liquido al tempo dello smartphone. Congresso Internazionale SIPPR 6-7-8/5/2016*. Accesses July 2, 2017, from https://www.slideshare.net/taraporcupine.

Pinsof, W., & Wynne, L. (1995). The effectiveness and efficacy of marital and family therapy. *Journal of Marital and Family Therapy, 21*(4), 341–343. https://doi.org/10.1111/j.1752-0606.1995.tb00169.x

Saul, L. J. (1951). A note on the telephone as a technical aid. *Psychoanalytic Quarterly, 20*, 287–290. PMID: 14844547.

Selvini Palazzoli, M., Boscolo, L., Cecchin, G., & Prata, L. (1978). *Paradox and Counterparadox. A new model in the therapy of the family in schizophrenic transaction*. Lanham, MA: J. Aronson.

Smith Benjamin, L. (2003). *Interpersonal reconstructive therapy: An integrative personality-based treatment for complex cases*. New York: Guilford Press.

Stern, D. N. (2004). *The present moment in psychotherapy and everyday life*. New York: W.W. Norton.

Titov, N., Andrews, G., Schwencke, G., Solley, K., Johnston, L., & Robinson, E. (2009). An RCT comparing effect of two types of support on severity of symptoms for people completing internet-based cognitive behaviour therapy for social phobia. *Australian and New Zealand Journal of Psychiatry, 43*(10), 920–926. https://doi.org/10.1080/00048670903179228

Vallario, L. (2012). SMS e terapia: le relazioni pericolose. *Ecologia della Mente, 2*, 240–252. https://doi.org/10.1712/1205.13352

Van Straten, A., Cuijpers, P., & Smits, N. (2008). Effectiveness of a web-based self-help intervention for symptoms of depression, anxiety, and stress: Randomized controlled trial. *Journal of Medical Internet Research, 10*(1), 25. https://doi.org/10.2196/jmir.954

Watzlawick, P., Beavin, J. H., & Jackson, D. D. (1967). *Pragmatics of human communication*. New York: W.W. Norton.

Part III
Systemic Interventions in Different Contexts

Future Strategies on the Treatment of Drug Addiction. Psychotherapeutic Work with the Families of Substance Abusers. Thoughts from Europe

Juan Antonio Abeijón

WE RESIGN OURSELVES TO SEEING OURSELVES THROUGH THE OTHER'S EYES

(J. P. SARTRE)

Introduction

"We are indebted to our past"; this statement, so pertinent in terms of human beings' individual and collective realities, also applies to the recent history of drug consumption and the evolution of the way we deal with the consequences of substance abuse, whether on the level of treatment or in terms of preventive policies. Being indebted does not mean we are condemned to repeat ourselves without any possibility of change, but instead that we evolve in an ongoing dialogue with a reality that feeds off its own history. When we refer to drugs we are talking about individuals and substances within a context of constant interrelation and dynamism, of individuals from an inner perspective (their personal stories, the building of their personality) and from an outer one (their transformative action), our internal selves and that of others, contemplating it and setting it in time and space; in history.

The models of care in drug addiction, as well as our profound understanding of the phenomenon, have evolved in step with the social perception of drug use.

The goals pursued in treatments overlap with the expectations that drug users attribute to the use of substances.

J. A. Abeijón (✉)
Vasco-Navarra School of Family Therapy, Bilbao, Spain

R. Pereira, J. L. Linares (eds.), *Clinical Interventions in Systemic Couple and Family Therapy*, European Family Therapy Association Series,
https://doi.org/10.1007/978-3-319-78521-9_10

In this inter-relational process between the outside and the inside, it is important to remember the adage that "suffering is part of human experience"; an experience that one cannot escape from however much one tries.

Modifying the experience of suffering is part of everyday life. The consumption of drugs may for many people become a way of coping with the experience of suffering, controlling it, silencing it, ousting it… Yet the management of suffering is not the only way drug use manifests itself and is experienced, with the other involving the right to have fun; drugs within the realm of pleasure.

The right to have fun reflects the need to find a pleasant way of coping with reality. Reality, the search for well-being, and the struggle against suffering are some of the major concerns that underpin human existence. The individual and social perception of drug use is informed by these concerns.

Since the appearance of drugs, the "pharmakon," in primitive societies under the ritual form of the sacred, the divine, through to their experience in our soulless societies, of what we lack and of what is needed to fill the vacuum; something that may be a substance, which is experienced as a passion, which we consume, and which in turn consumes us.

To paraphrase M. Foucault (1961) when he refers to the madness in human beings today, drug addiction is an experience you come out of as a different person to the one that went in.

When there has been a cry for help—a vital and necessary step for helping a patient with a drug addiction—dealing with the roots and consequences of the user's experience with the substance requires addressing the relationship between the drug addict and their therapist, the experience of what has been gained and the emptiness, of well-being (pleasure?) and suffering. Drug use should be read as a behavior, a message from the individual that tells us key things about them and their context. As recent studies have reported, there are genetic and neurophysiological roots present in drug use behavior, yet this conduct is nonetheless expressed as behavior with consequences for the individual and for their immediate and distant relational medium.

The possibility of interfering in relational mechanisms significantly modifies the meaning and development of drug use behavior. This involves therapy, namely, the ability to organize and structure certain interferences in a manner agreed by both therapist and patient.

Therapies are organized into complex interventions that involve the duality of the necessary intensity of the ongoing care and the search for a causality in diversified and changing programs.

The balance between abstinence and damage limitation in caring for drug addicts today is the outcome of professional development and the tailoring of care programs to the tension existing between the individual that suffers and the one that seeks well-being.

The professionals that work with drug addicts have endeavored to understand the changes arising in the needs of users of services, adapting care programs and their goals to best practices, and using considerable creativity to deal with the ideological tensions that have revolved around the proposed ways of treating addicts, as well as following the criteria put forward by international organizations and the different schools of thought.

There is no pleasure without suffering and there is no suffering without pleasure. Pleasure and suffering are the two sides of the same coin; we are capable of perceiving pleasure when we can feel its boundaries. To speak of pleasure is to do so implicitly of suffering, in the same way that speaking of suffering is to do so of pleasure without actually naming it. In the use of drugs that act upon the central nervous system, the search for well-being though presence or absence is part of the story of our lives: I gain that feeling, I avoid that other one, I manage to feel better, stronger, braver, more open and also less tired, less anxious, less sad, etc. And then we come up against the consequences of drug use.

Freedom of choice does not remove the need to attend to the consequences of drug use, and perhaps the most interesting example regarding this statement is the development of the phenomenon of tobacco addiction in western society: its consumption is relatively modern, dating back barely a couple of centuries. It has seen a change in its appreciation that has shifted from individual to collective consumption, from encouraging its use to its active restriction, from the development of tax policies to awareness of its effects on public health and healthcare spending. Care for health issues in societies based on social welfare systems has become universalized and democratized, whereby access to it is one of the quality parameters of care itself.

It is not ethical to leave drug users to their own devices; a drug addict's quality of life needs to be improved, even though they have "freely" chosen to become one. The tension, often creative, that is developed in programs treating drug addiction, especially those managed by public health services, is directly related to this specific situation.

Therapeutic Care in Drug Addiction. Complementarity in Treatments: Psychotherapeutic and Psychopharmacological Programs

There are two basic lines involved in treatments: psychotherapy and psychopharmacology.

Psychotherapeutic interventions focusing on the word as the vehicle for understanding and expression of the personal difficulties according to the individual stories of the patients-sick arise from the relational dialogue between the drug addict and their milieu.

As regards those interventions of a psychopharmacological nature, many of which focus on damage limitation programs, they respond to a need to minimize the negative physical, mental, and social effects linked to drug use through a series of individual and collective socio-healthcare measures. In short, the aim is to improve the quality of life of the patient-consumer, for the individual, on the one hand covers cognitive judgements on satisfaction with life, and on the other, affective evaluations on mood and emotions.

A study by Markez et al. (2000) reports that the opinion of the users of the various damage limitation programs improved in the following ambits of a drug addict's life:

Reduction in drug use and risk behavior
Reduction in delinquency
Improvement in relations both at home and at work
Improvement in perceived quality of life

The treatment (from its different perspectives: individual or group, maintenance programs with substitutes, healthcare policies, prevention policies, etc.) becomes the modulator of the tension existing between freedom, drug use, and its consequences.

The egocentric nature of an individual with problems of drug use is related to their ability to cope with the tension between suffering and pleasure.

Suffering for an individual means "the burden of reality"; suffering is a feature of everyone's lives without them looking for it, and is the result of physical pain, losses, and the awareness of one's limitations. Suffering is juxtaposed with happiness, in which pleasure is a major component. Escaping, finding a meaning, transforming, or ignoring are ways people have of coping with suffering.

The building of intervention strategies in socio-healthcare areas involves an interaction model that contains all the elements noted, classifying them into four spheres that dynamically organize the intervention, as shown below:

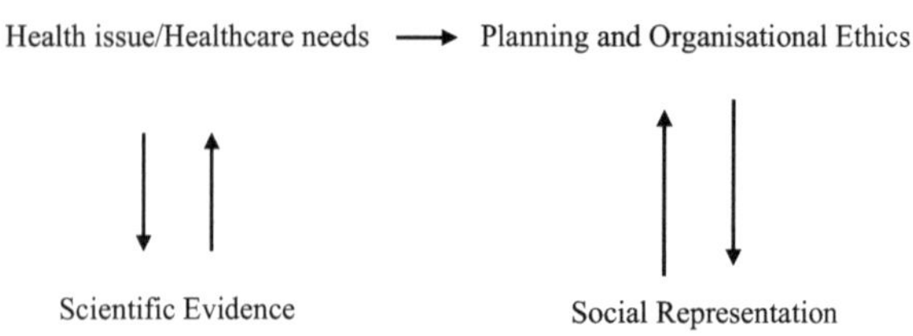

The tensions existing between a drug user's needs, their reference systems as a family, the educational system, their peer group, etc. and health issues at both a physical and mental level create a therapeutic arena in which to develop the intervention strategies required in each case. The social representation of a drug user and of the consumption itself, that is, the way in which over different periods in history societies have defined drug users and/or addicts and related to them (a good-for-nothing, a delinquent, a sick person, someone that has chosen to consume, etc.) has undergone a major transformation in recent years, as have the care responses that have been organized, with correlative patterns.

POSSIBLE DEVELOPMENTS AFTER FIRST DISCOVERING DRUGS (Source: L. Cancrini, 1996)

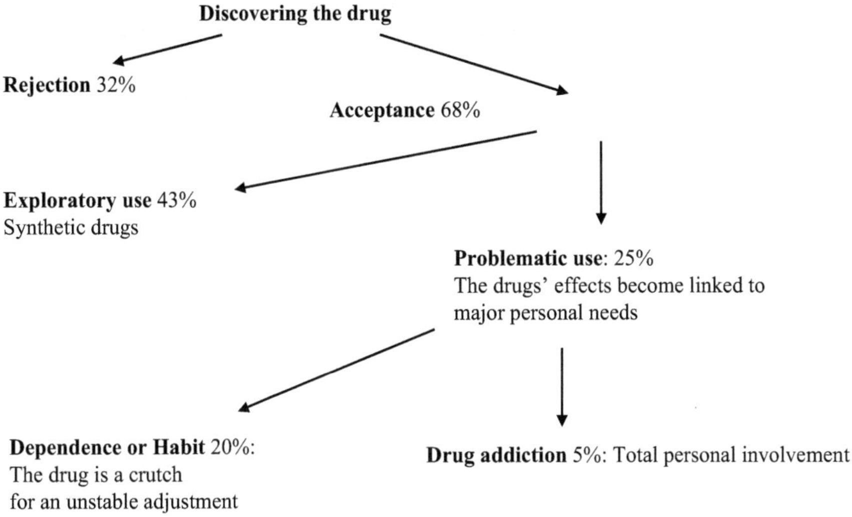

Problems do not currently arise when treating drug dependents (20%) or addicts (5%) according to Cancrini's graphic; that is, those that propose a demand for treatment because they are experiencing a loss of control over their use and the situations of suffering that accompany them; organic or mental illnesses, problems of disaffection at home and at work, loss of personal self-control. The problems arise when we are called upon to help that vast majority of experimenters that make no demands at all, many of whom are not going to turn their use of substances into a problem, but tolerate the difficulties of their different contexts until they assimilate them: the aggressive behavior of certain users of cocaine, the concern some parents have over the lack of interest and apathy of their children that use certain substances and are completely unaware they have a problem.
Current situation:

Working with a group of chronic patients.
Use is spreading.
New patients are appearing in the services.
There is a tendency to isolate the services.
There is above all a concern for the changes in behavior linked to drug use.
There is a crossover of interests between the healthcare and legal systems
We are moving towards a new relationship with substances characterized by the following:
Acceptance of drug use as a personal right
Substances are part of everyday life
The use of certain kinds of drugs is a rite of passage into adolescence among Spanish youth

Psychotherapeutic Work with the Families of Drug Users

We are now witnessing the start of a new cycle in the use of addictive substances by one sector of the population. Drug usage is now seen as an everyday event and as an individual right in which each one of us should decide and take responsibility for our decisions, protected by the safety net of the institutions that will shield us from the greatest risks of drug use.

Substances change, with the emerging use of cocaine set to increase considerably, as the drug of "happiness" and "success"; the use of marijuana has been trivialized to become the right of passage into adolescence, and the spread of stimulating drugs linked to the recreational side of the weekend. Treatments also change, adapting to each individual's circumstances, aiming to become incisive, fast acting, and very closely related to the context in which they are used.

Yet how can the therapeutic treatment of a patient's family address these changes?

Insofar as families are concerned, and conducting an analysis that moves from the general to the specific, we may note the following:

1. On a sociological level, all the surveys conducted on Spain's youth reveal that their family comes first in the evaluation made by the country's young people. What's more, they live in the family home longer, delaying the time they leave until the age of 29.5 on average, with the most common reason for becoming independent being setting up their own home and family, and not for reasons of studies or work. Spanish families have relaxed the rules regarding sexual mores and house rules (timetables, household norms, etc.), whereby both the young people themselves and their parents consider this greater experience of temporary cohabitation to be highly positive and much easier.
2. On an epidemiological level, the study conducted by the State System for Information on Drug Addiction of Spain's National Drug Plan reveals that 75% of the drug addicts treated by the different outpatient care services in Spain live at home with their family of origin, whereby we may affirm that drug addiction as a pathology goes beyond personal boundaries and becomes a situation of widespread consequences in the different systems in which it develops, and especially within the family.
3. Furthermore, according to studies conducted by Basque Mental Health Clinics, 30% of the working time of the care services for drug addicts is used by patient-related systems, and not directly by the patients themselves.

This aspect requires us to conduct a specific analysis of the characteristics of the demand for treatment in the case of drug addiction, above all from a systemic-relational perspective.

The Demand for Treatment

Demand is a key feature of the work of a professional team that looks upon it as the point where two systems meet:

- On the one hand, that which belongs to the set of relations in which drug addiction manifests itself, and which gives rise to the demand.
- On the other, that other one whereby through its members' ability to listen and their professional training it seeks to provide an effective response (Abeijon, 1986).

Demand has sometimes been described as an inter-relational challenge with obstacles to be negotiated, as tests the one expecting the care places in the path of their interlocutor. The latter will require skill to overcome them, and this will determine the possibility of establishing a relationship that will allow a change to be made, or else prolong the conflict and the symptoms.

We are moving towards an ever more complex process, as there is an increasing number of people demanding treatment, and each one has their own specific needs. This intersection of expectations and needs may even lead to pathologies that have a bearing on the treatment's final prognosis.

The context seems confusing and muddled. Who is more interested in solving the problems? The doctor, the patient, the family, the judge...? What do you need to be to solve the problems: doctor, social worker, psychologist, behaviorist...? Can you say everything you know?

This confusion means that demand constitutes a power struggle, like a relationship ensnared in one of its characteristics that needs to be clarified before the treatment proper begins. If the therapist or carer does not consider this aspect, they will provide answers formulated within the drug addiction's time and space, that is, within distorted time and space.

It is important from the start to present the treatment program as an integrated provision of the different resources available, and which will seek to address all aspects of the drug addiction, adapting to each specific case, even when we can only provide a partial aspect of the entire process.

It is true that the therapist will not be able to address all aspects and will need to call upon other services and other professionals to complete the process. If in this first stage of the relationship with their patient they are clear about the fact we are facing a lengthy process, this will change the nature of the relationship, knowing that the process may encounter all kinds of pitfalls. Despite everything and if the drug addict wants, the evolution of their treatment can be pursued in the same way as a long carpet is rolled out, and if the addict is willing, each one in their own space will be ready to engage in the series of situations that can arise.

Presenting the Care Offer

When a drug addict attends a service, they are presented with a proposal that they are going to work on in a dialogue with the service's staff within a setting defined by freedom and responsible commitment, and not what often happens, which is that when the addict attends the service they manage to create their own treatment proposal. What ultimately happens in these cases is that the solution becomes the problem.

The therapist's stance should be to consider all the factors involved in the problem presented, assuming the burden of anxiety they reflect and demarcating the areas for the relationship they have with their patient throughout the entire process, in which certain "about-turns" are possible and constitute messages on the decisive outcome of the entire problem.

The Drug Addict and Their Family

Although the family is one of the key players in problems of alcoholism and drug addiction, addicts often seek to exclude it from the treatment. It has been found that developing techniques that allow including the family in the therapeutic process significantly improves the prognosis in each case. It also tends to be the case that when the family attends the care service it does so with the designated patient and seeks to remain outside the understanding and consideration of the solutions.

These two situations are common when meeting the professional responsible for treating the addict.

It is frequent to hear such statements as the following:

- my parents don't know anything
- my family are sick and tired of this
- I don't want my family to get involved
While family members say:
- we're not getting anywhere with him
- his friends are to blame
- he goes crazy when he's on drugs or drinking
- you know what needs to be done

Is it advisable to include the family in the treatment when both parties are against it? What is the nature of the relationships established between addicts and their families? The traditional hypotheses refer to a drug addict as a "sociopath" whose allegiance is basically to the members of his group, his "peers"; however, increasing importance is being given to the contributions that deal with the evidence of the relationship of dependence between the addict and their family of origin. Most addicts maintain very close family ties.

Goldstein (1999) has reported that addicts generally use their parents' home as a constant refuge throughout their lives to the extent that the relations between the married addict and their family of origin have turned out to be more important than those with their spouse or partner. These relationships with the family, which are so close, may or may not lie at the heart of the addiction, but it is more than likely that they may indeed have a bearing on their condition as addicts. It is often observed that many families seem to excuse their addictive behavior, even withholding information about this conduct from the actual doctor and their care team.

On the other hand, once a family is included in the treatment, and according to the patients themselves, it becomes the best aid for helping to stop taking drugs. The statistics provided by care services in addiction show that addicts not only attend the clinic accompanied by their family, but also in a high percentage of cases the decision to go is made by the family itself, with this being much more the case among teenage patients, and especially in contacts with the GP.

Characteristics of an Addict's Family

As regards the nature of the relationships that an addict has with their family, they are so peculiar that specific traits may be identified in the structure of the family map. The structure of this family map reveals an alliance between the addict and one of the main parental figures, often of the opposite sex, and against the other parental figure. Given the high percentage of single-parent families among addicts, the relations with the parental system are applicable to those established with pre-eminent members of a preceding generation.

An addict wields a special power over parental figures, who need to focus their attention on them to establish a relationship. In the event of a looming separation, parents often come together using the drug problem and, at least at first, put off the resolution of their own problems.

To maintain this triangle, one of the parental figures needs to take the addict's side, providing protection and safety.

This is the case of Sara, who is 24 years old, with a record of addiction that has been developing over four years, with long and irregular periods away from her family, with a history of prostitution and delinquency. Her family consists of three siblings and the parents. The father has a serious problem of alcoholism that has required treatment, and begins to improve just when his daughter begins her addictive behavior. She is currently the reason the parents have stayed together, with a mother that has protected her, finding excuses for her, and resolving the various crises her daughter has gone through.

It seems that the addict needs to take drugs and pursue delinquent behavior to justify being given protection and safety. The ramification of this process is a reversal of the family hierarchy insofar as one of the two parental figures is placed at the same generational level as the addict.

Parental figures cannot proceed in a coordinated manner to look after the addict and change their behavior, and in turn the addict cannot become independent and leave them. There are alliances between the members of the family, crossing the lines that separate the generations, as well as a reversal of the family's normal hierarchical structure, whereby the two parental figures would not be in a higher position than the younger members. This means that in addicts' families the two parental figures and the addict may be involved in hierarchical reversals in which one parental figure is located below the other in the family structure.

As a rule, the addict does not outrank the parental figures when these hierarchical reversals take place. The reversal involves demoting one of them to the level of their offspring. The addict does not endeavor to gain power in their family, as it seems that it is offered to them.

Generally speaking, parental figures reverse the other person's position in the hierarchy and not their own position, thereby appearing to obtain a position of power and finding themselves alone on the family map. The members of these families are involved in intergenerational alliances rather than within their own generation.

Once the treatment process has begun, and all these difficult situations have been overcome, it can be seen how the initial reticence turns into progressive interest in taking part in the proposed treatment program, whatever it may be.

The User of the Services: The Carer-Intervener

In the process of treating addictions, we should consider that the field of operations is the relationship established between the user of the service and the intervention team. The field of intervention is designed by the array of information shared between the user and this team.

But Who Uses the Services?

Virginia phones the Primary Care Centre, the former Public Health Surgeries in towns and cities, which provide sectorized care for the Spanish population. They are staffed by GPs, pediatricians and gynecologists, and nurses, and they provide a patient care service and emergency services. Virginia wants to talk to her GP, who she tells about her son's addiction problem. She wants to know what to do with him because he always arrives home wrecked. She is advised to talk to him, and ask him to come along to an appointment, as it is very difficult to follow a course of treatment over the phone, as no medication can be prescribed without seeing the patient... but she says that is impossible because her son would never agree to see a doctor. The conversation with the doctor lasts around twenty minutes. In the end, the doctor wonders whether what he has said to the woman will be of any use.

In another case, Antonia talks to her doctor as an afterthought, after collecting a new prescription for lowering her blood pressure. She says: "By the way, could you see my husband? You see, he drinks a lot, it's nothing new, he's been doing it for years, but it recently got much worse, he can't control himself anymore, and we have a lot of rows at home. I know he won't want to come, but if I tell him it's about his heart...Could you talk to him about his drinking with that excuse?"

A dialogue is established between the doctor and the woman. The doctor tells her it would be better to convince her husband to come to the surgery. The woman insists: "If I tell him why he won't come." In the end, the doctor gives in: "Tell him to come and I'll see what I can do." The conversation has lasted fifteen minutes.

Many of the services involved in problems of alcoholism and drug addiction realize that an important part of their work does not take place in direct interventions with the user, but instead with a series of people around them that ask for information and their intervention, who feel just as affected as the actual user and have major burdens of suffering.

Depending on the quality of the care provided with this group of people, there is a change in the prognosis, the evolution of the use itself, and the treatment will be more or less successful. If we work with the medium, the changes in the patient will adapt to the changes in their milieu (in their system), with the change moving from level 1 to level 2; in other words, not only do the intervention and change affect the very act of usage (level 1 change), as the intervention and change also affect those functional situations related to the meaning of the drug use in their system (level 2 changes).

Changing the functionality of the symptom means restructuring the entire system, which prompts a change in the development of the behavior of each one of its members. The user of the service is not just the actual consumer, as instead the user, going beyond the boundaries of the actual consumer becomes the group of people around them and which are involved in their problem. This situation will require the professional to develop strategies that include these people in the solutions.

Who Is the Carer-Intervener?

One tends to think that the carer-intervener is the doctor or therapist that directly attends to the user and upon whom and upon whose training the results of the care will depend, yet the truth is somewhat more complex. The doctor or therapist is part of a team within a context that is constantly sending the patient messages. These messages are explicit and implicit, verbal and non-verbal, and define the sequence of the relationships that will take place between them and the patient.

The doctor at the neighborhood surgery could not understand why young people were coming just before closing with sleep problems, asking for "something to help them sleep." She was tired by that time and the appointments with these young people often ended up becoming tense and angry. One day, she discovered that the nurse responsible for making the appointments had a drug addict neighbour that caused a lot of problems in the area. So without meaning to, the nurse left those young people that "looked like drug addicts" to last, to stop them causing problems in "the vicinity of the surgery."

There is a well-known case involving a service whose waiting-room was in the main corridor in the care center. Patients hurried along without stopping, as they were on some specific errand, attending an appointment, getting their medication, and then they left. This service was the scene of numerous violent situations and confrontations when people were not immediately given their medication or when someone tried to get a patient to slow down a bit so that they could understand their situation better and receive a better diagnosis. The context sent out messages on the entire service's operation that had an impact on the relationship between doctor and patient. It is difficult to do a job calmly when everyone is passing through in a hurry.

The carer-intervener is therefore not only the doctor, the nurse, or the therapist, but also the team within its setting and its structure, which sends messages to the user of the service that will inform the style of the relationship. From the moment the patient arrives through to when they leave, it is important that both the user and their family or referents (educators, tutors, teachers…) feel welcome at the center, that the therapeutic activities programmed, whether these are doctor's appointments, group or family therapies, nursing care, or specific programs such as the one for adolescents, the one for methadone, the one for alcoholism, or the one for chronic cases can be held in an efficient and respectful manner, given that the request for treatment is the result of the interaction of many of these systems that make up the specific situation of drug addiction for each case and in each context.

The Patient's Arrival

We will never tire of stressing the importance of this moment in the intervention, as a decisive one in the development and prognosis of the treatment in drug addictions. Many of the issues that subsequently arise during the course of the treatment can be traced back to the difficulties in the management of that moment of interaction.

It is obvious that the patient's arrival at the service is conditioned by numerous factors. Some of these are of an individual nature and are related to the actual process of drug use, with the meaning that such use has for the patients themselves; in other words, with the experiences that the repercussions of drug use have for each person, whether on an organic level (physical health), psychologically (how they see their drug use), in terms of their family (how the family is responding), or at work (impact on their ability to work). Other factors stem from the context in which their drug use take place: legal pressures (a sentence to be served or a fine to be paid), a job ultimatum (involvement of the company doctor, threat of dismissal), proposals made by the school, etc.

It is nonetheless important to consider these factors conditioning the request in order to clarify the response. At this moment, when the patient arrives at the service, there are three circumstances that may complicate the relationship with the doctor, who needs to consider them to avoid being enmeshed in a process that is becoming increasingly confusing.

Triangulation Processes

As we said before, in the demand for treatment the relations between the patient and their context constitute a coherent whole. Triangulation processes refer to the inclusion of the doctor or their team in the network of relationships existing between the drug users and their context, forming part of the fabric of ambiguous interests that in themselves restrict the possibilities of change existing in the demands for treatment.

"Say something to my son or to my husband," "I'll bring him here so that you can convince him," "so that you can treat him and help him to become his old self, as I want him to be."

The therapist or the team become one side of the triangle made up of the relationships between the patient and their context (family, judge, school, social services, etc.), whereby whatever we do we will always be confronting someone and standing beside someone else, and whatever we say it will be contested by one of the system's components.

Ultimately, our options for intervention will be weakened and become paralyzed.

Processes of Confounding Expectations

There are contradictory phenomena in the expectations with which a patient or their family visits a service, and these contradictions have often been induced by the actual user:

"This treatment will enable me to clear up my problems with the law," "I'll stop my drug use if they give me this or that medication my friend has told me about," "I'll be able to rebuild my life here."

These and other examples enable us to see that what the patient expects from the treatment process hinders the possibility of creating an original space or area of therapeutic work for each case, focused on resolving their problems of drug use, and which in some way always has an unknown outcome for both patient and therapist, and which will also fall short of the expectations built up in the patient.

Processes of Contamination in the Demand

These processes refer above all to those situations in which patients and/or their families cause such a number of tense situations in certain services that in a more or less conscious manner these decide to cease treating the patients, either by finding reasons for expelling them and their families or by transferring them to other services for the sole purpose of seeing the back of them.

"If they don't give me this medication I'll create a scene."
"Doctor, give him what he wants, otherwise he'll just go out and steal."
"What kind of doctor are you?"
"You have no idea what this is like."

These situations contaminate the demand to such an extent that the ability is lost to clarify the real possibilities for change that the patient and their family have, falling more often into situations related to the intervention's limits.

In a lecture delivered in Madrid, MacLeland has proposed three conclusions forthcoming from a study on the efficacy of treatment involving drug addicts:

Addicts that attend a treatment program improve their prognosis compared to those that do not undergo any care program whatsoever.

Addicts that attend a treatment program with a multiple range of resources improve their prognosis compared to those that attend a treatment program with a single therapeutic offer.

Addicts that attend a treatment program that manages to involve the family improve their prognosis compared to those that attend one that does not manage to do so.

These three conclusions guide many drug intervention policies and are a vital referent for the building of intervention lines by a care service for drug addicts.

The addict experiences their addiction in a constant dialogue with their own context, and this alters the perception they have of their addiction. A circular relationship is established in which the proposals for treatment become yet another part of the context.

As we can see, the family is also part of this context in which addiction is experienced, and it becomes a necessary resource for the favorable development of the treatments, regardless of whether their level of engagement is the simplest or the most complex.

The family maintains a structure, proposes a model of communication within it, evolves through adaptive processes upholding a constant dialogue with the outside, and being capable of telling its own story both to itself and to others. These elements will be the benchmark for building the interventions.

Drug consumption should be understood as a form of behavior although if the genetic and neurophysiological roots are present in this behavior then the meaning for this conduct needs to be found in the individual and in their context, especially the family. Understanding the meaning of this behavior in each case will enable us to properly formulate the diagnosis of situations of drug addiction over and above the consumption of such-and-such a substance and connect with the characteristics that such consumption has at the level of the drug addict's personality and of the involvement of the different systems in which they live the experience of drug consumption. Without these analyses, it is impossible to formulate a treatment that is not purely symptomatic.

Therapy is the ability to organize and structure certain interferences in a manner agreed by the therapist and their patient. The possibility of interfering in relational mechanisms makes a major alteration to the meaning and development of drug use behavior; in other words, it induces the possibilities for change. Bringing about this change requires using a method for reading situations and therapeutic interventions with precise rules for building those interventions. It has always been considered that the following are the three key points for interventions with the families of drug addicts:

1. Work on the family structure, in other words, break up destructive alliances and propose a united front between parents that facilitates mutual cooperation.
2. Situate the intervention in relation to the family's life cycle, in other words, work to help build up the children's autonomy and that of the family, helping to cope with the family's "empty nest" syndrome.

3. Modify the communicative model in which the family has given a role to drug use behavior, in other words, avoid facilitating any sense of victimization among family members, remove contradictions in language and attitudes, and stop using the consumption of drugs as a weapon against the other partner.

The most important thing is not the change concerning the symptom, but the changes following on from the initial change. It is not enough to stop consuming, but what happens when this occurs and is built up on the basis of this change.

The consequences of these changes will define addicts' relationships with drugs and their families, as well as with the treatments. For many years, intervention with drug addicts more or less explicitly proposed a change in the object of the addiction. Many treatments created new addictions without substances; even methadone substitution programs proposed this same swap. Autonomy is a complex process, a development that involves families and treatments on the same level as substances.

Situations experienced in the complicity of the aforementioned triangle involving substances, families, and treatments are more important among patients that have so far been, and continue to be, the main users of our services: among these three components of individual-family-treatment, a major relationship is forged through which there will be a sharing of expectations, needs, desires, frustrations, relationships of dependence, etc. which will determine how each case develops on a personal level, while also always establishing a relationship of dependence that will require finding one's own process of personal autonomy, which becomes more important in step with the greater success of the treatment.

Evolution of Patients' Profile

The current profile of the patients being attended to at the clinics is as follows:

1. **Chronic patient**
   Male (8 out of 10)
   Average age 29
   Low level of education
   Unemployed
   Polyconsumer (with heroin as the main drug)
   With experience of numerous treatments
   Very close relations with their family of origin
   Nevertheless, we are now dealing with new emerging profiles in patients that are asking to begin a treatment:
2. **Young adult**
   Young adult that has recently left home
   Well integrated socially and at work
   With a partner
   The relational medium is very important in their drug use
   Very little awareness of the problem

Uses stimulating substances
With very little involvement of their family of origin
Recreational use of drugs
With serious financial problems related to their drug use

3. **Adolescent**
   With either non-problematic use or highly problematic use, no middle ground
   There is a family background of related psychological problems
   Considerable family involvement in the search for solutions to their drug use
   Uses stimulating substances
   With difficulties both at school and with social integration
   Recreational use of drugs
   Very little awareness of the problem
4. **Consumer of legal drugs**
   Average age 50
   Consumer of alcohol
   Suffering organic complaints such as hepatitis, polyneuritis, etc.
   With a family background of alcohol consumption
   Family involvement in the search for solutions to their alcohol consumption
   Little awareness of the problem
   Good prognosis
5. **Mental illness**
   Young
   With a history of psychiatric admissions
   Consumer mainly of psychodysleptic drugs and stimulants
   With a family background of mental health problems
   User of medications
   Isolated and individual consumption
   Major user of Mental Health and Drug Addiction Services

These new users featured in groups 2, 3, and 5 require a differentiated treatment given their specific characteristics, and one customized to their own context, avoiding the risks of replacement or substitutive proposals, which may simply be a major initial supplementary step towards others that will be made through the building of a long follow-up for the patient in which affective sexual areas, autonomy processes, situations of pathological grief, and the preparation of socio-work plans will provide the fulcrum for the therapeutic relationship.

Family Perception of Treatments

The changes brought about by the treatment lead (according to the families themselves) firstly to an improvement in family relationships, secondly to greater personal responsibility, and thirdly to higher personal self-esteem and greater personal acceptance.

It is of interest here to see in the changes the pre-eminence taken by the family, whose changes prevail over the individual's improvement. Indeed, the family is the principal factor of protection against a relapse because it helps to identify the early warning signs and delay its onset. Mother and siblings are the first line of defense, being the first to recognize the alarm signals. When the father is roused, that is, when he ceases to be an observer and starts to say what he thinks, forging an alliance with the mother to set out rules of conduct regarding consumptions, etc., and does not let others be the ones to express his opinion, the scope for preventing the relapse is even greater.

The view taken by professionals also has an influence on families' level of participation in the treatment. Professionals agree that family data are essential for understanding the addict's situation although many professionals still see the family as an obstacle in their way. Considering the changes in families in recent years (smaller families, emergence of new family models, such as single-parent or reconstituted or blended households, change in the woman's role in the family, less contact with the extended family, etc.), there is a need above all to seek the family's cooperation in the treatment. Nevertheless, most of the professionals involved in the treatment of drug addiction in Spain's public services have no systemic family training.

There has also been a change in families' capacity for treatment. There has been a normalization of the social conditions of drug dependents, and many families no longer see their involvement in the treatment as being essential, delegating this responsibility to the intervention teams. In turn, successive relapses wear families down, and damage limitation programs mean that many of them are not prepared to restrict the goal of the treatment to anything other than abstinence.

We should include families in treatment processes in any way we can: as key players in the treatments as well as a supporting cast, as agents involved in parts of the treatment or as active companions in them. The individual may change, but so must their context. If there is even a slight change in the context, this will help to consolidate the corresponding change in the individual.

References

Abeijon, J. A. (1986). Los sistemas en la demanda del toxicómano. Comunidad y Drogas, Monografía n° 1.

Cancrini, L. (1996). *La Psicopatología de la Drogadicción: una revisión*. Madrid: Itaca.

Foucault, M. (1961). Histoire de la folie à l'âge classique—Folie et déraison Gallimard, Paris.

Goldstein, A. (1999). *Adicción*. Barcelona: Ediciones de Neurociencia.

Markez I, Iraurgi I, Polo M, Ordieres E, Del-Arco J, Presser E, Linaza I, Menoyo C, Diez M A, Ruiz J, Zapirain E, Ortega B, Ruiz-de-Apodaka J.(2000). Programas de Mantenimiento con Metadona en la Comunidad Autónoma Vasca. Consejo General de Colegio de Farmacéuticos de la CAPV. Secretaria de Drogodependencias del GV. Plan Nacional sobre SIDA, Bilbao. ISBN 84-921852-3-6.

The Multi-problem Family Generating Multiple Problems

Maurizio Coletti

Introduction

The multi-problem family (MPF) is a difficult, tough client.

Professionals working in the Social Services quickly learn to know these chaotic, redundant "family systems", that ask a lot. Or vice versa, they don't ask for anything, at least they don't ask what could be considered, generally speaking, as an advantage.

They often refuse job offers, chances for training, sometimes also occasions to improve their living conditions. They pitch, sometimes with violence, against the chance for younger family members to improve their living conditions, in more welcoming and protected contexts, with better prospects. Or to simply go to school to learn and socialize.

At the same time, they ask. They ask for direct economic support; or also indirectly, through the covering for their rent's debts, electricity, gas, fines. They ask nappies, food, and clothes for the children. But, most of all, they seem to have a violent aversion for structural changes. Or changes tout court.

On the one hand, they strongly cling to lifestyles that seem mostly chaotic, dysfunctional, lacking, often crossed from violence, problems, abuses, sexual habits that go from "poor" prostitution to sexual violence (also towards children), sexual intercourse without precautionary measures, with more than one partner or in any case without any privacy.

If we would try to suggest changes or improvements, we would face refusals, negations, and escapes.

M. Coletti (✉)
European Institute for Systemic Training and Counselling (I.E.F.Co.S.), Rome, Italy
e-mail: coletti@iefcos.it

R. Pereira, J. L. Linares (eds.), *Clinical Interventions in Systemic Couple and Family Therapy*, European Family Therapy Association Series,
https://doi.org/10.1007/978-3-319-78521-9_11

The MPFs are difficult not only because rigid (in regard to lifestyles and "deviant" behaviours), but also because they suddenly disappear without an ostensible reason. And, then, they reappear with new requests.

They are "flooding" systems that turn to everyone and to all the services and the agencies. They involve hard work from the caregivers and put a strain on the same agencies.

The systemic thought and approach have also been strongly challenged by the MPFs; we were used to deal with, for example, "enmeshed" and "disengaged" families, and then we faced disasters in terms of emotions and organization, education and social. And, at the same time, we faced systems with a nucleus able to develop a strong, exclusive, dramatic, and senseless membership. Besides, the conditions of life and relationships, apparently so unlucky and depressing, rarely change into coherent requests, in ambitions for great changes, in a commitment to improve something.

And, as it is known, the professional who has a systemic education desires to create new conditions in the systems that he has in charge. Overtaking the crisis "moving forward", using the family systems as resources to make the individuals feel better. The systemic professional is satisfied if he is able to create the conditions to move forward.

In the first cybernetic setting, two opposite "states" were set: the homoeostasis and the change. The first was the enemy of the systemic, such that the second was considered the highest point of a professional ambition in the work with the families. Even if the following epistemological thought has broadly gone beyond this hasty and Manichaean division, it always remains a bitter feeling when you face the immobilism and the resistance even to the smallest step ahead. The systemic therapist greatly suffers of these situations. And, on the other hand, if Athens cries but Sparta doesn't laugh: also other professionals, with different approaches from the systemic one are in an extreme difficulty in these type of cases. I will return later on the topic of the emotions of whom faces the MPFs, on the consequences of the emotions, on how recognizing and face them.

General Definition and Authors and Quotes: MPF in the Literature, in the Research and in the Clinic

Regardless of the beginning phase of the systemic thought and its evolutions, it's possible to state that the MPFs are one of the first fields of intervention of Social Services (SS).

As happens in several fields, the terminology is various[1] and, sometimes, muddling.

[1] We could make reference to the same terminological problem, referring to the different terms used for the drugs: addiction, dependence, use, abuse, misuse, consumer, path consumer, etc.

- Multi-problem families (Cancrini, 1994, 1997)
- Families with social problem
- Marginalized families
- "Asocial" families (Voiland, 1962)
- Disorganized, chaotic families (Minuchin et al., 2007)
- "Unstable" families
- "Sub-organized" families (Aponte, 1976, 1981)

All these terms can be referred to similar situations.

Luigi Cancrini (1994, 1997) proposes an MPF's definition based on five elements:

1. Presence at the same time of symptomatic behaviours in one or more family members.
2. Serious lacks in the emotional and organizational functions.
3. Mutual reinforcement between the point one and two (if one indicator increases, also the other increases).
4. Fragility of boundaries.
5. Relation of chronic dependence from assistance's services.

Cancrini adds the following characteristics to these points:

- A very limited exchange of information between the members and a basically undifferentiated cognitive and emotional experience.
- A predominant use of pre-verbal channel of communication.
- In the majority of the messages, aspects regarding the relationship have more importance than the ones related to the contents.
- A communicative chaos is perceived and this is an indicator of relationship disorder and structural disorganization, which in turn contributes to reinforce it (Malagoli Togliatti & Rocchetta Tofani, 2002).

At this point, it could be clear what is the difference between the dysfunctional families and the MPFs: while in the first (dysfunctional families) the symptomatic behaviours are usually useful to produce a balance for the emotional difficulties of the other members of the family and for the whole system, in the latter (MPFs), the symptomatic behaviours work as an additional factor of difficulty and disruption for the other members of the family system (Cancrini, 1997).

We know that the family system evolves through consecutive phases and that the passage from a phase to another of its life cycle (McGoldrick, Carter, & Garcia-Preto, 2010) is or could be characterized by crises, that allow the family members to experiment with new behaviours, new relationships, new achievements regarding the relationship of each member and the system in its entirety with the microsystems and the macrosystems external to the family itself.

Cancrini (1987) states that in MPFs, the appearance, the stabilization, and the increase of symptoms constantly occur in the first phases of the stage of life cycle: the construction of the couple, the children's birth, the children's adolescence and that, if symptomatic behaviours are capable of literally stopping the passage to the following phase, they are not so effective in the maintenance of the balance of the previous phase; the symptoms produce more disorganization and disruption of the family system, acting in a way in which they constitute:

- A dysfunction of the family that is not able to cover in a satisfactory way the organizational aims (sufficient economic resources, accommodation, children's instruction, growth and support, protection of the weakest members of the group), and the emotional aims (stress management, children's emotional nourishment, guarantee of individual and couple's privacy, emotional stability of the members).
- A continuous and hard research of external people able to give answers to the problems of the previous point. This research (when completed) progressively and inexorably reduces the competences of the members of the family system.

The symptomatic behaviours (as already stated) are multiple and various. They may vary from ineffective or non-existent care and support of minors to family violence, psychotic behaviours, use of alcohol and drugs, prostitution, physical and sexual abuse, problems in obtaining and keeping jobs, inability or refusal to respect authority and institutions, criminal behaviours such as thefts and stealing.

Always Cancrini (1987) insists on defining the MPFs depending on the following specific and general aspects:

- The social level: in the large majority, the social level of the MPFs is low and humble. Characterized by conditions of economic and cultural deprivation, the condition of misery hugely increases the risk factors of the symptomatic behaviours. They often belong to immigrant's families, families with one or more members with institutionalization, or families that can be considered as multi-problems families. Irregular and, at the same time, annoying in the help's research, they don't normally benefit from economic helps even if reiterated. Several characteristics of the MPFs can be found also in family systems of the middle or even upper class. They are isolated and serious cases, hard to be taken in charge.
- The dimensions: there does not exist a standard dimension of the MPFs, also it is very frequent to bump into very numerous nucleus with many children, also because of the incapacity to avoid undesired pregnancies. These multiple and continuous births are intended as a "strong" signal, against the persistence of the services when they intervene and inform about the practical impossibility to cure and nourish all the children. It is as if, especially the mothers, they want to express in this way their "generating potentiality". Almost always, the attempts to proceed with a withdrawal of the parental responsibility (when put it into practice: as explained later on, these people are not able to follow the institutional and legal procedures) produce opposition and violent reactions.
- The styles of life: they are the clear mirror of the relational and practical disorganization. Dirty houses, with furniture and bits and pieces piled up in order to block the passage, missing or unusable sanitary services, open doors. Inside, it is quite clear the boundaries' lack of physical spaces and the definition of their

specific function (bedroom, dining room, the room in which the TV could be seen that is, instead, always present!). The relationship between MPF's members is often in danger of incest and sexual abuse, carried out without any regards for the children or other family members' presence. The concept of time is ephemeral, or totally missing. This aspect is also reflected in the relationship with professionals and services, with the unavoidable consequence of missed, postponed, cancelled appointments. The same chaos can be found in the nourishment, both for the quality and the quantity of the food. The educational and school attendance's needs are not recognized. Clothes are poor, dirty, and strongly inappropriate. This is valid both for the adults and the children. The lack of economic resources plays an important role, and the MPF faces it in a uncertain and vague way, with illegal activities (see later) and with continuous, external requests for economic support.

- The relationship with legality: this aspect is also a mirror and a consequence of the chaos of MPF. There isn't attention either for the legal recognition of the couples, nor for the official registration of the new-born children. The latter frequently result totally unknown to the authorities, without identification documents, and without possibilities (because unknown or not registered) to access the public service, even the emergency room. Illegal activities (usually, petty crimes) are the standard; in case of legal consequences, the members of an MPF are not interested in following the legal procedure. In this way, the legal procedure continues on its own, without any forms of defence; and the consequences of the decisions are often very serious, more serious than what could be with just a little attention from the defendant. An assured consequence is the "the absence to avoid the arrest" or the "contumacy" of the alleged guilty. Often, the members of the MPFs are imprisoned and they spend long periods in jail. They are the typical subject that, in a detention condition, gain a more criminal experience.
- The children: usually quite numerous, they are the bridge for the pressing requests to the Services. Their conditions (both the ones related to practical lacks and the ones related to functional lacks, such as the poor or absent coverage of the parental responsibility) are always the first and main reason that causes an intervention of the Social Services. As explained later, the images of undernourished children, exposed to violence or workload totally inappropriate, roughly dressed, without instruction, smile or vitality, they are always aspects that impress the professionals and that drag them into attempts of practical and emotional substitution of the discovered lacks.

I consider useful to report here a sort of classification of the MFPs proposed by Luigi Cancrini (1984). Even if the typologies of the systems (and the dysfunctional systems) open to differentiation and to cases showing characteristics common to different case-typology, the proposal is interesting, current, and valid.

- The peripheral father: described effectively by Salvador Minuchin and others (Minuchin, Colapinto, & Minuchin, 1967) and based on pioneer experiences in the black and Puertorican ghettos of Philadelphia is a typology quite frequent also in family groups different from MPFs. In the latest, it could be found father

without (or limited) instruction, with no or occasional and various jobs, these men haven't any relevant roles within the family system. Often, they come from long and reiterated jail experiences, which raise the extraneity and careless level towards the children. In this case, this is what Gilbert Pregno (1998) described in his work: a distant, absent, and non-relevant figure; when someone in the family speaks about him, often it is said "the father is in jail". In relation with the mother, the profile is that of a violent man, often alcoholic, unfaithful, and incapable of taking care of the children and the family, even only from the economic point of view. With all these preliminary remarks, it is very easy that the father doesn't go to the services together with the mother, when she asks for help. And this absence becomes a huge problem during the intervention. At the same time, the mother occupies all the scenes and plays (at her best) all the roles. In case of an "official" marriage, the peripheral, absent, non-relevant position of the man doesn't produce legal consequences such as separation or divorce even if the wife-mother finds a new partner and starts a cohabitation. Another curious repetition is the one related to the father's absences at the family meeting: in rare cases, the mother doesn't offer a sort of "excuse" for the absent father. She will say that he is at work and he cannot lose time. The mother doesn't openly recognize the peripheral position of the father, but she seems to give it a certain, theoretic importance. Actually, the absence of the father (also at the meeting with the Social workers) allows the mother to cover the entire field to decide and count always more and more. A sort of reinforcement of the family system organization based on the condition described above.
- The unstable couple: here there are two young subjects, sometimes very young. Because of behaviours such as reiterated school failures, use of drugs, petty crimes, and inclination towards every kind of excess, the two subjects don't create a wise and responsible couple. Almost always, there are undesired children. Then, the couple is forced to take some responsibilities; but, because they are not able to do that, very strong fights rage, which can involve also children and that reduces the space for a life sufficiently balanced. At a certain point, one of the partner leaves and who stays should take charge of the children. In this situation, it is frequent to run to the origin family as "substitute family"; usually, it is the mother of the person who hasn't left to take charge of them, while the son/daughter tries (without great success) to find a job. The partner who left can, sometimes, come back asking for economic support or for parental responsibility; often with the support of his own origin family. This brings conflicts that could be really strong, with the involvement of Minor's Court. The configuration that provides the partner's mother who stays with children playing a sort of maternal role, reminds the configuration of the "absent grandmother" (Minuchin, Montalvo, et al., 1967); so called because, in reality, it is the job of the grandmother to take care of nephews (and also of the son or the daughter), fully acting as a mother and creating the conditions for the role and function's absence typical of the grandmother.

- The alone woman: here is a nucleus that rotates around a single feature: a woman that has often suffered in the past of long institutionalization periods, who decides to bring up children completely alone. These have usually been conceived with different partners. The partners of the "alone woman" are a fleeting presence that don't establish a stable bound. The advantage of these partners, sometimes, is having a bed to sleep and something to eat. The advantage for the woman is having a provisional presence at home that can give to her the feeling of a couple. The occasional partner is often violent; he maltreats and sometimes abuses the woman's children. They are situations in which the limited incomes can be guaranteed from prostitution, often exercised in the same place where woman and children live.
- The "petrified" family: in this last kind of multi-problems family is a family system affected by a dramatic event, often para-normative. A family in which symptoms could have a "classic" role in life's cycle, a sudden and unexpected event (accidental death, disappearance of an important member, an untimely intervention of the justice) causes the condition for the creation of the vicious cycle between disorganization, presence of symptomatic behaviours, incapacity to cover the typical function in a group like this. The family appears "petrified" around the events and things can only get worse. It should be noted that the starting conditions of these families are clearly more favourable than the ones of the families (or systems) previously described. This kind of family is more infrequent and this has been recorded during the project's activities "Viva Palermo Viva": Cancrini (1994) links them to the mafia's crimes, in which a member of the family disappears; it is considered that he has been killed in a brutal way, but the fact that the body cannot be found doesn't allow the processing of burial and funeral rites with the deceased, that (especially in the South of Italy) have a strong symbolic value, liberator in a certain sense.

The MPF When Appears to Professionals and Services. The Multitude of Services

As already stated, the arrival of a signalling involving an MPF is almost always received with worry, sometimes with anger or disappointment. This emotion is mostly present when there is information of maltreatment or inacceptable conditions involving the weakest subjects: women and minors.

Usually, MPF's members rarely turn to services to report their difficult conditions. This is valid especially for the first contact.

They are reluctant to recognize themselves as dysfunctional members or individuals, not interested in entering into training and refresher circuits that could improve their instruments and skills for the research of a job and therefore an improvement of their economic conditions, but they are competent in the various requests of material and economical supports.

According to Gilbert Pregno (2016): "they seem to ask nothing that can permanently improve their situation; on the contrary the feeling is that they ask for everything".

One of the aspects, quoted several times in this chapter, is the one related to the non-spontaneous sending to the competent services: they present themselves (or are contacted) without an attitude for the help's research.

Several authors insisted on the particularities and difficulties of being involved with the human systems, with individuals, parents, members of MPFs that show a deep lack of interest, if not an open hostility, towards intervention offers (but also judicial impositions) that can structurally improve their conditions.

According to Coletti (2001), these premises could create another huge problem that is an oscillation between an intervention purely helping-pietistic and an intervention that could be defined sadistic-collusive. The first includes the typical substitutive proposals, as the ones represented by donations of different kinds of economic supports, accommodations and working facilitation, crèches, organized socialization's moments, offers of domestic help; in the second are found "punitive" interventions such as children and teenagers' removal because they are at risk of maltreatment and all the forced interventions with the participation of the Court.

In this "forced to cooperate" situation, families quickly develop a growing competence to turn to different services.

It is extraordinary how people surely without a solid base's instruction and away from the usual sources of information are able to understand the specificity of the competence of the different welfare's agencies, avoiding the offers involving commitments considered useless and, on the contrary, asking specific requests in the "appropriate" context.

G. Pregno (2016) states that he discussed a case in which the agencies involved and active in different ways were the exceptional number of 25.

It's more frequent to find MPFs that turn into a number of welfare's agencies that are around ten. Social Services, Specialized social services, mental health's institutes, charity agencies, district's agencies, parish churches, and local social centres are the most frequent.

Something is asked to each of them, and MPF mobilizes all sort of resistances if different requests are suggested. This scenario includes the most varied requests and, usually, a kind of behaviour based on the presumption that this is their right.

The MPFs don't tell at all that they turned to other agencies to ask some economic help or other kind of support. So, the agencies and professionals involved in the interventions find out that other organizations, other colleagues are active on the management of bill and residual aspects.

One of the most repeated "mantras" in the psychosocial intervention is the one of coordination. The coordination has, or should have, the following advantages:

(a) Saving resources.
(b) Do not duplicate actions.
(c) Harmonizing strategies.

From the moment that there doesn't exist an "integration's science", with specific parameters, indicators, universally applicable protocols and that the actual protocols and the guidelines enormously vary from situation to situation, the integration is a movement left to the professionals, coordinators, and manager's responsibility and interpreted differently case by case.

No matter of the great efforts that sometimes are put forward, getting together in a single network 10 or 20 agencies of different dimensions, missions and competences, availability (hours, office, rules for taking in charge), is really a huge and quite impossible aim.

People who had the experience of participating at meetings and reunions know well the risk that defensive[2] and/or accusatory[3] positions prevail; this makes these occasions frustrating, distressful, and less effective.

The characteristics of MPFs stress the difficulties, moving naturally between the agencies and imposing their chaotic dysfunctionality as driver for the relationship with centres and professionals.

It seems, then, that the organizational chaos of MPFs has the power of reflecting on the centres and professionals who meet it, making it really difficult to reach the same goal that should be reached for the MPF: organizing in a rational, non-chaotic, regular way.

Notes for the Intervention

The work with MPFs has to do, in the first instance, with the setting.

Systemic therapists learnt that counting on certain "home rules" (rules that are connected to the therapeutic context) gets some advantages. For example, booking the appointments, defining who is the most appropriate to participate, defining a known and prearranged length of the meetings, be able to lead the conversation (avoiding, for example, that someone speaks for too long), etc., these are all actions that facilitate the therapist in leading the interviews. Clearly not all the things are predictable and it's reasonable that the intervention in its entirety cannot always go in the expected direction.

With the MPFs, excluding that it would be possible to count on the acceptation of usual setting's rules (previously indicated) the professional hasn't the security represented by proposing some rules and negotiating them with their patients.

He has to get used to booking the meetings and finding out that no one is coming, or that not all the participants are coming that (according to the professional) would be useful they participate.

With infinite patience, he should take contact and book another appointment again. Also the meeting's length is uncertain.

[2] "it isn't our competence ..."

[3] "should be a task of ..."

As much as the place where the interviews take place; often, it's useful and advantageous to do brief interviews in the corridor, maybe standing up.

A Setting: Non-setting, in Conclusion

A second point involving the interventions has to do with the characteristics of the little or non-existent cooperation between the families and the professionals and the centres.

Taking for granted that treating this aspect as offensive, reacting with anger, making them feel guilty are (all) useless interventions that could even make the situation worse, it is very important to try to intervene on this aspect; first of all, defining it without any fear, putting it on the light, not ignoring it.

Gilbert Pregno (2016) insists on the work's possibility in the lack of cooperation based on a creative and open form, proposing a series of unusual interventions that try to approach the adverse situation in a less losing way.

According to the author, it is necessary "to use a clear language, without excesses of interpretation, tactics, and strategies. It is possible to use a direct form of humour, with no regards but without irreverence".

For example:

> "In my experience I verified that if a family cooperates, the length of my intervention decreases".

Always according the same author, it is suitable to openly evoke the limits of the professionals and propose to the family a sort of cooperation:

> "I am not very efficient in my job but I would like to improve myself: what do you think could be done?"

Or, "supporting" the resistances that MPF shows in the work:

> "Let's try to shorten the length of my intervention so that I can set you free".

Or, also:

> "I imagine that you would be happy if my intervention ends here, but for the moment that is not possible".
>
> "I understand that my work bothers you. Do you have any ideas on how these meetings could be more pleasant?".

Also the positive redefinition could be a useful instrument:

> "I am interesting to observe how you educate your children. You are original, and you do different things from the usual way of doing …".
>
> "May I ask you to give me an advice for my future work with the families? In particular if there were things that you didn't like or others that you would say this has been very useful? These kinds of things interesting me a lot because in this way other families could take advantage of them".

Also the desperate lack of temporal references is so redefined by Pregno: "Oriented on hic et nunc, they manage the time with a great flexibility".

Accepting, then, the most part of challenges to the setting and use them for a reasonable path.

As stated later on, working with subjects that recognize neither their own situation as problematic, nor the competence of the person in front of them, nor the obligation to change some risky behaviours (especially regarding the minors) is deeply frustrating.

But it is also possible to use this scenario in a therapeutic form. With obvious and frequent exceptions, it is possible to redefine the relationship with the MPF as "mandatory for all; therefore, It is convenient that everyone conforms to that". This kind of intervention could allow to lower the sensation of "being controlled, judged, sometimes punished", of having in front of them professional that "oblige". Furthermore, it would allow to reach a sort of "alliance" between the acting subjects.

In the end, the already mentioned feeling of judgement and penalization.

The MPF (as the huge majority of the human systems) has a bad reaction to the sensation of being judged: one of the most recurrent and reiterated aspects of the work with this kind of family is focused on defensive attitudes, detachment, aggression focused on the sensation to be perceived as "wrong" and waiting for a punishment for that.

If the professional is able to reduce this reactive feeling, commenting on it directly and openly, the meeting's atmosphere could be really improved. "I/we am not/are not here to judge you; most of all we don't judge your feelings and intentions. We know that these are positive. We want to support you in the attempts of "improving the situation".

The Emotions

Many years ago, when I was working in training and supervision of Social Services of Ciutat Vella in Barcelona, one Social Worker told me during a GROUP SESSION one of her recent experiences.

She was following a curious "family" system made of two adult women, both of them with children, who found it useful and convenient to share a dirty shack in order to keep staying together the two sons of one (5 and 3 years old) and the three kids of the other (one daughter of 9 years old and two twins of four). The women had the children from occasional relationships, when they lived by various expedients, among them prostitution. Therefore, there weren't either men or fathers. Also the origin families were absent: one was in Andalusia, the other was made of the father of one of the woman (the mother was deceased) and the brother; both of whom didn't care for their relative. Between the two women there was nothing more than a friendship relation and sharing of the "house".

The case was brought to the Social Services' attention because of a exantematous disease of the eldest daughter and her hospitalization and, later, because of a signalling of the Local Police authorities who stopped and identified one of the two adult women while she was exercising prostitution with one occasional client.

The following interventions and home visits found out that the daughter had several tics and the 2 years old son seems not able to speak, except with gestures.

On two previous occasions, the Social workers had already opened a file for the withdrawal of the parental responsibilities due to a clear inability to act as parents and supposing a quick assignment of all five children to Institutes and/or foster families. Towards this option, the two women had a strong resistance and an absolute contrariety, stating that "children get along well together" and that they were providing all they need.

However, the judicial procedure was still in place and the Social Assistant went to the shack to understand if something was changed.

The professional, during one of the case SUPERVISION meetings, says:

> *"I opened the door of the shack, children were on the floor, a floor of dirt. There wasn't any adults with them. The eldest daughter was dealing with a pot and a cooker, probably preparing something to eat. But I didn't see anything, except for some leafs of verdure, dry bread and a fistful of rice. The other children were lying on the floor, playing with pieces of wood and iron. One was continuously sneezing and his nose was running. The hygienic conditions were extremely bad; there were dirty straw mattresses on the floor. At a certain point, I saw in a corner one of the twins playing with a big rat and the animal was nibbling one of his fingers. I felt bad, I run out and I vomited in the street".*

At this point, a heavy and dramatic silence has crossed all the group. A long silence. Suddenly, it has been interrupted by an intervention of a worker who screamed:

> *"Now we all go out from here, we call the police and we go to take these children!! Now, immediately!!"*

A very animated discussion began, in which everyone expressed his pain and disgust. Several of them reacted with verbal violence against the "two mothers". Someone proposed to interrupt the supervision and go to the Police to report the situation. The Police would interrupt that situation and put the children in safety. Others expressed criticisms against the colleague as she didn't decide to call immediately the authorities.

The Social worker listened to the discussion very tensed. Then she started an uncontrollable fit of weeping; all the others tried to console her and increased the number of people that thought reporting the two women to the Authorities was the right thing to do. The woman, among the sobbing, stated that that evening she was on the point to ask a job's change (she wanted, she said, to work in the adoption field). The day after (1 week before the supervision session) she has had an interview with her area manager who asked her to wait some time before taking her final decision. A lot of colleagues expressed criticisms towards the manager because, according to them, he didn't defend the woman enough and he just took time. For a quite long period of time, the atmosphere of the group changed: the discussion was on the "limited" protection for a job like this, about the indifference of managers and politicians, of the injustices suffered during the work. She has been advised (by the supervisor and all the group) to go and speak again with the manager; this time, about the specific case and proposing to him to go together and report the situation.

A supervision session conducted 2 months later after this session allowed to gather the feedback on the case: the Social worker spoke with her manager, who agreed to go together to report the situation to the authorities. The Minor's Court disposed, at the beginning, another inspection at the shack. The Police, this time, found the two women: they reacted with violence when Police arrived. According to them, nothing was wrong: children felt good, they were nourished, and they don't complain. The neighbourhood arrived when the women screamed and they confirmed that the children were often alone while women exercised prostitution. At this point, the policemen took the minors and brought them to an Institute. They also reported the mothers.

The Judge had quickly expressed a withdrawal measure of the parental responsibility and the two women have been arrested. The Social worker when told the fact really tensed, but in a less dramatic way than the first time.

This example (extreme, but not too much) shows how working with these client is risky both for the emotional system and the human dimension of the professional.

Compared to other interventions, the one on the MPFs is characterized by widely penalizing and dramatic conditions that tested very hard the professional operator.

There are five aspects that attack the emotions of the operator:

1. The already mentioned (sometimes extreme. As in the case reported) gravity of the situations. Even if it is possible to find family systems with the typical characteristics of the MPF also in cases belonging to the middle or upper class (Coletti, 2001), the majority of the cases belongs to the lower class. Poverty, lack of economic resources, lack of acceptable work conditions, unstable (or worse) accommodations, lack of education, and basic social skills greatly increase the previously described processes. The interventions are difficult also for these aspects. The more the situations is serious, the more the operator is in difficulty.
2. The attitude to the delegation and to continuous, insistent, requests of every kind. Usually, in the field of direct or indirect economic requests. They could be utility bills to pay, the rent to pay, nappies for the children, a car ride, or tickets for public transport. The competences of these families in dealing with the services and the operators is so elevated that, often, the same support is requested to different organizations. It is quite frequent that the behaviours of the family system's members are claiming to obtain what they ask as if it is an acquired right. If we think that, at the same time, the professional faces a wall regarding the offers that would involve efforts and behavioural changes from the system's members (for a job, to accompany children at school, to keep a sufficiently hygienic level at home, to remember the appointments and arriving "quite" in time, for example), it is quite logical that the operator thinks that "they" want

only to have practical advantages, but they don't do anything to change. The most frequent emotion, in this case, is anger.
3. The previous point brings us to the infinite expectations of enough consistent changes. It is very difficult to adjust ourselves to the exhausting slowness of the modifications of the behaviours and relationships, also when there are minors. Besides, when these changes take place, they are not stable, they haven't coherence, they vanish soon. The most frequent feeling is an immense frustration. The waiting (generous) for decisive changes, in comparison to the umpteenth request for nappies, could be too much.
4. The relational, organizational, emotional, social conditions of the MPF have a strong feature of chronicity. The extreme severity previously mentioned is perpetuated for a long time. Those that could be considered "errors" from outside (do not take enough care of the children, do not resort to alcohol and drugs, do not resort to violence) are sometimes endlessly perpetuated in the MPFs. The chronicity of the situations, the so-called relapses creates very frustrating conditions for whom is dealing with them.
5. The generosity (sometimes the inexperience) of the operators puts them frequently to face the failures. A failure on a specific intervention, or a general sense of failure, that involves both the intervention on a specific case, and the entire work done. The utility of their own efforts, of the structure, and of the entire system could be doubted; or also being adequate for this kind of work. In the conclusion of this chapter, the problem of burn out will be mentioned.

What could be done to face these emotional storms?

The instruments to mitigate a sense sometimes dramatic of being inadequate, of anger, are not miraculous. And they are based on the work on ourselves and with the staff.

First of all, the professional must have adequate instruments to know himself/herself, his/her reactions to stressful pressures as the ones previously described. In fact, only a patient, focusing on the emotional reactions allows to search and find the indispensable lucidity for interventions that are not only reactive interventions. Recognizing his own fragility, his own subjective critical points in work with the MPFs is essential.

Beyond the individual efforts, there are essential other instruments.

The individual supervision allows a deep work on the meaning of the reactions and the feelings for who works with the MPF. But it is also possible to call on resources of the internal staff: an expert and competent colleague could act in this role.

The group's supervision detects another level: the collective dynamics that develop around the private and lived emotions with the MPFs. It is clear that the dimension of the group has an auto-referential level, in which the followed cases could be the starting point to develop or underline aspects of a group dynamic independent from the discussed case. In this situation, it is appropriate that the supervisor is external and, if it is possible, chosen with the agreement (or, at least, without disagreement) of all the members of the group.

The group's supervision is also useful to identify, debate, and recalibrate the emotional feeling related to the proper running of the staff system in the situation as institutional, modification, hierarchy changes of above systems.

Conclusions

As it becomes clear, the interventions in case such as those of the MPFs are extremely difficult, long, and full of obstacles.

The most relevant aspects that we wanted to underline are:

1. The approach to organization with high dysfunctionality, very self-referenced, little cooperative is often carried out through a forced sending. This aspect makes difficult an intervention (as the systemic one) that is actually based on a meeting based on collaboration and availability.
   A requirement put into the light at various times and repeatedly is that of the essentiality of the maximum integration between the competent services or those that play a role in it. This aspect is widely important. But very difficult to achieve. Centres and structures with different mission, organization, dimension, leadership are not themselves, easy to coordinate, and ready to collaborate. The steps back are more frequent than the steps forward.
2. The work with the MPFs makes visible to the systemic operator new universes, challenging him to accept those of the setting's modifications and non-common techniques that need training and updating.
3. The work with the MPFs, by its own nature, involves in an extremely relevant and dramatic way the emotion system of whom works with it.

Apart from asking for great investments on the field of training and supervision, it would be necessary to use studies and researches having as subject the operator and the staff submitted to this kind of stressful and absorbing events.

In a study on a significant sample of professionals of the Italian Treatment Centers for drug use (SerT, SerD, Dipartimenti delle Dipendenze, residential or semi-residential treatment centres—TCs) of addiction in Italy (Coletti & Gaudio, 2008), there was the attempt to estimate the working stress and the risk of burn out for the professionals working with them with different competences.

The study provided some interesting clues, and at the same time, the operator risking burn out could be estimated in 15/20%.

According to the surveying, risk factors for burn out and work disease are considered:

- Gender's factors (especially for married women)
- Kind of services (for the public treatment centres for addiction)
- Excess of work
- "Evanescence" of professional role
- Weak management of the human resources (training, participation, …)

It appears less relevant for the disease's risks:

- The "material work" conditions (not adequate spaces)
- The relational system (inside the staff, with the clients)

From the research: the self-perception of the critical conditions signals as important:

- Users: a sense of detachment in the help's relationship; little expectation of the results
- Staff: professional integration; common approach and practice
- Organization: strategic management; participation; personnel's politics
- Professional feeling: qualitative (aims' difficulty, heterogeneity) and quantitative (excess of work) overloaded

The researchers conclude signalling the essential importance of some strategic priorities that can reduce the risk of burn out and stress and work diseases.

- The participation of all the professionals to the strategic choices of the services
- The clarity of the used procedure and the individual professional aims
- The investment in advice, training, and refreshing

These choices, these priorities are reasonable, not expensive and in the range of the sector's policies.

This study has been mentioned because both the analysis of the problems and the conclusions reached from the research have huge analogies with the intervention with the MPFs.

The multiple problems that MPF create to the services and professional can be faced not only by adopting innovative techniques, but with a deep and continuous revision of the intervention's setting, with a particular attention to the professional as a person, with choices adequate to the general system.

It seems necessary, most of all, to underline the importance of the supervision's intervention and case's discussion, seen as an option to support both a different and integrated reading and a decisive support to the professional involved.

The systemic approach helps in better understanding the mechanism, conditions, and paths. But, also, in using interventions with a bigger level of complexity (the individuals, the system, the systems), and in better understanding the process.

References

Aponte, J. H. (1976). Under-organization in the poor family. In Guerin, P. J. (Comp.), *Family therapy: Theory and practice*. New York: Gardner. ISBN-10: 0470150890.

Aponte, J. H. (1981). Structural family therapy. In Gurman, A. S., & Kinskern, P. (Comp.), *Handbook of family therapy*. New York: Brunner-Mazel. ISBN-10: 1138917621.

Cancrini, L. (1984). Quattro prove per un insegnamento della psicoterapia. Roma: Carocci Editore. ISBN-13: 978-8843006502.

Cancrini, L. (1987). La psicoterapia: grammatica e sintassi. Roma: Carocci Editore. ISBN 8843021060.
Cancrini, L. (1994). *W Palermo viva. Storia di un progetto per la prevenzione delle tossicodipendenze*. Roma: Carocci. ISBN: 9788843001316.
Cancrini, L.(1997) Lezioni di psicopatologia. Torino: Bollati Boringhieri. ISBN-13: 978-8833955858.
Coletti, M. (2001). Famiglie multiproblematiche, servizi sociali e approccio sistemico. In O. Cellentani (Ed.), *Lavorare con la famiglia. Manuale ad uso degli operatori dei servizi sociali*. Milano: Franco Angeli. ISBN: 9788846407467.
Coletti, M., & Gaudio, F. (2008). *Lavorare con i tossicodipendenti. Complessità. Sfide, rimozione sociale*. Milano: Franco Angeli. ISBN: 9788856803860.
Malagoli Togliatti, M., & Rocchetta Tofani, L. (2002). *Famiglie multiproblematiche*. Roma: Carocci Editore. ISBN: 9788843057009.
McGoldrick, M., Carter, B., & Garcia-Preto, N. (2010). *Family life cycle: Individual, family, and social perspectives* (4th ed.). Boston: Allyn and Bacon. ISBN-13: 978-0205747962.
Minuchin, P., Colapinto, J., & Minuchin, S. (1967). *Working with families of the poor* (2nd ed.). New York: Guildford Press. ISBN-13: 978-1572304062.
Minuchin, S., Montalvo, B., Guerney, B. J., Jr., Rosman, B. L., & Schumer, F. (1967). *Families of the slums. An exploration of their strucure and treatment*. New York: Basic Books. ISBN-13: 978-0465023301.
Minuchin, S, et al. (2007). Assessing Families and Couples: From Symptom to System. Boston: Alyn & Bacon. ISBN: 9780205470129.
Pregno, G. (1998). *Les enfants, orphelins de droits*. Luxembourg: Editons Le Phare. ISBN: 2-87964-036-2.
Pregno, G. (2016). *Le famiglie multiproblematiche ... o quando le famiglie non chiedono niente: Come soppravivere*. Roma: Workshop agli allievi di IEFCoS.
Voiland, A. (1962). *Family casework diagnosis*. New York: Columbia University Press.

The Multifamily Group in Severe Psychiatric Pathologies

Norberto Barbagelata

However the madness is, I don't know if a death in life or a revival. In any case, is a human process and not martian. And psychiatry is non human consideration of the human.
Leopoldo Panero. Cursed poet, schizophrenic. (Interview published in the Madrid daily El Pais, on Saturday, October, 27 2001.)
When psychotherapy has no social purpose, it has no reason for being.

N.B.

Introduction: Brief Theoretical Conceptualization of Identity Development

In the twentieth century, between 1940s and 1960s, came a conjunction of ideas in the scientific world that countered the ideal of the "individual created himself." It was the appearance, or rather, the reappearance of the belief that things, objects, individuals, are connected with each other in a complex way. This, which was present in the hard sciences (the General System Theory was known), was revolutionary for the analysis of serious psychiatric pathologies, as well as to have a new vision of the development of the normal psyche.

In what sense was it revolutionary? In helping us to ask some fundamental questions in our clinical world: How does the mind show up? Where is it located? How does identity develop? What is necessary to allow the individual to live a moderately successful life? and so on.

On the other hand, what we have learned over time is that the subject, the child, without ties, dies; understanding ties as the affection he or she needs, the physical

N. Barbagelata (✉)
Zurbano Group of Family Therapy, Madrid, Spain

R. Pereira, J. L. Linares (eds.), *Clinical Interventions in Systemic Couple and Family Therapy*, European Family Therapy Association Series,
https://doi.org/10.1007/978-3-319-78521-9_12

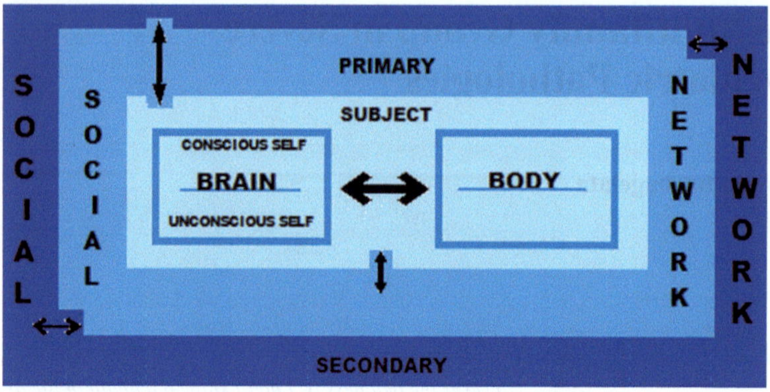

Fig. 1 Self-made

care, feeding, etc. (Spitz, 1999). In 1977, Rene Zazzo published in Spanish "La vinculación" (in Anzieu, 1977), a proposal to child psychiatrists, psychologists, ethologists, and psychoanalysts, involving paradigm change, which had caused a certain commotion in the environment "psi." He essentially proposed the concept of tie, as a primary impulse, rooted biologically. This statement broke with the classical psychoanalytic perspective according to which the primary impulse was that of self-maintenance and places the need to bond as the core of identity's constitution and development.

Earlier, in 1956, anthropologist G. Bateson (1976), a scholar of communication in humans and animals, observed, based on an analysis of the relations of mothers with children who were diagnosed with schizophrenia, a component that he called "double bind." He also conceptualized and described the human mind as a continuous feedback loop (between the subject and the environment) that does not reside in the brain. External and internal stimuli create a never-ending circle which is always being disturbed by new information coming both from the outside and inside.

The diagram, developed by us and based on Bateson's ideas (1976), expresses the above graphically in Fig. 1:

That the mind does not reside in the brain, or was born in the brain, is easy to check. Children who are born in a context where a language is spoken, think, talk, and know themselves in that language. In other words, the brain is "loaded" with information from the outside world. We know that the brain carries a genetic underpinning with a set of impulses (such as the tie impulse) and that it will be found in and it will have to adapt to a particular context.

To accept that we are not isolated, separated, independent, that we do not begin or end in our skin, we will look at a paragraph of the *Tibetan Book of Life and Death* (S. Rimpoché, 1994):

> Nothing has an "inherent" and own existence when it is examined carefully, and this absence of independent existence is what we call "vacuity". Think of a tree. When you think of a tree, you tend to think in a clearly defined object, and in a certain way, like the wave, it is so. But when you contemplate the tree more closely it shows that it ultimately lacks an

> independent existence. When you examine it, you will find that it dissolves itself into a very subtle network of relations that encompasses the entire universe. The rain that falls on their leaves, the wind that shakes it, the land that feeds it and holds it, seasons, the weather, the moon, the stars and the sun light… All of them are part of the tree. When you start to think more and more about the tree, you will discover that the entire universe contributes to make the tree what it is. In no moment could it be isolated from any other thing and at all times its nature is subtly changing. This is what we mean when we say that things are empty: that lack independent existence (p. 62).

In another order of things, but in this context, Pichon-Rivière (1978, 1977a, 1977b), proposed in his *Social Psychology*, that all subjects are subjects of the need, that we have for food, affection, sex, protection, etc., and that these needs will unquestionably be provided for socially.

If we put together, hypothetically, that the impulse to bonding of Zazzo (1977) is a primary impulse in the individual, which is determined by genetics, which will allow the survival of the infant, that this infant from birth required to satisfy his social needs, we can deduce that society is constituted not only by the prohibition of incest (Lévi-Strauss, 1994) but by the fundamental need for bonding.

In this set of ideas that underlie the scientific world of the time, we have to acknowledge a linkage with ethology, using animal behavior as a way to find the similarities and differences with humans (do not forget than our genetic similarity with certain primates is of 99%).

In our view, this approach of the ethologists, psychoanalysts, psychologists, and vice versa led Bowlby (1989), with his Attachment Theory, to demonstrate the importance of a mother-child tie (attachment) as a central factor in the healthy development of all the individuals. This is not a place to highlight his immense work and that of his followers, but at least to place on record that bonding between a child and his or her caregivers will mark, in part, his future psychological development and his or her integration into society.

In short, the mind does not lie in the brain; the brain develops while being sustained and nourished by the body, but needs society to survive and develop Barbagelata (2005). The identity of the subject is constructed and evolves in continuous interaction with the environment.[1]

In this conceptual framework, severe[2] mental pathology would appear due to an unfortunate encounter between the genetic (brain or body) and the environment. So certain "encounters," do not favor the development of an individual with psychic abilities or "genuine ego resources," in the words of J. García Badaracco (2000), enabling it to integrate into a society which it depends on.

---

[1] Faris and Dunham (1939) says: "the work suggests that social isolation is the biggest risk to develop a mental disorder." In *Mental disorders in urban areas: An ecological study of schizophrenia and other psychoses.*

[2] WHO (1976), conducted an international study on the prognosis of schizophrenia. The percentage of worse prognosis (24% versus 12%) in underdeveloped countries is higher than in developed countries. As well, the good prognosis is 41% in underdeveloped countries, versus 15% in developed countries. They concluded: Cultural factors have a statistically significant effect on the prognosis of schizophrenia.

Justification: Why the Multifamily Group in Severe Psychiatric Pathologies?

It is told in my home town that one day, a citizen was driving his car and he passed in front of the psychiatric hospital when suddenly a wheel comes loose. The good man, displeased, steps out of his car, lifts the car with a jack, puts the wheel on and desperately discovers that he has no screws to tighten it. Sensibly, he steps back on the road in search of the missing screws. He searches, but does not find any. Desolate, he suddenly sees from behind the gate of the hospital a patient looking at him who says: "Listen, remove one screw from each of the wheels and use them on the one which has none, with them you can continue your journey." Our man looks with astonishment and asks: "Why are you there?" After a moment of silence the patient responds: "because I am crazy, not because I am a fool."

Why do I tell this apocryphal story of my home town? Because the axis of these reflections is focused on trying to recognize the subject with severe psychiatric pathology as it is, an individual with an intellectual capacity as "any of us." This individual, like the rest of us, needs to stay within the social link to follow their evolution and development in life. From our point of view, the important question is: what happens to a seriously ill psychiatric patient when he starts his first psychotic episode? What is it what fractures and bursts, besides his "self," when he is invaded by a great sadness, voices, and delusions that confuse, frightened, and alienate him?

The theme we are following is that this subject had his connections with the common world distort and destroy a little or much of the social network that he had before the psychotic burst. Thus, the intervention must have a fundamental and essential axis: to try not to break this social link or, when that is not possible, rebuild it as soon as possible, to prevent the arrest of the individual evolutionary process (cut out of the social world).

The importance of the previous statement is that the brain is nourished by two sources. The most well known is the one which comes through the body, that is to say, the physical, the material, the energy that carries the blood. The other source, the most ethereal but also more meaningful and fundamental for the survival of a functional brain, is the information that comes from the social world. Without this second "fuel" the brain deteriorates so much that it is similar to the deterioration that ateromas of the arteries that do not allow the food to reach the brain and is even measurable with the Wechsler (1999) test.

Seen from this perspective, we can represent the psychotic episode of the subject in the dialectical evolutionary spiral of Pichon-Rivière (1978), as a break from the cycle of the spiral and the therapeutic act, as an attempt to mend this split as soon as possible, with an approach that keeps the subject in the social network.

We cannot forget, on the other hand, what the breakdown of the Self means for the subject. Things like deep depression, self-destructive desire, voices, and delusions invade the mind. It is another disaster for himself, given the difficulty to comprehend all the unheard of things that are happening (or that he is perceiving) as healthy individuals usually do. Precisely it is in this process, where the theory and the methodology underpinning the multifamily groups make sense. The individual pathologies of each participant are underestimated in favor of listening to the group's speech and finding a joint solution for the difficulties of life for every one of the attendees.

In the multifamily group, society can rescue the subject from his or her pathology. The focus changes and moves from illuminate psychopathology to looking at the social life of the subject, that is, friends, work, family, etc. And where does that leave psychopathology? It is clear that you cannot abandon it. If there is much delusional activity, hallucinatory, etc. the therapeutic work is impossible. On the other hand, if the subject does not understand what is happening in their intrapsychic world, social reintegration is questionable and incomplete. As we believe will be shown, the multifamily group can resolve the contradiction precisely by those characteristics that are inherent to it: the cure of mental pathology through relational, the intersubjective, that is, the group helps the subject to solve its problems and to understand its intrapsychic world. In this way, mental pathology relieves itself.

A Brief History of the Multifamily Group

All history is a series of events that orders and links, in a comprehensible and logically coherent form, dates, documents, analysis of the contexts, etc. It looks like the narrative of a historian based on verifiable elements that give it a certain likelihood. We will build a similar story with the facts that, in our view, led the way which ends in the multifamily groups with serious psychiatric patients.

In the beginning of the twentieth century, Freud, with the creation of psychoanalysis, provide us with a new view of mental illness, showing that some psychopathological pictures are understandable, accessible, and treatable by the word. From this teachings have emerged some psychoanalysts that created different schools and trends approaching the social. Among them, Erich Fromm (2008, 2011) and Karen Horney (1993). Others, such as Virginia Satir (1964) or Enrique Pichon-Rivière (1978), began to treat psychiatric patients, interviewing them and their families. A milestone in this process was Bateson (1974), who moved the gaze definitively from the individual to relational, thus expanding the vision of mental illness and its treatment to the relational connectedness[3] and has been considered one of the most important founders of family therapy.

Influenced by social and cultural movements of the twentieth century and derived in part from constructivism (Maturana & Varela, 1990), (Maturana, 1997),

[3] Mauricio Kartum (2014), dramatist, in his work *Terrenal*, writes a scene where God complains to his son Cain the murder of his brother Abel in the following words: "Misery is to kill the pair. One grows to two. The two fighting is harmony. It is flying. Only one, growing Monster. A single wing bird. Like you. You cut yourself a wing. Together could be angel and look at you, you finish hen bataraza. One is the tragedy, Cain…"

(Watzlawick & Krieg, 1994) arises (Gergen, 1992) Social Constructionism (Gergen, 1996), (McNamee & Gergen, 1996a, 1996b) as a theoretical support that allows, in part, the evolution of family therapy to multifamily groups.

Previously, Maxwell Jones (1970), had created the Therapeutic Communities, further into the world of rational community but without abandoning the theoretical axis of psychoanalysis; and later allowing, García Badaracco (1990) to create the "multifamily psychoanalysis groups" which definitely linked the relational with the intrapsychic aspects.

We should not forget in this brief history of the multifamily groups, the relevant importance of the work done by the Finnish school in the early 1980s, and also the Finnish National Project about Schizophrenia, led by Alanen. It was he who developed the Approach Adapted to the Needs (2003), from which, Seikkula, Alakare, and Aaltonen (2001) developed another innovation they called "Open Dialogue approach." What is new is that therapeutic intervention of the psychotic patient is addressed, first of all, by gathering together the family, the patient, his closer social network and professionals who will be in charge of the case.

What Is a Multifamily Group?

The question refers to thinking about a definition, which is encompassing and represents the multifamily group. Many have been given and we will not track them. For us it is a meeting of several individuals of different families which are experiencing difficulties in some area of their life, which leads them to seek help from other people, including the group coordinators. It is a micro-society, in which the voices of all attendees have value; where the coordinators' task is to promote the horizontal dialogue among the people who compose it. In this dialogue, many ideas should appear as well as understandings and various analyses that help to increase the number of possible types of difficulties that the members have. All psychiatric disorders fit in this context, from the less severe to most severe psychopathological pictures whenever they allow the type of dialogue mentioned above.

Our vision of the multifamily groups has certain connections or attachment, with the model of intervention, quoted above. The Perspective of the Open dialogue (Seikkula, et al., op. cit.) where, in the treatment of acute psychotic episodes, the patient is invited from the beginning to gather together his family, his closer social network, as well as all professionals or technicians who will intervene throughout the treatment. In the meeting everything is decided: from the patient admission to the psychopharmacological treatment. The connection with multifamily groups is in "that open dialogue" and giving validity to the word of "all" members of the group, and "respecting" the value and authorship of who says it, no matter who says it. Looking for the understanding of what each member says explicitly.

In short, the multifamily group is a collaborative group, which tries to correct, as far as possible, social failure (familial and contextual) trying to rebuild a subject who is able to fulfill himself or herself in life. A subject having "proper mental health" so he or she can survive in society while maintaining individuality.

The Theoretical Foundations

How did it start? One of the pillars of the multifamily group, from a theoretical point of view, is Social Constructionism (Gergen, 1992, 1996; McNamee & Gergen, 1996a, 1996b among others) as mentioned above. One of its tenets is that "knowledge" is not only for the experts. Think of one neighbor meeting another and them talking of their economic difficulties, of disputes with their husbands and life in general. When one tells to the other that her son has been diagnosed with schizophrenia and the other expresses what she thinks, both do not know that they are possibly continuing, what Laqueur in 1951 began to practice on Sundays with his psychotic inpatients and their families, bringing them together to talk about the disease, treatments, and concerns. This practice led to, what he called "Multifamily Therapy," which he worked with for years and which consisted of (defying the accepted practice of that time), weekly meetings forming groups of four or five inpatients along with their families and relatives. Initially, there were only inpatients but sometimes even families and patients already discharged participated in the meetings (Sempere, 2015).

What is psychotherapy for the social constructionist? For H. Anderson (2012), it is simply a type of social situation that occurs in a particular environment with a specific agenda. It resembles the way in which we interact and speak in everyday life. Anderson proposes that psychotherapy in this perspective is an "interactive conversation that occurs naturally (through which people live their lives and conducts his daily business)" (Anderson, op. cit. p. 257).

What we want to highlight about the theoretical foundations is to show (or prove?) that psychotherapy began many years ago. Even before the term was established, it had begun under another name, "to converse" (to go around), quotidian action we do since childhood. "To converse," said Maturana (1991), carries the "lenguajear" (to talk with an emotional feeling) and "excite," that is, "to converse" implies to share the hardships of life, cooperate with each other trying to help with problems and thus, increase the visions about the setbacks and to elaborate traumatic situations, suffering, losses, etc. As the philosopher Adela Cortina said, any society with a minimum of intelligence is able to "realize that the core of social life is not composed of isolated individuals, but groups of people, bonds of mutual exploration. People who charge their self-esteem from the respect that others show them" (2017).

If to overcome difficulties of the life, sufferings, and losses, it is necessary to resort to an "expert" that helps us, how do the seven billion subjects who do not receive psychotherapy overcome all its problems? why we do not recognize the social network as a therapeutic element, knowing that it is this which builds the identity of the subject, along with himself, as well as any possible mental pathology?

As mental health professionals, we say that psychotherapy is a "very difficult" specialty, and perhaps it is; where much still remains to be study and read. Learning about the brain, the development of the psychic apparatus, having complex thought Minuchin (1985) would say in any of his multiple seminars; living your life, having experiences, being a parent, knowing English—as Maldonado said in a course (1982)—having a partner and be more or less happy, being sexually and emotionally satisfied. Also having a thorough understanding of himself, having made a personal analysis, be supervised by more certified therapists, have participated in a workshop of the family, and so on. It is partially true, the fact remains, that as we have already said, all humans take part in a receive "psychotherapy" in the social world, in conversation, in being part of the sufferings and joys of life with others. In the multifamily group, we cooperate, share, reflect, and participate "in society," the difficulties of the different stages of life. We tried to partly recreate, a micro-society coordinated by professionals where the knowledge of all members of the group surface, in the analysis of the various difficulties arising, in order to help other families and helped themselves in a mutually supportive way.

We present the multifamily group as a "micro-society" where new links will be found which, in certain ways, favor the reconnection with the wider social world. A space where the family pattern is not reproduced but a space that opens the subject to the possibility of generating different links in addition to those established in the family.

Constitution of the Multifamily Group

There is a great diversity of multifamily groups. The one that we propose and that has existed for years is constructed in the following manner: it is free; anyone who needs it can come. Their interest must have something to do with a personal preoccupation. They are not obliged to talk and they can attend anytime. The group meets weekly and there is no age limit.

The group has not fixed end point, it is founded with the idea of having continuity in time, or "infinite," so those who attend find in it a place, a context, which is always available and can be used as a resource for their whole life. That is why continuity in time must be an essential factor. Free service is another feature that allows its "use" without discrimination.

From our point of view, the multifamily group is an instrument at the service of the community that, without a fixed end point, works as a way of support, analysis, and understanding of the problems, in parallel to the life of the families and the social network.

The Coordinators

We believe that it is essential that coordinators have a framework that involves some theoretical paradigms that must sustain the look and performance of the multifamily group. The framework of complexity often becomes necessary to assume theories that to some extent are contradictory, like someone is always connected to the environment and at the same time it is an independent subject. This is a contradiction that resembles the problem of quantum physicists, depending on which the observation instrument employing get the knowledge that light is corpuscular or wave, what is an insoluble contradiction. So the coordinators of the multifamily groups need individual and systemic theories knowledge and about the structural determinants that organize people experience (social class, labor, economic situation, etc.). Perspectives that at some point are connected and in others are contradictory, but in any case are necessary to understand the internal and relational reality of the people.

Thereby, coordinators must know the different paradigms in depth. Firstly, the systemic model and within it the Social Constructionism. Secondly and equally important, the psychoanalytic model in its various developments and thus it is gaze towards the intrapsychic world, the defense mechanisms, resistances, and a long etcétera. Also, everything developed by multifamily psychoanalysis, like concepts such as "pathogenic intersubjectivity," and "virtual health." (García Badaracco, 2006).

On the other hand, it is essential to know the various pathologies described by psychiatric phenomenology in their main sections. The interest of this knowledge is motivated because these diseases involve specific dynamics relations: communication quality (Wynne, Ryckoff, Day, & Hirsch, 1974), degrees of difficulty in rational individualization (Stierlin, 1997), the differentiation (Bowen, 1991), to name a few.

It should be noted that in the former paradigm, the systemic, the therapist has to handle maps of the family structure that Minuchin identifies in his work (Minuchin, 1977; Minuchin & Fishman, 1981; Minuchin & Nichols, 1994; Minuchin, Lee, & Simon, 1998). We should also underline in the second paradigm, the psychoanalytic, the manner that Wahlberg et al. (1997) present about the communication quality in families who have a member that has the features of the diagnosis of schizophrenia.

If the reader knows these paradigms, you can quickly notice the presence of many contradictions between the diverse theoretical models. Indeed, the proposal we make is that each coordinator will perform a personal synthesis of the contributions offered by all these models to understand that within the family structure, each individual possesses an intrapsychic world that feeds itself and at the same time modifies the family and social context.

Therapeutic Aspects

In this section, we attempt to expose the therapeutic aspects of multifamily groups, as well as the most outstanding elements. The question is, what is it that the multifamily group offers which is therapeutic and promotes change? First of all, respect and acceptance a priori to any of the arguments exposed by its members. It also allows them to have alternative views about themselves, their problems, and their definitions of reality which come from other members of the group and from the coordinators. At the same time, other testimonies evoked by each narration multiplied these narrations exponentially. On the other hand, it offers a listening, without moral judgment (as far as possible), confronting with the tips, full of certainties type of "what you have to do...," which are not welcome in the group (and that at one time could join the group as part of the group ideology and could be transmitted among the members).

The group is also a privileged space for the identification of other members with similar problems. It offers an intimacy which favors the expression of trauma and suffering that tend to be difficult to tell if the context does not offer an atmosphere of solidarity between all members. As Sennett suggests (2012), rivalry and competence exist in society, but also cooperation and collaboration that favors codependency and solidarity.

A brief example of the functioning of the family group to try to illustrate the above is described below.

Earlier on we attended a multifamily group of about 70 people, coordinated by two therapists. One of them began the session inviting the newest member to participate in the proceedings. A man took the floor and he told the group of his recent medical discharge after a 3 months psychiatric admission. He had been diagnosed with depression with led to suicide attempts. The man explained that on previous occasions the episode had not been so prolonged. He thanked his wife and his children (present in the group) for the dedication and support he had received from them. He said that he had no desire for life that any difficulty seemed a mountain for him and that the idea of killing himself would not leave his thoughts. "I am good for nothing more than to make problems…" he would say.

When the therapist showed an interest in his story, the man told that in his childhood he was very unhappy due to the violence exercised by his father on his mother: "My father often beat my mom." Both he and the rest of the family always feared that these scenes would be repeated, and in fact many times they were. That went on until he turned 15 and another fight between his parents began, this time thought he could not stand it. He faced his father warning him that he would not allow him to hurt his mother anymore. The fathers arm fell, he turned', and left the home for good.

At that time during the group session, another participant took the floor to say that he did not understand why the man had such a bad opinion of himself. How was it possible that he did not want to live anymore when, at 15 years old, he had had the courage to confront his father to protect his mother. The other participant considered the man to be very brave to be able to face a very difficult situation at the age of 15. "I admire you" he said. "Facing your father down, at the age of fifteen, to stop him hurting your mother is very courageous." He concluded by saying, "don't kill yourself because you have a lot of worth." After a moment of silence, he added: "You remind me of my brother, and not only because you have the same name as him. He was also very depressed and he ended up committing suicide. He was 49 years old. How old are you?" The first man replied: "I am 49 years old."

A deathly silence descended.

For us, this brief conversation filled with such emotional intensity (which resulted from participation of other members of the group), brings many therapeutic[4] elements for actors, as well as the rest of those present. We summarize them briefly.

The words of the second participant benefit to the first one:

- To respect his frame of mind and his suicidal desire
- To emphasize and enhance a part of his identity where he has been powerful and has protected his mother from the paternal violence
- To authentically claim, not impose, that he should not kill himself
- For his solidarity with the man
- For the great emotional intensity of the entire scene that creates a link between them.[5]

The therapeutic effects for the second participant:

- He benefits by talking about his pain and the shame that his brother's suicide caused him.
- Feeling that what he is saying is helping another person (similar to his brother) who suffers.
- Receiving the blessing of the group by having designated the strengths of the first participant ("La virtualidad sana" of J. García Badaracco, 2000).

Reflecting on Theodore Zeldin (2014) and his book *Conversation. How the dialogue can transform your life* (2014), we can add some ingredients to make the conversation psychotherapeutic:

- Equal treatment, without condescending attitude (respect often cited in the article).
- The introduction of new subjects into the groups enriches it. On the one hand, there is a wish to know and understand the new member and to know his story which leads to an interested listener position. It is new lifeblood for the group. On the other hand, the one who tells the story is contained by the group in his suffering, listened with attention and interest.

---

[4] Norma Barbagelata (2017), in his book "Las infancias cuentan," talking about dialogue with children of the street, she says: "For this dialogue to happen, will have to break the rankings of knowledge...". The knowledge of each participant is as valid as the coordinators of and has the added emotional value of the experience of the story of both interacting subjects.

[5] "Independencia recíproca" J. García Badaracco (2000).

- “Other people are infinitely more interesting and have infinitely more things to say.” (p. 47)
- The conversation should explore new territories in psychotherapy. There is the coordinator, whose job is to give the floor to other non-members of the family that are describing at the moment and they will try to contribute with new view points of the problem. They, the outsiders, are not a part of the story and do not share in the difficulties that the family relate enabling the introduction of different points of view.
- When you give the floor and listen to a child, they bring a fresh and naive look about what they hear and see. They tend to transform the stories recalled by adults.

Epilogue

The multifamily group does not seek, in any way to solve all problems; it is only a framework that allows a dialogue where the psychotherapeutic novelty is the contributions of the others. We all know the old but current Socratic phrase: “I only know that I know nothing,” to which the multifamily group would add: “what I do know, is that the others know... that I don’t know.” The multifamily group can find the vein that leads to show virtual health of the individuals who compose it.

The multifamily group has the virtue of being a context of dialogue without a past and without a long history. The members of each family do not resemble the others; each family has its own story, with the emotional and own interaction guidelines. They have “their” story of conflicts, their frustrations, their pains, their envy, their rivalries, their jealousy that partly organized their life, their conversations, and the ways of understanding their conflicts. Therefore, the contribution that the rest of the group offers them, having no tangled past, can be heard in a different way, more crystalline, since comments are not contaminated by these stories.

References

Alanen, Y. (2003). *La Esquizofrenia. Sus orígenes y su tratamiento adaptado a las necesidades del paciente*. Fundación Para la investigación y el tratamiento de la Esquizofrenia. Madrid.

Anderson, H. (2012). Relaciones de Colaboración y Conversaciones Dialógicas: Ideas para una Práctica Sensible a lo Relacional. *Family Process, 51*(1), 1–20. https://doi.org/10.1111/j.1545-5300.2012.01385.x

Barbagelata, N. (2005). Nuevos horizontes en la terapia familiar de la psicosis: Biología, entorno y desarrollo de la identidad. *Redes* (15) Barcelona (pp. 26–33).

Barbagelata, N. (2017). Qué adulto para qué niño. In N. Barbagelata, E. Fraile, C. Mussi, & L. Pallero (Eds.), *Las infancias cuentan. Relatos del trabajo con niños y jóvenes* (pp. 33–47). Paraná: Fundación La Hendija.

Bateson, G. (1974). Hacía una teoría de la esquizofrenia. In VVAA. *Interacción familiar. Aportes fundamentales sobre teoría y técnica* (pp. 19–57). Buenos Aires: Tiempo Contemporáneo.
Bateson, G. (1976). *Pasos hacia una ecología de la mente*. Buenos Aires: Lohle.
Bowen, M. (1991). *De la familia al individuo*. Barcelona: Paidós.
Bowlby, J. (1989). *Una base segura*. Barcelona: Paidós.
Cortina, A. (28 de marzo de 2017). *La patología del odio*. El País. Tribuna. Retrieved from https://elpais.com/elpais/2017/03/16/opinion/1489679112_916493.html
Faris, R. E. L., & Dunham, H. W. (1939). *Mental disorders in urban areas: An ecological study of schizophrenia and others psychoses*. Oxford, England: Univ. Chicago Press.
Fromm, E. (2008). *El miedo a la libertad*. Barcelona: Paidós.
Fromm, E. (2011). *Espíritu y sociedad*. Barcelona: Paidós.
García Badaracco, J. E. (1990). *Comunidad terapéutica psicoanalítica de estructura multifamiliar*. Madrid: Tecnipublicaciones.
García Badaracco, J. E. (2000). *Psicoanálisis multifamiliar. Los otros en nosotros y el descubrimiento del si-mismo*. Buenos Aires: Paidós.
García Badaracco, J. E. (2006). De sorpresa en sorpresa. *Revista de Psicoterapia AnalíticaGrupal, 2*, 59–73.
Gergen, K. J. (1992). *El yo saturado. Dilemas de identidad en el mundo contemporáneo*. Barcelona: Paidós.
Gergen, K. J. (1996). *Realidades y Relaciones: Aproximaciones a la construcción social*. Barcelona: Paidós.
Horney, K. (1993). *La personalidad neurótica de nuestro tiempo*. Barcelona: Editorial Paidós. ISBN: 978-84-7509-096-2.
Jones, M. (1970). *La psiquiatría social en la práctica la idea de la comunidad terapéutica*. Buenos Aires: Americalee.
Kartum, M. (2014). *Terrenal. Pequeño misterio ácrata*. Buenos Aires. Atuel.
Lévi-Strauss, C. (1994). *Antropología Estructural*. Barcelona: Altaya.
Maturana, H. (1991). *Ontología del conversar. Revista Psicoterapia y Familia*. Asociación Mexicana de Terapia Familiar, A.C. ISSN 0187-7445 (pp. 19–28).
Maturana, H. (1997). *La realidad: ¿objetiva o construida?* Madrid: Anthropos.
Maturana, H., & Varela, F. (1990). *El árbol del conocimiento*. Madrid: Debate.
McNamee, S., & Gergen, K. J. (1996a). *La terapia como construcción social*. Barcelona: Paidós.
McNamee, S., & Gergen, K. (Comps.). (1996b). *La terapia como construcción social*. Barcelona: Paidós.
Minuchin, S. (1977). *Familias y terapia familiar*. Barcelona: Gedisa.
Minuchin, S. (1985). *Seminar organized by the team of family therapy at the University Hospital San Carlos*. Madrid Sercotel Conde Duque.
Minuchin, S., & Fishman, H. C. H. (1981). *Técnicas de Terapia familiar*. Barcelona: Paidós.
Minuchin, S., Lee, W. Y., & Simon, G. M. (1998). *El arte de la terapia familiar*. Barcelona: Paidós.
Minuchin, S., & Nichols, M. (1994). *La recuperación de la familia*. Barcelona: Paidós.
Organización Mundial de la Salud. (1976). *Esquizofrenia: Un estudio multinacional*. Ginebra. Retrieved from Cap. June 20, 2017, http://apps.who.int/iris/bitstream/10665/37874/1/WHO_PHP_63_spa.pdf
Pichon-Rivière, E. (1977a). *El proceso grupal. Del psicoanálisis a la psicología social II*. Buenos Aires: Nueva Visión.
Pichon-Rivière, E. (1977b). *El proceso grupal. Del psicoanálisis a la psicología social III*. Buenos Aires: Nueva Visión.
Pichon-Rivière, E. (1978). *El proceso grupal*. Nueva Visión: Del psicoanálisis a la psicología social I.Buenos Aires.
Rimpoché, S. (1994). *Libro Tibetano de la Vida y la Muerte* (p. 62). Urano: Barcelona.
Satir, V. (1964). *Conjoint family therapy, 1964*. ISBN: 0-8314-0063-3, Epi, 1971.
Seikkula, J., Alakare, B., & Aaltonen, J. (2001). El enfoque del diálogo abierto. *Sistemas familiares, 17*(2), 75–87.

Sempere, J. (2015). *Terapia interfamiliar: Análisis y descripción de la aplicación de un nuevo modelo de terapia multifamiliar* (Tesis doctoral, Universidad de Murcia).
Sennett, R. (2012). *Juntos*. Barcelona: Anagrama.
Spitz, R. (1999). *El primer año de la vida del niño*. Buenos Aires: Fondo de Cultura Económica.
Stierlin, H. (1997). *El individuo en el sistema*. Barcelona: Herder.
Wahlberg, K.-E., Wynne, L. C., Oja, H., Keskitalo, P., Pykäläinen, L., Lahti, I., et al. (1997). Gene environment interaction in vulnerability to schizophrenia: Findings from the Finnish Adoptive Family Study of Schizophrenia. *The American Journal of Psychiatry, 154*(3), 355–362.
Watzlawick, P., & Krieg, P. (Comp.) (1994). *El ojo del observador*. Barcelona: Gedisa.
Wechsler, D. (1999). *WAIS-III. Escala de inteligencia de Wechsler para Adultos-III*. Madrid: TEA.
Wynne, L., Ryckoff, I. M., Day, J., & Hirsch, S. (1974). Pseudomutualidad en las relaciones familiares. In C. Sluzki (Ed.), *Interacción familiar. Aportes fundamentales sobre teoría y técnica* (pp. 111–153). Buenos Aires: Tiempo Contemporáneo.
Zazzo, R. (1977). La vinculación. En Anzieu et al. Alcoy: Marfil (pp. 5–54).
Zeldin, T. (2014). *Conversación. Cómo el diálogo puede transformar tu vida*. Barcelona: Plataforma.

Family Therapy with Involuntary Clients. The Therapeutic Alliance as a Major Key to Therapy Success

Ana Paula Relvas and Luciana Sotero

"Mother: *We actually thought of asking for help, but now that we were forced to be here we don't want it anymore.*

Therapist: *What made you change your mind?*

Daughter: *I think that the more they want to help us the worse it gets... Too many people interfering with our lives... Here, at school, at CPCJ (Children and Young People Protection Centre), at the Health Centre... I am sick of people intruding in our lives and telling me what to do!*

Mother: *I agree.*

Father: *You can speak all you want, you will hear nothing else from me! Besides, I don't know what else we can do here in therapy.*

Therapist: *Believe me, your point of view and what you really want for you and your lives, individually and as a family, is essential to our work. The work of all of us, indeed. I still don't know how we can help and if we can at all, but I am certain that you, the family, can help us, therapists. How? By telling us with all honesty and no fear what you would like to happen. To all of you as a family and to each of you individually.*"

The Involuntary Family/Clients: Who Are They? Can We Apprehend the Specificity of Involuntary Families?

Although the recognition of an involuntary client would seem intuitive, the truth is that it is not so immediate or uncontentious, both in theory and in practice.

The original version of this chapter was revised. A correction to this chapter can be found at https://doi.org/10.1007/978-3-319-78521-9_16

This publication is the result of the Portuguese FCT support, in accordance with the Strategic Project (UID/SOC/50012/2013).

A. P. Relvas (✉) · L. Sotero
Faculty of Psychology and Education Sciences of the University of the Coimbra, Researcher at Center for Social Studies, University of Coimbra, Coimbra, Portugal
e-mail: lucianasotero@fpce.uc.pt; aprelvas@fpce.uc.pt

R. Pereira, J. L. Linares (eds.), *Clinical Interventions in Systemic Couple and Family Therapy*, European Family Therapy Association Series,
https://doi.org/10.1007/978-3-319-78521-9_13

The first point to consider is the way in which the involuntary clients are seen by the receiving institutions and by specialized literature. Terms such as involuntary, mandated, and non-voluntary are frequently used as synonyms with little conceptual rigour. However, they carry distinct meanings. Involuntary client refers to a wide group of cases where there was clear external pressure by an entity (e.g. School, Child Protection Services, Employer, Health Centre) or a helper to enforce therapy (Sotero & Relvas, 2012). Mandated client refers to cases where there is a legal mandate or court order to enforce the client(s) therapy intervention; they are therefore a subcategory of the involuntary client (Sotero & Relvas, 2012). The non-voluntary client was first described by Rooney (1992) as the "invisible involuntary" client and refers to those clients who are in therapy due to informal pressure by family members, neighbours, work colleagues, etc. Accepting Rooney's categorization, involuntary clients are in therapy because they face legal and judicial consequences (mandated) as well as personal consequences (non-voluntary), if they decide not to participate in the therapeutic process. Within this logic, it is the very fact that leaving the therapy will lead to legal or personal repercussions that create in both scenarios an environment of coercion. This coercion immediately makes it impossible to opt out of the therapeutic process, which leads to a specific framework in the relationship between therapist and client that must be understood (Rooney, 1992).

The second point to consider relates to the way in which the clients see the psychosocial support institutions, the therapy, and the therapists. We consider in this perspective the importance of the motivational factor (Sexton & Alexander, 2003), associated to the desire for change, the engagement in therapy and the recognition of its usefulness. In this regard, the clients can be positioned in a continuum that goes from not wanting to participate in the therapy at all and the opposite pole in which, even though they did not request therapy, they desire it and see it as a good opportunity (Relvas & Sotero, 2014).

In sum, when defining and identifying involuntary clients, one must articulate and match these two aspects: the referral made by a third party and the unwillingness to participate in therapy (the former being a particularly evolving and dynamic aspect, as we will see next). We can therefore suggest a flexible approach to the involuntary client's circumstance subject that will place the clients in a continuum and not in rigid pre-defined positions.

If we look at a family that non-voluntarily (or even voluntarily) arrives at therapy, we can see that the above-mentioned aspects become more complex. Frequently, the degree of motivational and voluntary engagement and participation, as well as the specific demands for each element of the family, are not clear. More than that: these demands are multiple and diverse and, as is known, in most cases there is no consistency amongst the family members' ones, not even an agreement or congruency. Sometimes they can even be antagonistic. On the other hand, when we work in therapy with families, we deal with different levels of development (youngsters, children, adults, elderly, etc.) and different levels of power (which are related, for example, to the roles of each element within the family system or with the gender).

In the case of involuntary families, all this is amplified first at the referral stage, and then during the actual therapeutic process.

Often, it is the deviant behaviour of one element of the family (i.e. the recognition of one or even more than one identified or designated patient) that leads to referring the family and to impose therapy externally. It is therefore expectable that this "designation" brings a degree of internal aggravated blaming of that element, as well as coalitions, which undermines the possibility of the family getting involved as a whole in the therapy (Escudero, 2009). This makes it harder to establish common family goals for the process. When the family is referred for therapy after being referred by a public institution, this means that the social context has rendered it incapable of fulfilling its roles and tasks, for instance with regard to parental role when the referral comes from child protection services. In these cases, there is a kind of extension of the sanction and social control (Cingolani, 1984) of one individual to the whole family group and its capacity to function and respond to the psychosocial demands of society.

When we think about a family in therapy placed in the voluntary pole of the continuum mentioned earlier, it is easy to imagine that the active search for support was probably carried out by one or several of its elements, but not by all. This is why, at our therapy service (Family Therapy Centre, Faculty of Psychology and Educational Sciences of the University of Coimbra—CPSTF/FPCEUC), from the beginning of the process and with the completion of the appointment demand form, the degree of agreement, and knowledge of the family members about the demand is always assessed. Secondly, it can be assumed that the motivation for therapy and the belief in its value and effectiveness is different from individual to individual and, thirdly, there can always be one or more people who are in therapy under some kind of pressure. Regarding the opposite involuntary pole, with the exception of the first aspect, an almost mirrored situation can be observed: even though the active search for support is external to the family, the motivation for the therapy continues to be different from individual to individual. Besides, there can always be one or more members of the family that are in therapy with no feeling of pressure. Therefore, we can conclude that both voluntary and involuntary families are distributed throughout the continuum and very rarely are they positioned, as a group, in one of the extremes (Relvas & Sotero, 2014).

In addition, wanting therapy and considering it useful are dynamic feelings; consequently, during the therapeutic process, this stance varies. In this regard, let us look at the case of a family who came to therapy referred by the Children Protection public services (CPCJ) due to the adolescent daughter's behaviour (missing school, taking psychoactive substances, disobedience). Even though they were referred, the elements stated that they needed help as they did not feel capable of dealing with the problem by themselves. After missing two consecutive sessions, the family reappeared, and the mother indicated it was due to pressures from CPCJ's social worker. The family therefore came to the session with a very distinct attitude, the family members were angry and not collaborative, the mother having stated: "We were coming here because we wanted to. Now we are forced and the therapy no longer makes sense!" However, the opposite also happens.

Therapeutic Challenges. How Do These Families Challenge Their Therapists?

Based on all the aforementioned information, the involuntary families in therapy challenge their family therapists at three main levels: (1) Recognizing the usefulness and kindness of the therapy and the therapeutic environment; (2) Creating a therapy request co-constructed by the family and the therapists within the therapeutic process; (3) Establishing a good therapeutic alliance.

First Challenge: Why Family Therapy?

Concerning the first challenge, frequently these clients define or present themselves as (a) not having any problem; (b) not needing therapy; (c) being in therapy only because they were forced to do it. With such a stance from the clients, some therapists feel they are not qualified in their skill and function, or classify these families as "resistant" or, in a closer approach to the receiving institution or the referencing entity perspective, as "non-cooperative". This posture from the therapists does not seem very useful (e.g., Miller & Rollnick, 2002; Rosenberg, 2000). In many cases, the family reactions described are common and expectable, and the therapists should be able to anticipate these initial attitudes and develop strategies and skills which allow them to deal with them in an efficient manner, as we will see further on. To understand the context that "explains" the "lack of collaboration" is a fundamental first step, even to prevent false interpretations (e.g. "what I know of family therapy cannot help this family"; "families or clients I work with are very disturbed or limited", etc.) (Escudero, 2009; Relvas & Sotero, 2014).

Second Challenge: Co-construct Shared Therapy Goals and a Broader New Request

The most frequently used solution to face this challenge and ultimately reduce or even eliminate the feeling of disqualification and almost therapeutic impotency is to co-create with the family a joint demand that can be transformed into goals shared by the various members of the family as well as by the therapist.

The respect for the dignity and rights of the person, as well as promoting the client's autonomy, are some of the fundamental principles of the psychological intervention that cannot be jeopardized. However, there are cases where the individual autonomy and the interests of society clash, and the professional can easily get triangulated. In effect, the therapist working with involuntary families (particularly mandated families) has probably two clients: the client making a request or mandate—"the referencing entity"—and a client that is the target of the intervention—"the client-family". One of the two clients often represents the interests of society, the social norm, and the other is a unique system, different from all the others and with its own will that urges to be respected and promoted in the therapy. Thus, the therapist must be very clear and transparent about his/her contacts and the information shared with the referencing entity. It is therefore easy to conclude that in these cases there is a relational triangle constituted by referencing entity/client(s)/therapist(s), in which the client and therapist apexes are subjected to pressure (Relvas & Sotero, 2014). Clarifying the norms regulating the relationship between therapist and referencing entity as well as respecting the ethical and deontological principles are fundamental aspects. In our clinical practice, we establish certain rules, which we reveal to the referencing entity before accepting the process and to the family on the first session. These rules can be summarized as follows: (1) the intervention goals proposed by the referencing party are considered, but their exact definition is carried out with the family within the therapy context; (2) the information sent to this entity can only contain data related to the attendance, conclusion or need to proceed with the process, with no justification regarding the contents of the process; (3) all material related to the contents of the process/sessions is confidential and cannot be passed on to the third party; (4) when the family explicitly requested that additional information be reported, or when the therapist considers this advisable, the matter is discussed in the therapeutic system, where it is also analysed and the content and form of such report is decided.

Thus, at the initial stages of therapy, therapists must create a safe environment in which all members of the family can express what they hope for the future in terms of change, both individually and as a family. Then, always in cooperation with the family, the therapist must articulate the different proposals in order to create a new integrative request. In all this process, the therapist's interventions must work towards getting the client to recognize that the disagreement within the family can be approached without damage and, as such, there will be common goals that can benefit all without having to eliminate individual goals and needs (Ausloos, 2003).

Third Challenge: Building a Forced Alliance. The Role of the Therapist

One of the singularities in involuntary client's intervention is the complexity of co-creating the therapeutic alliance (Friedlander, Escudero & Heatherington, 2006; Honea-Boles & Griffin, 2001; Snyder & Anderson, 2009). In family therapy, the alliances are simultaneously developed at an individual level (family member—therapist; family member/family member) and at a group level (family—therapist), so it is important to consider the alliance established by the family members amongst themselves. The alliance, in terms of the family as a whole, has been alternately conceptualized as allegiance (Symonds & Horvath, 2004), within-family alliance (Pinsof, 1994), and shared sense of purpose (Friedlander et al., 2006), referring not only to the willingness to collaborate in the therapy but also to the emotional bond between the family members (Friedlander, Escudero, Heatherington, & Diamond, 2011). Keeping this in mind we developed a set of studies that allowed us to define some specific profiles of the problem, as well as note some implications for therapy (Sotero, Cunha, Silva, Escudero, & Relvas, 2017; Sotero, Major, Escudero, & Relvas, 2016; Sotero, Moura-Ramos, Escudero, & Relvas, 2017).

Based on a comparative study between voluntary and involuntary family-clients on building the therapeutic alliance, we conclude that the two groups significantly differ in all dimensions of the therapeutic alliance observed on the first session.

Specifically, and according to the Transtheoretical Model of Therapeutic Alliance (Friedlander et al., 2006) assessed with the System for Observing Family Therapy Alliances (SOFTA) (Friedlander et al., 2006; Portuguese version in Sotero & Relvas, 2014) at the beginning of the therapy (first session), the involuntary clients show: (1) less engagement in the therapeutic process than the voluntary ones [they do not consider treatment as important and do not engage as much in therapy regarding the work carried out with the therapist in defining and negotiating goals and tasks]; (2) less emotional connection with the therapist and less safety within the therapeutic system than the voluntary clients [respectively, they do not see the therapist as such an important person in their lives and they feel the client–therapist relationship is less based in trust, affection, interest, and belonging; they also consider to a lower degree that the therapy context can be seen as a place where risks can be taken, where one can be open and flexible]; (3) as a group, the involuntary families have a lower shared sense of purpose within the family with regard to the therapy [the members of the family, amongst them, are less united and supportive in therapy, and find it difficult to see themselves working together to improve family relations and reach common goals] (Sotero et al., 2016). The other relevant point, shown in the first session, is the fact that only negative therapeutic alliances were observed in the involuntary client group, particularly in safety within the therapeutic system and shared sense of purpose within the family (Sotero et al., 2016). These results sustain the hypothesis advanced by Friedlander et al. (2006) that the safety and sharing goals within the family are two of the most affected alliance's dimensions when working with involuntary families. By comparing the two groups at the fourth session, it was clear that these differences become dissipated, with the only exception being engagement. In terms of the therapy practice, this result confirms the importance of what was said regarding co-constructing a joint demand at the very beginning of the therapy because obtaining the involuntary clients' engagement in therapy is an additional challenge for therapists (Relvas & Sotero, 2014; Sotero et al., 2016). Summing up the main conclusions of this study, it can be stated that, despite the lack of unity within these families with regard to the therapy (shared sense of purpose) and the weak values of the alliance dimensions on the individual side (engagement, emotional connection), the beginning of therapy is crucial to establish the commitment because there is certainly the possibility of positive evolvement of this aspect with time. In fact, the opposite happens with the dimensions particularly related to family therapy (safety and shared sense of purpose), whose values decrease in the middle stage of therapy (although the differences with the voluntary family-clients disappear: the values decrease in both groups).

Let us now analyse what we know from our studies on the role of the therapist in building the therapeutic alliances while working with involuntary families. Based on the results of the comparison between involuntary groups and voluntary groups, it can be stated that, particularly in the first session, therapists try to build and reinforce the therapeutic alliances, especially with involuntary families. To do so, they foment the engagement and the family unit, as well as the shared goals related to the therapy, through more numerous contributions in these dimensions (Sotero, Cunha, et al., 2017). It therefore seems that the therapists recognize the greatest difficulty areas of the therapeutic alliance with these kind of clients and realize the need to give them an intense and direct response (Sotero, Cunha, et al., 2017). After engagement, the emotional connection dimension was found to have more contributions from therapists in both groups, both on the first and fourth sessions. The therapists participating in this study gave preference to strategies that promoted the therapeutic alliance by endorsing the engagement (explaining how therapy works, encouraging the definition of goals, asking what they want to discuss during the session) and establishing a good emotional connection with the clients (expressing trust in the clients' skills, using sense of humour, using self-disclosure) (Sotero, Cunha, et al., 2017). It can be said that the therapists choose contributions that increase the active participation of clients in the therapy and that leads to a positive affective and emotional connection with them. Surprisingly, therapists' contributions for the safety dimension are almost non-existent in both groups although slightly higher in the voluntary group. This result shows that the management of conflict and intrafamilial hostility seems to be one of the areas that therapists probably find harder (Relvas & Sotero, 2014; Sotero, Cunha, et al., 2017), which is particularly relevant both from a clinical point of view and as regards the therapists' learning and training (Sotero, Cunha, et al., 2017). In sum, and recognizing that on the first therapy session the alliances with the involuntary families are weaker, this study shows that therapists seem skilled enough to recognize the alliance problems and focus on creating strong therapeutic alliances by establishing differentiated behaviour patterns in response.

The Therapeutic Work with Involuntary Families: What Effects Does the Initial Condition of Families Have on Therapeutic Outcomes? How Can Family Therapists Work Hopefully and Successfully with Those Clients?

The success of the therapy with involuntary families is a question that often comes up. In fact, the therapeutic change with these families is seen as hard and difficult to achieve.

In order to assess the effect of the families' involuntary condition on the therapeutic outcomes and considering the lack of consensus noted in literature on the matter (e.g. Burke & Gregoire, 2007; Snyder & Anderson, 2009), we designed a study to compare the therapeutic outcomes of voluntary and involuntary clients, trying to understand as well the influence of the alliance in these results (Sotero, Moura-Ramos, et al., 2017). The results obtained led to the following conclusions: (1) there is no statistically significant difference in therapeutic outcomes; (2) only safety and shared sense of purpose at the fourth session have a significant effect on the final therapy outcomes, and (3) there is no differential effect in the relation between safety and the outcomes and between the shared sense of purpose and the outcomes, considering the two groups of voluntary or involuntary families. So we came to a conclusion that, despite the initial difficulty in establishing the therapeutic alliance, involuntary families can (or cannot) change as much as the voluntary ones. Thus, it seems that the clients' safety in the therapeutic process and the shared sense of purpose within the family in an intermediate stage of therapy (fourth session) are more relevant to the final therapeutic outcomes than the voluntary or involuntary condition. In other words, a reliable therapeutic environment, in which the family-clients feel they can take risks, may lead to better therapeutic results. Additionally, with such conclusions, it can be stated that the first four sessions, and particularly the process of alliance co-constructing during this period, are valuable because they can determine the extent of therapy success (Sotero, Moura-Ramos, et al., 2017). These results somewhat support the importance of what Flaskas (1989) designated as "de-centred" alliance in conjoint therapy. This means that, contrary to what happens in individual therapy in which the alliance is centred on the client–therapist relationship, in family therapy the alliance is de-centred because the alliance amongst the family members is equally or more relevant than the alliance between client and therapist.

Although prior engagement and client motivation are essential to therapeutic change, what therapists do (or not do) during therapy has an important impact on the way in which clients get engaged in process. So, therapists are responsible and must be capable of adjusting their intervention models and strategies to the characteristics of the clients they work with.

Following the conclusions of the previously presented studies, in the case of involuntary families, a first aspect worth highlighting is that therapists need to define, as a central goal of their interventions, helping the clients to see their problems in a less personal and more interpersonal way. This transformation involves challenging the points of view of each client regarding the problem, offering a new unifying perspective of that issue so that each member relates to the problem (Sluzki, 1992). This change therefore implies transforming individual goals into family goals (Rait, 2000). From this new point of view, clients start to recognize that everyone needs to contribute to a solution. To do this, therapists can use strategies such as: incentive family dialogue; deliberately involve the quieter or less participative clients with questions or showing empathy; validate the different points of view; promote the establishment of agreements amongst the clients; encourage the clients to question each other on their points of view; point out what is common in the various perspectives on the problem or on the solution (Friedlander et al., 2006). As a way to help clients recognize each other as a family unit, therapists can draw attention to what is shared between the various elements in terms of values, experiences, needs, or feelings, for example.

A second aspect implies the need to accept the clients' initial negative stance, but also find strategies to reframe and redefine it. The lack of involvement or the refusal in accepting the therapeutic process can arise from the very intrafamilial conflict or the lack of trust in the services (and the professionals), sometimes originating from previous experiences (Friedlander et al., 2006; Imber-Black, 1988). Listening to each family member separately at an initial stage can be a good alternative when significant conflict is noted. When the lack of trust in the services and professionals is evident, therapists must genuinely try to understand where that lack of trust comes from. In fact, when a family has a tense relationship with the referring entity, clients frequently see therapists as an extension of that entity. As a priority, therapists must then try to understand the different points of view of the family members regarding the value and the goals of therapy, and explore their previous experience with other services and institutions. From our experience, clients usually respond positively when therapists show that they understand the reasons for the clients' lack of trust. In this sense, there is a number of simple but effective measures that the family therapist can adopt (Sotero, Cunha, et al., 2017): (1) avoid interventions that can increase pressure in the family that feels forced against their will to be in the therapy, for example, moving too fast into defining goals or trying to convince clients of the need or advantages of therapy; (2) show kindness towards the negative emotions regarding therapy or the professionals, accepting these as part of the job; (3) avoid blaming the clients for their lack of collaboration or making hasty interpretations of the case; (4) show interest and curiosity regarding what originated the request for therapy, exploring the different points of view of the family members on the request and referral, trying to clarify what each member thinks and feels about the current situation; (5) understand with the family the factors that may be influencing their initial negative attitude.

A third aspect is related to the model adopted by the therapist. With regard to involuntary clients, literature points to a very consensual way in which therapists can adjust some therapy models. In individual psychotherapy, the awareness of the need to adapt intervention strategies in terms of client motivation led to the development of several intervention models, namely the Transtheoretical Model of Change (Prochaska & DiClemente, 1984) and Motivational Interviewing (Miller & Rollnick, 2002). Literature on family therapy with involuntary clients often describes as "good practice" the collaborative approaches, especially Solution-Focused Therapy (TCS; De Jong & Berg, 2001; Osborn, 1999; Rosenberg, 2000; Tohn & Oshlag, 1996), Multisystemic Therapy (TMS; Tuerk, McCart, & Henggeler, 2012; Henggeler, Schoenwald, Borduin, Rowland, & Cunningham, 2009) and Functional Family Therapy (TFF; Sexton & Alexander, 2003; Sprenkle, Davis, & Lebow, 2009). In our clinical practice, we use the model we developed at the Family Therapy Centre in FPCEUC, where we work, entitled Curiosity Therapy (Relvas, 2003), an approach which also has collaborative characteristics.

This model was not designed specifically with involuntary family therapy in mind. It is a brief therapy model, usually with seven sessions and two follow-ups [or brief-long therapy, according to Ausloos, 2003, as the spacing between sessions is normally 3 weeks to 1 month]. In formulating the therapy demand (completing a phone form), one investigates the reason for the appointment and obtains a preliminary description of the problem, trying to understand the precedents and consequences, as well as the involvement of each family member and other significant elements (e.g. teacher, extended family, doctor or the individual or institution that referred the family). The degree of knowledge and acceptance of the different family members concerning the therapy request will also be verified. Even in the case of families referenced by a third party, the therapy team always asks for one of the family members to complete the phone form as indicated before, which will give a preliminary overview of the points of view of the family on the problem and on the referral.

The therapy process involves joint interpersonal sessions in a classical family therapy setting: two adjoining rooms separated by a unidirectional mirror, equipped with an audio and video system. An important aspect is the establishment of a therapeutic contract. Normally, after one or two sessions, the therapeutic contract is established with the clients. This is an agreement in which the therapeutic goals, co-created in therapy, are established, as well as the number of sessions considered necessary to reach them (between 7 and 10), and the spacing between sessions. The contract is conceptualized as having both therapeutic and pragmatic value in itself, redefining therapy as co-participative and co-liable, creating a positive expectation that the problem has a solution. It must always include the possibility of renegotiation or the establishment of a second contract with new goals.

Conceptually, this is a meta-model, framed in a systemic perspective and using a post-modern integrative therapy approach: it articulates core ideas of different family therapy schools and proposes a new epistemological view. In therapeutic terms, the focus is on the meaning (and not on the pathology) and on the dialogue or conversation (and not on the technique). It is intended to approach therapy as a process of construction and deconstruction of the problem by means of client–therapist recursivity. The therapist places his/her clinical stance on "curiosity" (Cecchin, 1987) and never believes he/she "already knows!" managing the therapeutic dialogue in a way that will articulate multiple points of view (dialogic), generating new descriptions of the problem and the solution. The therapist accepts and is interested in all possible descriptions of reality. These principles, jointly with the model structure, make it particularly adapted to work with involuntary clients. Actually, the work of therapists is fundamentally based on creating hypotheses and adjusting and transforming them in a collaborative way with the clients, encouraging the change of the system (Relvas, 1996, 2003). These hypotheses must be systemic, promoting a wider understanding of the problem, from the personal to the interpersonal level, as well as to increasingly vaster contexts (Relvas, 2003). It is through the co-construction of systemic hypotheses between therapists and family that data gets transformed into information and a new "story", "narrative", "map" or "perspective" emerges which relieves the family's discomfort. When working with involuntary families it is fundamental to keep an epistemological positioning allowing the respect for the ecology of the system as well as for the client–therapist relationship, conferring to the client an active role as responsible for the possibility and meaning of change, from the definition to the attainment of goals.

About the learning, training, and supervision of family therapists, it seems important to highlight two points. Firstly, we believe that the specificities of therapy with involuntary families should be approached throughout the family therapists' learning and training (Sotero, 2016). As far as we know, this does not form part of most of the family therapists' educational curricula; the development of clinical skills and knowledge based on the research findings of the therapeutic process with these families is extremely important, considering the frequency with which family therapists work in such circumstances. Secondly, apart from covering several theoretical models, the family therapists' training and supervision should also cover the complex process of building therapeutic alliances in family therapy (Sotero, 2016).

Conclusions

A 25-year-old mother with four minor children arrived in therapy referred by the court and very much against her will. The need to supervise the reintegration process of the family's minors after institutionalization, the mother's unemployment and the recent divorce after the mother's complaint of domestic violence were some of the reasons worrying the court and were the basis of the family therapy referral. During the first two sessions, work had to be done on helping the family to formulate its own request for therapy. According to the mother, the psychiatric support that she had been receiving for almost 3 years was enough to feel supported, so she could not understand why the court insisted on family therapy. After this initial work, however, both the mother and the remaining family discovered sense and usefulness in family therapy, which allowed them to engage and continue the process. This had a successful outcome in the opinion of all persons and institutions involved.

References

Ausloos, G. (2003). *A competência das famílias: Tempo, caos, processo* (2ª ed.). Lisboa, Portugal: Climepsi.

Burke, A. C., & Gregoire, T. K. (2007). Substance abuse treatment outcomes for coerced and non-coerced clients. *Health & Social Work, 32*, 7–15.

Cecchin, G. (1987). Hypothesizing, circularity and neutrality revisited: An invitation to curiosity. *Family Process, 26*(4), 405–413.

Cingolani, J. (1984). Social conflict perspective on work with involuntary clients. *Social Work, 29*, 442–446.

De Jong, P., & Berg, I. (2001). Co-constructing cooperation with mandated clients. *Social Work, 46*, 361–374. https://doi.org/10.1093/sw/46.4.361

Escudero, V. (2009). *Guía Práctica de la Intervención Familiar I*. Junta de Castilla y León. Retrieved from http://uiicf.net/wp-content/uploads/2014/06/Gu%C3%ADaPrácticaIF_VEscudero.pdf.

Flaskas, C. (1989). Thinking about the emotional interaction of therapist and family. *ANZ Journal of Family Therapy, 10*, 1–6.

Friedlander, M. L., Escudero, V., & Heatherington, L. (2006). *Therapeutic alliances in couple and family: An empirically informed guide to practice*. Washington, DC: American Psychological Association.

Friedlander, M., Escudero, V., Heatherington, L., & Diamond, G. (2011). Alliance in couple and family therapy. *Psychotherapy, 48*, 25–33. https://doi.org/10.1037/a0022060

Henggeler, S. W., Schoenwald, S. K., Borduin, C. M., Rowland, M. D., & Cunningham, P. B. (2009). *Multisystemic therapy for antisocial behavior in children and adolescents* (2nd ed.). New York, NY: Guilford Press.

Honea-Boles, P., & Griffin, J. E. (2001). The court-mandated client: Does limiting confidentiality preclude a therapeutic encounter? *TCA Journal, 29*, 149–160.

Imber-Black, E. (1988). *Families and larger systems: A family therapist's guide through the labyrinth*. New York: Guilford.

Miller, W. R., & Rollnick, S. (2002). *Motivational interviewing: Preparing people for change*. New York: Guilford.

Osborn, C. J. (1999). Solution-focused strategies with "involuntary" clients: Practical applications for the school and clinical setting. *Journal of Humanistic Education and Development, 37*, 169–181.

Pinsof, W. B. (1994). An integrative systems perspective on the therapeutic alliance: Theoretical, clinical, and research implications. In A. O. Horvath & L. S. Greenberg (Eds.), *The working alliance: Theory, research, and practice* (pp. 173–195). New York: Wiley.

Prochaska, J. O., & DiClemente, C. C. (1984). *The transtheoretical approach: Crossing traditional boundaries of therapy*. Homewood, IL: Down Jones Irwin.

Rait, D. S. (2000). The therapeutic alliance in couples and family therapy. *Psychotherapy in Practice, 56*, 211–224. https://doi.org/10.1002/(SICI)1097-4679(200002)56:2<211::AID-JCLP7>3.0.CO;2-H

Relvas, A. P. (1996). A co-construção da hipótese sistémica em terapia familiar. *Análise Psicológica, 14*(4), 563–579.

Relvas, A. P. (2003). *Por detrás do espelho. Da teoria à terapia com a família* (2ª ed.). Coimbra: Quarteto.

Relvas, A. P., & Sotero, L. (2014). *Familias obligadas, terapeutas forzosos: La alianza terapéutica en contextos coercitivos*. Madrid: Ed. Morata.

Rooney, R. H. (1992). *Strategies for work with involuntary clients*. New York: Columbia University.

Rosenberg, B. (2000). Mandated clients and solution focused therapy: "It's not my miracle". *Journal of Systemic Therapies, 10*, 90–99.

Sexton, T. L., & Alexander, J. F. (2003). Functional family therapy: A mature clinical model for working with at-risk adolescents and their families. In T. L. Sexton, G. R. Weeks, & M. S. Robbins (Eds.), *Handbook of family therapy: The science and practice of working with families and couples* (pp. 323–348). New York: Brunner-Routledge.

Sluzki, C. E. (1992). Transformations: A blue print for narrative changes in therapy. *Family Process, 31*, 217–230. https://doi.org/10.1111/j.1545-5300.1992.00217.x

Snyder, C., & Anderson, S. (2009). An examination of mandated versus voluntary referral as a determinant of clinical outcome. *Journal of Marital and Family Therapy, 3*, 278–292. https://doi.org/10.1111/j.1752-0606.2009.00118.x

Sotero, L. (2016). *Clientes (In)Voluntários em Terapia Familiar. Aliança terapêutica e resultados* (Unpublished doctoral dissertation). Universidade de Coimbra, Portugal.

Sotero, L., Cunha, D., Silva, J. T., Escudero, V., & Relvas, A. P. (2017). Building alliances with (in)voluntary clients: A study focused on therapists' observable behaviors. *Family Process, 56*, 819–434. https://doi.org/10.1111/famp.12265

Sotero, L., Major, S., Escudero, V., & Relvas, A. P. (2016). The therapeutic alliance with involuntary clients: How does it work? *Journal of Family Therapy, 38*, 36–58. https://doi.org/10.1111/1467-6427.12046

Sotero, L., Moura-Ramos, M., Escudero, V., & Relvas, A. P. (2017). *When the family doesn't want to come to therapy, is there any hope? A study focusing on outcomes and alliance with (in) voluntary clients*. Submitted for publication.

Sotero, L., & Relvas, A. P. (2012). A intervenção com clientes involuntários: Complexidade e dilemas. *Psicologia & Sociedade, 24*, 187–196. https://doi.org/10.1590/S0102-71822012000100021

Sotero, L., & Relvas, A. P. (2014). Sistema de Observação da Aliança em Terapia Familiar, Versão Observacional (SOFTA-o). In A. P. Relvas & S. Major (Eds.), *Avaliação familiar—Funcionamento e intervenção* (Vol. I, pp. 121–149). Coimbra: Imprensa da Universidade de Coimbra.

Sprenkle, D. H., Davis, S. D., & Lebow, J. L. (2009). *Common factors in couple and family therapy. The overlooked foundation for effective practice*. New York: Guilford.

Symonds, B. D., & Horvath, A. O. (2004). Optimizing the alliance in couple therapy. *Family Process, 43*, 443–455. https://doi.org/10.1037/a0022060

Tohn, S. L., & Oshlag, J. A. (1996). Solution-focused therapy with mandated clients: Cooperating with the uncooperative. In S. D. Miller, M. A. Hubble, & B. L. Duncan (Eds.), *Handbook of solution-focused brief therapy* (pp. 152–183). San Francisco: Jossey-Bass.

Tuerk, E., McCart, M. R., & Henggeler, S. W. (2012). Collaboration in family therapy. *Journal of Clinical Psychology, 68*, 168–178. https://doi.org/10.1002/jclp.218

Systemic Intervention on Disabilities

Javier Bou

Introduction

Disability, handicap, subnormality... These are all words that have been used to describe, in different periods of western culture, how that culture viewed the fact of human differentiation with regard to people's ability to adapt to, and handle themselves in, the society of their time.

The terms that were used in each period reflected an attitude and entailed a way of acting on the part of society and the public bodies. These attitudes and behaviour have changed with the times and with social consciousness. These terms indicated the consideration warranted by the differential fact of people who, usually due to disease or alterations, behaved or performed in such a way that did not fall within "normal" standards.

Difference, that which is different, is, on many occasions, a generator of unease in society, something that helps conceptualizations of such differences to emerge and that consequently promotes the development of the attitudes and policies that have faced the issue in different ways down through the ages.

Ever since classical times, disabled people had been considered "abnormal", defective, and as a result, solutions had little to do with rehabilitation or integration.

> *...One starts from the idea that a person with a disability has nothing to contribute to society, that he or she is an unproductive being and, not only that, a burden that must be endured, either by the parents or by the community itself.*
>
> *However, within this model of abstention, it is deemed possible to distinguish the existence of two sub-models: that of eugenics and that of marginalization. This distinction is based on the various implications that may arise from the condition of "being unnecessary"*

J. Bou (✉)
Dictia Valencia (Systemic Training Institute), Valencia, Spain
e-mail: xavibou@cop.es

R. Pereira, J. L. Linares (eds.), *Clinical Interventions in Systemic Couple and Family Therapy*, European Family Therapy Association Series,
https://doi.org/10.1007/978-3-319-78521-9_14

> *that characterizes people with disabilities. Thus it will be seen - although both sub-models dispense with the lives of these people - that in the former, the solution is pursued through the application of eugenic policies, while in the latter, the objective is achieved through marginalization.* (Palacios, 2008, p. 37)[1]

In the Greco-Roman period, the balance of the bodily humours or the lack of such balance represented the onset of difference or madness. In medieval times, the mentally ill or the psychically disabled (someone different) were conceptualized as being possessed (the Ship of Fools) and consequently isolated.

Many years ago, Europe began addressing these differences when the state began assuming a certain degree of responsibility for the problem and the concept of disability emerged, based on an interpretation of difference from an essentially medical point of view. That difference is due solely to the flaw that the subject has in his or her body, which leads to an alteration in their behaviour and in how they adapt to their environment. From that perspective, the only solution lies in rehabilitation and economic or residential support. In certain cases, the latter is centred on segregation, the exclusion of someone who is different in specific centres, whether these be psychiatric hospitals, asylums or residences for the insane. The problem pertains to the individual and only to the individual. Society merely attempts to mitigate the consequences of his or her problem, but is in no way responsible. We are dealing with a policy of charity. What Palacios (2008) called the rehabilitation model.

Subsequently, following the development of ideas such as the Warnock Report (1981) in the United Kingdom, which defends the educability of all children, education as a right and that educational needs are common to one and all, the concept of disability emerges and, in its wake, that of disability (the deficiency-disability-handicap axis) which, although still based on a defective organ or function, did nevertheless introduce a social response to such disability and the limitations to social adaptation which correspond to society itself with all its barriers and its vision of uniformity. Now, a person who is different begins to be the subject not of charity but rather of rights. Although the medical model of rehabilitation continues to occupy a space, politics and the transformation of cities, businesses (with jobs) and social awareness are important factors in the approach to the problem. See the introduction of the concept of participation by W.H.O. in the international classification of disability and health.

Finally, and as a further extension of the above, the idea of functional diversity emerges. That is to say, we humans are diverse in our functionality; no one is functional in every aspect and we all have areas in which we cannot handle ourselves as we do in others. The goal is to transform society rather than the individual who is different; to generate structures and changes in society that allow for the adaptation of the enormous variety of people with their diverse functionalities: adapted jobs, ad hoc training curricula, barrier-free cities and public transport, the integration of the mentally ill within the community, etc.

From this perspective, the method of curing is no longer medical-biological, rather it is fundamentally political. In fact, the latest ideas in the assessment of

---

[1] Literal quotes are all translated.

disability focus more on limitations to participation and on contextual elements than on the individual (IMSERSO, 2017; OMS, 2001).

In the light of this evolution, we can see how the process has gradually transformed itself from an individual gaze of scrutiny directed at the interior of the individual and their deficits, to one that focuses on the context. It is, to a certain extent, ecosystemic: the problem belongs to society as a whole.

The Systemic Model and Disability: A Delayed Relationship (the Influence of a Deficitary Scrutiny as Opposed to an Appreciative One)

The systemic model has been slow to approach disability, usually circumscribing it to an intellectual deficiency, which could not be the muse of the relational model. If neurosis was psychoanalysis' most worshipped and studied pathology, the systemic model emerges in the most serious pathologies such as psychosis, while intellective deficits are belatedly contemplated therein on their own.

Even so, 27 years ago, Fishman (1990) talks about how the way in which the family and the intervening systems that revolve around disabled children make up with their somewhat forlorn scrutiny what he calls the "room of mirrors", something similar to what Rolland (2009) describes as the cycle of limited expectations. Ever since the 1990s, texts have been published that deal with families with children or adults with disabilities. Particular mention should be made of Ana Mª Sorrentino (1990) and her book "Handicap and Rehabilitation: a Systemic Compass in the Relational Universe of the Child with Psychic Deficiencies".

Coping with Disability and Its Impact on the Family

Rolland (2009) tells us that the arrival of any important disease represents an impact which necessarily affects the entire family and the roles of each member, changing its interactions, expectations, structure and, in the final analysis, becoming part of the family as yet another element, one that is going to modulate relations and probably generate situations of dependence with respect to professionals and institutions. In this sense, the professionals who intervene in this situation may be seen as allies or as rivals or obstructers, which may also be the case with the institutions that are involved. This will inevitably affect the development of the disabled person and his or her family. How often do we come across families who place all the "blame" for the handicap on how the institution or the professionals involved in the delivery or in the first few months of the child conducted themselves? As he says, the system will comprise the interaction of the family, the disease, the institution and the patient.

A disease, a pathology, does not affect every individual in the same way. The reaction to the disease, not only that of the patient, but also that of their relational context, is going to be critical in determining the degree of impact and thereby the disability generated. We are all aware that when faced with a banal infection such as a cold, how we handle it and how interested we are in the activities we have to carry out are going to determine our reaction to the cold and how much we allow it to affect us. Our reaction does not dependent absolutely on the bacterial or viral load, rather it is something personal and relational.

As Rolland points out, in the presence of a child with difficulties, not only does the family face the anguish of the future, but also the risk of being trapped in one of the following two attitudes:

- They either consider the person they have to take care of as a sick person, which will not allow him or her to develop to their full potential.
- Or they consider them to be the eternal child, thereby deferring or preventing their integration.

The way in which the family faces up to the arrival of the child, the information and advice they receive, the first messages received from, and the relationship established with, the professionals who interact with the family from the outset are going to modulate the expectations of the family as well as the likelihood of a cooperative interaction among all of the affected system.

All of this represents a period of mourning the family has to endure, during which "it is necessary to adopt behaviour that defends the integrity of the system. The family sets in motion a series of defence mechanisms, reinforced culturally, that have as their objective the maintenance of the family". (Pereira, 2002, p. 2)

Sorrentino (1990) refers to the different stages a family goes through as they attempt to adapt to the arrival of a child with difficulties, a child with a disability.

1. Every pregnancy involves expectations and a desire. The parents imagine that it'll be a boy or a girl (until the routine ultrasound test), how much it will look like you or me or the grandmother, what size it will be...
2. When the time comes to give birth, frequently if it is a congenital or perinatal pathology, the defect is discovered or revealed by the professionals. How this is handled and how they treat the family is of crucial importance.
3. Unless the problem is self-evident, the first reactions typically involve surprise, stupor or even a denial of the problem. The family then begins a tour of different professionals in search of evidence to discard what they dread.
4. With time and as the problem is accepted, emotions such as anger, grief and guilt appear, guilt that can be externalized onto the health institution, the professionals, the families of origin (genetics) or the care received or implemented: "It was the doctors, you didn't look after yourself, you upset me, he's just like your deficient cousin, etc."
5. That is when the mourning process begins, for the loss of prior expectations and the assumption of new ones that are not always quite so full of hope.

6. Over time, family roles are restructured and readapted, and it adapts to and makes space for support structures.
7. All things considered, each member of the family must give up certain things although, at the same time and unevenly among all members, they also obtain secondary benefits.

It is therefore important to note how the illness or disability brings about changes in each family member: Who is affected and in what way? What other conflicts is it masking or what conflicts is it causing? Who gains power and influence? Who is overburdened with tasks? Etc.

Important elements will have a role to play in this adaptation, such as the primary social network of the family and the resources it has; if there are other children or not; whether this child is the first one; if the defect is obvious at birth or if it gradually becomes apparent, generating growing uncertainty; previous experiences with respect to diseases, etc. The family has its own history prior to the birth and circumstances that will mediate the effect of the problem (Ríos González 1994).

Impact on the Parents

They are the ones who have taken the decision to have another child, albeit, as is always the case, with a different degree of enthusiasm in either one, but they are the first to suffer the disappointment and the first changes. With the discovery or unveiling of the flaw, the parents and not only the parents—(let's not forget the grandparents), face a period of mourning that is renewed with each changing stage of the life cycle and the difference between what they had expected and the actual reality (Leal, 2008).

One of the disputes they will have to deal with is how they handle guilt. This is where elements are deployed that have to do with the care received or with the legacy of the families of origin.

The first changes are in the roles and tasks, since the arrival of a disabled child always entails extra chores and how they are distributed always creates controversy, if not a crisis. The mother may become overinvolved in caring for the child, with more or less enthusiasm, which in turn will allow or require the father to be peripheral. In some cases, the father will welcome this given that he will be released from a daunting task which at the same time keeps his companion busy (which is an advantage in the case of jealous husbands), but it can also be most unpleasant for the father, who may interpret that the child is "mama's boy", distancing himself from raising the child and also, secondarily, from the marital relationship.

The high demands implied by these parenting tasks usually involve considerable commitment from both parents (although with differences) and give rise, as a result, to a predominantly parental bond as opposed to a marital bond (which tends to be reduced, especially in the most serious problems). How often a couple forgets that they are a couple, and oh, the price they pay in the future! There may be (Núñez,

2003) situations in which the parental couple is strengthened by the problem, maintaining their alliance in the struggle to care for the child. In any case, previous problems within the couple can be key elements when it comes to coping with the new difficulty.

The parent who normally looks after and is more involved in care tasks is going to suffer delays or loss of professional and social expectations due to his or her dedication, which in the long run can lead to their resenting the other partner.

We all know well how delicate a couple's relationship with either partner's family of origin is. Well, the arrival of a disabled or problematic child usually creates movement in one or other family of origin as well, with the consequent sensation of being invaded on the part of one or other or perhaps both parents. There may also be a distancing but, in either case, the influence they exert is clear.

If the impact of the arrival and the coping with all this is not properly handled by the family and by the systems involved, the couple may suffer distance and coldness, with a growing decline in the more playful and complicit aspects of their relationship, including under this heading sex, which is so necessary.

In the final analysis, it is the couple's affections and their social relations that may be most affected.

Parent–Disabled Child Relationships

As Núñez (2003) says on the relationship between parents and the disabled child:

> ...countless ambivalent and extremely intense feelings are unleashed, from the very first moment that the disability is discovered: confusion, estrangement, insecurity, disappointment, pain, guilt, fear, rejection, anger, etc.

These negative feelings may be combined with other positive ones, all woven together in complex interactions: feelings of tenderness, of love and even of pride in the child; a desire to compensate them and eagerness to put a lot of effort into making things work out for them, giving them the greatest possible chances to get ahead; feelings of joy and delight over their achievements; the feeling of facing a permanent challenge; etc. (p. 136)

On many occasions, there is real fear about expressing these feelings, given they may be contradictory—not to mention that feelings of despair, weariness and tiredness are very negatively seen socially, which means they are left to simmer in silence, without catharsis, making them even more powerful.

Stemming from the guilt mentioned earlier, the same author infers that these parents may feel indebted to the child, because of what they did or did not do, on occasions plummeting into invalidating and ultimately negligent overprotection. However, they can also consider the child as a debtor who has made their lives and their personal and social achievements much more difficult. As Núñez says (2003):

> *The child usually feels that he has let his parents down. His experience is that because of his disability, they are dissatisfied and disappointed in him insofar as he is a long way from*

being what they desired. He feels guilty about it. This is linked to the conscious or unconscious attitude of his parents who burden him with the blame for their failure. (p. 137)

The opposite position is to not demand anything from the child at all and, full of pity, not to expect any progress and to therefore focus more on his or her less skilled or sicker aspects, neglecting the skills that they do have. These are parents who expect little of their children, other than providing them with affection. In the worst scenario, they may feel that he or she is a gift from heaven. Parents for whom the diagnosis represents a burden that may not be avoided.

Other parents deny the differences, either unconsciously as a defensive mechanism in the face of the pain of the handicap, both in their narcissistic pride and in their concern over the difficulties they will have to face.

Another tendency is to turn the disabled child into the depository of all the family defects, splitting the family between the healthy and the sick (Núñez, 2003):

Parent-child bond in which the differences are highlighted. Excision: healthy-sick. The disabled child, and only that child, is the king of the castle of failure and becomes the depository of all the disabilities and limitations of the other family members. He or she is the family buttress. The others are freed from their own limitations, and, in this way the differences within the family are strongly demarcated. (p. 137)

Finally, to summarize their attitudes towards the child, his or her disability and exercise of power, parents may take up a position that oscillates between total permissiveness, granting their each and every whim as a way to compensate for their failure, which will turn the child into a despot or, on the contrary, making occasional attempts to control this attitude through aggressive responses which, secondarily, lock the family into an impulsive and not at all flexible game, and into a bipolarity that will not be easily structured in the mind of the disabled child.

Towards the Other Children

The same author (Núñez, 2003) argues that, due to the disabled child's abundant demand for care, fatigue can lead to the other children experiencing that their parents or either one of them is no longer interested in them. Such children go unnoticed in front of their sibling, nor can they demand clearly or at least without feeling guilt, that much-needed attention that has been usurped from them by the exacting centre of attention that is their sick brother or sister. In this context, they lack those moments of intimacy with and the exclusive attention of their parents; they don't get to play the games their parents have been busy playing with the disabled sibling; the economic investment that sibling implies may have led to a fraternal economic injustice that cannot be disputed or claimed under penalty of their being considered ungrateful and selfish. I remember Emili, a 48-year-old man who came over as being particularly demanding of one of his undoubtedly anarchic children, while he would remember with pride, yet also with a certain sense of fatalism, how he had to help his deficient sister to dress and then take her to school every day, and how he had to forget about all the games his friends would play along the way.

It is easy for parents to fall into the parentification of one of their healthy children, setting them tasks and responsibilities that go far beyond what might be desirable for their age, which may consequentially cause early maturation, the loss of childhood and the impulsiveness that goes with it. On other occasions, these children can also be overprotected, an extension of the overprotection extended to the disabled sibling, but in my opinion these cases are less frequent.

The decline in expectations as far as the sick child is concerned, can mean that the expectations placed on the healthy ones, or, more frequently, on one of them, may be excessive, as a way of compensating for the other ones. Parental narcissism also plays a role in this, as does the desire for compensation on the part of the healthy child. I recall the case of Cristina. All her life she was told she should take care of her useless brother. That was all she ever heard. All manner of tasks were demanded of her, too much was expected of her and she faced considerable difficulties when it came to rebelling in her teenage years. Now, with her small son, whom she associates with the indolence of her useless brother, she swings between a critical attitude (probably more than deserved) and excessive protection.

As Núñez says (2003), the opportunities, achievements and the development of potentialities that are made available to the other children may be curtailed or otherwise affected in order to reduce the differences with the sick child, conditioned by the parentification that, generally speaking, only one of them endures. This may or may not coincide with the assignment of the family legacy, that is to say, with making one of the children (usually a sister) responsible for the future care of the disabled person when the parents are no longer around. This is something that may cause parents to fear that the legate may leave or move away from the family environment, with the consequent threat to its individuation. These delegated siblings often feel trapped by this mandate. In many cases, they require treatment as a last-ditch therapy through which to achieve the greater autonomy of the disabled person and a more stimulating and less protective educational style in the parents.

This can cause early maturation in the siblings, or in one of them, if not quite the contrary through a compensatory and balancing overprotection of how care is distributed by parents among the members of the siblings. If the former occurs, it is not uncommon for inordinate expectations to be deposited on that sibling, to compensate for the limitations and frustrations generated by the flawed disabled child, but this can make the differences between them more visible and, secondarily, it can affect the latter's self-image, while the other brothers and sisters are left on the sidelines, between two differentiated poles: the incapable disabled sibling and the mature and responsible sibling. Finding a place between the two can be difficult.

And Among the Siblings?

It is common, as noted by Sorrentino (1990), that siblings initially act with absolute normality with the disabled child. His or her appearance and their difference is treated as if it did not exist, but with the passage of time, they may begin to copy the overprotective attitudes of their parents, either through observation or by the direct messages they receive from them. At this point, in childhood, other attitudes such as jealousy, rage and competition can arise, and there may be symptoms that require the attention of the parents so that they can be balanced. The loss of expectations and experiences does not just affect the parents; the siblings have lost someone with whom they can compete and brawl without remorse, someone with whom they can share confidences and secrets that they keep from their parents. In short, a peer.

Later, as they grow, their awareness of the difficulty their sibling faces grows, and with it a clear contradiction between the anger and discomfort referred to in the previous paragraph, and the guilt that comes from feeling that way, from knowing that they are privileged, that a different future awaits them and that, unlike the disabled sibling, they are in possession of all their faculties. This guilt can be linked with what we mentioned earlier with respect to the parentification that parents can impose on a healthy sibling, encouraging parental responsibilities to appear in him or her and calling the process of the child's empowerment into question. In addition, as indicated by Núñez (2003):

> *These concerns and excess responsibilities are also present in relation to the parents who are felt to be vulnerable and wounded in their narcissism. The sibling is left exposed to bearing the weight of supporting these parents. He or she feels compelled to comply with the heroic mission of compensating them for their hurt and pain, through permanent achievements and satisfactions. He or she seeks compulsively to be mature, competent, bright, intelligent.* (p. 138)

A clinical case will serve to illustrate this: Ana, 30-years-of-age, has a 25-year-old brother who has suffered from cerebral palsy from birth, with moderate to severe mental retardation and occasional bouts of aggression. Her life has been characterized by unsuccessful attempts to break free from the family, attempts which in a more or less subtle way have gone hand in hand with reproaches from the mother for her having ignored her brother. This causes a mixture of feelings in her, among which anger and guilt struggle for prominence. Add to this the anxiety caused by the uncertainty she feels as to what will become of her life, and how on earth any young man might possibly accept the burden she bears in her backpack. She knows what is expected of her, that she will inherit her brother and that conditions her future. The mother's marital relationship is not as successful as might be expected and so, in that context, Ana's presence and her remaining are clearly comforting for her, although this does not always facilitate her independence. Is the disabled brother therefore a way to hold on to her?

Intervention and the Needs of the Family

Rolland (2009) emphasizes the importance of working with various aspects of the interaction between the family, the intervention system and the disease:

- The family's belief system as far as the disease is concerned, its previous experience and how that has shaped its vision and emotions with regard to being sick in general, will have a lot to do with the significance the family has granted over time and down through the generations to the fact of being sick. For some families, sickness is one of life's temporary conditions that can be overcome with a certain degree of acceptance, albeit with a desire for improvement. For others, sickness is something to be feared, something that can lead to a crisis that may disorganize the family and give rise to the onset of symptoms in several of its members.
- The way in which a family has responded, throughout its history, to crisis situations, to losses and to the evolution of each member in relation to such situations and losses. How each individual in the family has constructed his or her personal development in relation to the critical situations they have gone through, how they have acquitted themselves in such situations and what capacity for change and adaptation they have developed.
- Preparing the family for medical crises as well as its ability to regulate home healthcare, to adapt to it and to deal with the demands of the interaction with medical or rehabilitative services, including placing its trust in them, the relational skills with the professionals, the possibilities of time and activity management, etc. Families who manage to establish cooperative relationships with the intervening systems ensure a better prognosis in their adaptation, while at the same time they gain a greater sense of being cared for properly.
- The social network, the sources of support and help as well as the ability to use and interact with the resources that the community makes available in relation to the disease.
- And of course, the functions and skills that any family—in crisis or not—must have to negotiate an effective and healthy course through life: clarity in communication, the avoidance of triangulations, the ability to confront and solve problems, the commitment to fondness among its members and the expression of that fondness, the ability to adapt and change the roles of each member on the basis of the problem, etc.

As Rolland himself well summarizes (2009), it is important that both professionals and families can come to realize what the family's vision and beliefs about disease are, down through the generations, and those of the professionals and the healthcare systems. To which we might add the importance of the social and cultural scrutiny at any given moment.

According to the author mentioned above, families need to reach, and professionals should help them to do so, a clear understanding of how, over time, the disease (or disability) is going to ask foreseeable questions of them, questions they will have to answer in an effective manner. An understanding that will allow them to better prepare for them. At the same time, it is of vital importance that they can also understand themselves as an interactive and mutually influencing system, coevolving together and subjected to a lifetime experience in which the construction of significance is of vital importance.

Finally, the author raises the question of how important it is that they should understand how they will be required to adapt to the changes in both the individual and the family life cycle brought on by the various demands that the disease, the disability, will require over time, and how this is going to cause changes in the development of and interaction within the family and in each of the members with respect to the other members and to the social environment.

Verdugo (2000) argues, with ideas not far distant from those reflected above, that families and professionals have a range of needs that are set down in his compilation for FEAPS (the Spanish Federation of Organisations in favour of People with Intellectual Disability):

- *The need to adopt an ecological and cultural perspective of the family.*
- *The need to adopt a work model with the parents based on collaboration between equals.*
- *The need to implement a rigorous and individualized process to assess the needs of the family.* (p. 11)

From this perspective and in line with Sorrentino (1990), the objectives to be considered for intervention would be the following:

- Prevent disability from becoming a dormitive principle that can, per se, justify any conduct or event in the interaction of the disabled person, which would dramatically help to reduce the chances of his or her recovery, while at the same time leading the family to a situation of surrender in the face of the chances of recovery.
- Help the family to overcome that feeling that usually arises, whereby a difficulty is going to bring in its wake and justify the occurrence of many other difficulties, what he calls the cycle of limited expectations. In short, ensure that a decline in one skill is not extrapolated to many others as a kind of snowball effect, increasing a negative, conformist attitude.
- Collaborate in creating support systems, not only within the extended family or professionals, but also and especially with other family members, other parents whose experience can help the new parents to feel accompanied and to convey calmness and a desire for effort and struggle.

An ecological perspective of the quality of life of children and families implies admitting that not all expertise resides in the professionals...; so it is that professionals definitely need not only the expertise of the parents but also that of other key members of the community (Turnbull, Blue-Banning, & Park, 1999). And as is also raised in the work for FEAPS compiled by Verdugo (2000) with respect to parent to parent support:

> *It is important to strengthen and if necessary, mobilize, this type of relationship in the family and in the community; the creation of groups of parents has been seen to be a good strategy for leveraging and nurturing natural groups.* (Verdugo, 2000, p. 24)
>
> *The Parent-to-Parent Program provides emotional support and information to parents whose children have special needs. To facilitate this support, there are veteran or welcoming parents (experienced and trained) who meet in one-on-one meetings with parents who are approaching the program for the first time (new parents). As veteran parents share their experience of disability in the family, they are able to provide support that only a parent who has "been there" can offer.* (Ponce, 2008, p. 23)

Sorrentino (1990) emphasizes the importance of a series of actions:

- When a disability is discovered, professionals and support organizations should act immediately to prevent any tendency to reinforce the disability and the crisis situation that may occur socially and in the thinking of the family. The drama they are experiencing may lead them to construct a reality that includes the perspective of a grim future and this will become more difficult to remove a posteriori; therefore, early intervention is needed, not only with the disabled person but also with the family and its environment. This means we should be aware of how applicable the classic saying "It never rains but it pours" is in this territory, that is to say, the disability itself generates a special vulnerability in the entire family group, with differentiated characteristics for each member as we have seen above, but all sharing what that author referred to as an intensification of vulnerability.
- Basically, searching for fields of competence, both in the disabled person and in the family, which we in systemics refer to as focusing on the positive, working from an appreciative perspective that rests on capacities and not on shortcomings. A basic rule in systemic work in any field.
- Another objective raised is that of contemplating and working on the aftermath it can generate for the other members of the family, at the spousal, fraternal, extended family level, etc.
- As in any situation of loss, work on the grief the family experiences will be essential. Both with respect to the expectations of the parents and the siblings, grandparents, etc. helping them to accept what has happened, but also to the struggle for the better development of all.
- Be aware that as professionals we become new relational elements that intervene in the family game, and that we do so with significant impact because they place their hope and wisdom in us. For some families, we will become a fundamental source of support, a relationship akin to an alliance, while for others we may be frustrating professionals to rail against. All of this from the awareness that both professionals and institutions generate attitudes in the family towards the biopsychosocial healthcare system that they either blame or thank.

Intervention with such families can take many forms: Information, advice, support, group or network therapy and as the case may be, family, couple or individual therapy. The first three, from the very moment of birth, using clear and precise language, without hiding from the truth but scaling the information to facilitate its acceptance, with a closeness and warmth that will allow the professional–family encounter to be collaborative and empathic. To achieve this, it is important that the parents and child have had a previously bonding contact. This initial information usually occurs in health centres primarily, which would therefore require hospital and primary care professionals to have received a certain degree of training.

Let's see what Ruiz Fernández and colleagues have to say in this respect (2011):

> *Training begins during the same stage of diagnostic information because, as we have mentioned, that harsh moment of emotional impact is mixed with the immediate consequence of seeking an explanation for what has happened and wanting to know about the suffering inherent in their child's disorder, its possible evolution and the prognosis. All the explanations for these possible questions, still within the confused framework of the crisis that the news has brought in its wake; together with additional information on the disorder itself, institutions, associations or resources to which the family can turn, are the first step of the training... The second step of the training is the qualified and specific help of professionals who are dedicated to working with children who suffer from this disorder and to providing care for their family members. In these associations or centres where these professionals work and collaborate, families are provided with broader advice on their children's problem through personal interviews with the professionals at the training centre, informative talks about the specific problem... while they also receive emotional support and guidelines on how to interact with their child.* (p. 346)

Accompaniment, although it can be provided by several different people including the professionals, is probably the intervention that can generate most calmness and empathy in the family, given that it is usually provided by other parents who have gone through similar circumstances, who have more experience, and who welcome and calm the family, transmitting to them an appreciative perspective of their situation and especially of the future. To this end, the selection of these parent chaperones is of enormous importance; they must be warm and serene, positive yet realistic at the same time, with the ability to listen and with knowledge of the problems inherent in each type of pathology. This accompaniment, generally in the hands of support associations for the disabled, also includes "Have a Break" programmes, in which families can be released temporarily from the responsibility of their everyday tasks. A format of vital importance is group dynamics, either with the parents, siblings or the disabled themselves, as mechanisms to ensure that those involved do not feel alone. They also facilitate not only comfort but also learning about how other people with similar circumstances have found answers and solutions to their problems. A well-known type of intervention in systemic therapy is the network therapy proposed by Elkaïm et al. (1995) in situations in which the family or any of its members (such as, for example, the disabled person him or herself) may require collaboration, the activation of community resources, that of the primary network or of people they know.

Finally, in those cases in which relational conflicts or unease in the family may require it, we may find that family therapy or couple therapy is indicated, especially when the impact on the family or the couple is greater than what might be expected. What is always needed here is that the professionals involved should not be the same ones that are providing information, accompaniment, or who are leading the group therapies; in other words, they should be professionals who are not involved in the associations that usually provide these services.

Some Paradoxes in the System

Society has gradually built up aid and integration systems for people with disabilities. Considerable progress has been made from the solution the Spartans found for these problems,[2] but these very helpful systems also contain contradictions for which it is not easy to find a solution. We could talk about support systems that, paradoxically, represent a burden for any therapeutic intervention.

Sometimes, as Pakman tells us (2011), accepting a serious diagnosis may have its advantages. Imagine a family with a member affected by a disability who, thanks to the seriousness of their condition, can obtain benefits whether economic or of another kind. If this family is economically dependent on these benefits, an improvement in his or her symptoms may represent a threat to their financial stability. In this context, professional psychotherapists are faced with a serious dilemma that is by no means easy to resolve. In view of the demand from users for them to issue certificates or reports that reflect a serious pathology so that they can maintain or obtain aid and benefits linked to the disease, therapists have to decide whether they support medicalization and stimulate a vision that is pathologizing and therefore alienates the psychic problems and "helps" their clients in their economic hardship, or whether they are reluctant to do this which means they may lose such aid and benefits.

> *Many psychotherapists found themselves trapped in this situation, in which denouncing medicalization might deny social benefits to people who needed them, while affirming it would perpetuate such benefits for them, even though it might help in that specific case. At the same time, not only did this process configure the subjectivity of the "disabled," through understanding the mental illness as something independent of all these considerations, but also that of the professionals who had been appointed to make a diagnostic decision with the consequences that that might imply for the lives of the people involved when determining the concomitant disabilities and indeed for themselves, left as they were in an uncomfortable position from which to practice psychotherapy on these clients who need the disease, the psychotherapist and the medication if they are to keep their social benefits. The supposed field of therapeutic work is thus on occasions transformed into a battlefield where the therapist represents a system that is going to grant or deny benefits through their power to diagnose, given their position in the healthcare system and their relationship with the disability and social benefits system.* (Pakman, 2011, p. 103 electronic version)

The pharmaceutical industry and mass media are also involved in this process, echoing new diagnoses and diseases that "need" new medications. All together, the pharmaceutical companies, the healthcare and the social systems and the professionals, in their interaction with families with disabled persons and their

---

[2] The precipitation from Taygetos Mountain.

organizations, generate this paradoxical situation where being sick has advantages and getting better can entail losing them. Obviously, all families want their patients to be cured or at least to improve, but the loss of benefits influences them and can leave families caught between their need and their hope.

Working with disability and families is a territory that is booming from the systemic perspective, in which more and more professionals rely on a relational scrutiny to meet the challenges for society and families that are inherent in disability. And we should be thankful that that is the case.

References

IMSERSO. (2017). *Borrador de baremo de evaluación de personas con discapacidad.*

Elkaïm, M., et al. (1995). *Las prácticas de la terapia de red.* Barcelona: Gedisa.

Fishman, H . Ch. (1990). Tratamiento de adolescentes con problemas, Paidos, Barcelona.

Leal, L. (2008). *Un enfoque de la discapacidad intelectual centrado en la familia.* Madrid: FEAPS.

Núñez, B. (2003). La familia con un hijo con discapacidad: sus conflictos vinculares. *Archivos argentinos pediátricos, 101*(2), 133.

OMS. (2001). *Clasificación internacional del funcionamiento de la discapacidad y de la salud.* Madrid: Ministerio de Trabajo y Asuntos Sociales.

Pakman, M. (2011). *Palabras que permanecen, palabras por venir.* Gedisa: Barcelona.

Palacios, A. (2008). *El modelo social de discapacidad: Orígenes, caracterización y plasmación en la Convención Internacional sobre los Derechos de las Personas con Discapacidad*, Cinca.

Pereira, R. (2002). Duelo familiar. *Sistemas Familiares, 18*(1–2), 48–61.

Ponce, A. (2008). De padres a padres. Madrid. FEAPS.

Rios González, J. A. (1994). Manual de orientación y terapia familiar. Instituto de Ciencias del Hombre, Madrid.

Rolland, J. S. (2009). *Familias, enfermedad y discapacidad: Una propuesta desde la terapia sistémica.* Barcelona: Gedisa.

Ruiz Fernández, M. I., Vicente Castro, F., Fajardo Caldera, I., Bermejo García, M. L., García Aparicio, V., Pérez Ruiz, M., et al. (2011). Discapacidad e intervención familiar. *International Journal of Developmental and Educational Psychology, 4*(1). http://infad.eu/RevistaINFAD/2011/n1/volumen4/INFAD_010423_341-352.pdf

Sorrentino, A. (1990). *Handicap y rehabilitación.* Barcelona: Paidós ibérica.

Turnbull, A. P. - Blue-Banning, M. - Turbiville, V. - Park, J. (1999) "From parent education topartnership education: A call for a transformed focus" en Topics in Early Childhood Special Education.

Verdugo, M. A. (2000). *Familias y discapacidad intelectual.* Madrid: FEAPS.

Warnock, M. (1981). *Meeting special educational needs.* London: Her Britannic Majesty's Stationary Office.

The Mourning Family: Diagnosis and Systemic Intervention in Dysfunctional Family Grief

Roberto Pereira

Introduction

The term "bereavement" and the emotions associated with it have not always meant what they mean today. Social and cultural reaction in the face of death has changed considerably throughout history (Ariés, 1977). Until not that long ago, death was commonplace, something that people accepted in a fairly resigned way as an unavoidable reality. Increasingly however, bereavement is no longer seen as something "normal", a more or less stressful circumstance of life; more and more often, it is acquiring a pathological connotation (Pereira, 2010).

The loss of an important family member is the greatest crisis it has to face. If it lacks the necessary resources to adjust to the new situation, the family system may well disappear altogether. This process by which a family adjusts to a new reality from which the deceased is absent is known as the grief process.

Grief also has an individual component and a major socio-cultural impact, which have been widely studied. The systemic dimension of grief however, has not been given the attention it deserves. Issues such as the evolution of grief within the family, the diagnosis of dysfunctional family grief, the risk factors for its appearance, the assumption of the role of the "mourner" within the family, or systemic intervention with the bereaved family are fundamental issues that the systemic model must incorporate into its therapeutic arsenal.

R. Pereira (✉)
Vasco-Navarra School of Family Therapy, Bilbao, Spain
e-mail: director@avntf-evntf.com

R. Pereira, J. L. Linares (eds.), *Clinical Interventions in Systemic Couple and Family Therapy*, European Family Therapy Association Series,
https://doi.org/10.1007/978-3-319-78521-9_15

Grief Within the Family

The reaction of grief, i.e. the pain and sorrow we feel when someone dies, primarily affects the relational network closest to the deceased. In most cases, this basically comprises the members of his or her family. From a systemic point of view, it is clear that the family plays an important role in the grief process (Moos, 1995). It is usually the family that accompanies the dying person through their illness and agony, and it is also the most impacted by their unexpected loss. It must reorganize itself after the loss of one of its members and that often calls into question the very viability of the system.

Traditionally however, the study of grief has focused on the individual grief reaction. Indeed, since the pioneering work of Freud (1915), Klein (1940), and subsequently Lindemann (1944), not to mention that of Pollock (1961), Clayton, Desmarais, and Winokur (1968), Parkes (1972), Bowlby (1980), Raphael (1984), and Parkes and Weiss (1985) to cite only some of the most significant, the grief process has been thoroughly studied: its different stages, symptoms, evolution and complications, the factors affecting the latter, normal and pathological types of grief, etc. However, the focus has always been on the individual process of grief. Nonetheless, we know that this individual grief is influenced by the cultural context in which it is lived, or by the presence or absence of social and family support, which can determine whether the grief process is functional or becomes more complicated, turning into chronic grief or some other type of grief (Pereira, 1998).

Despite this, it was not until the last quarter of the twentieth century that family inter-relationships during bereavement and the family grief process began to be studied. We can cite certain pioneering work by Paul and Grosser (1965), Jensen and Wallace (1967), and Bowen (1976), but generally speaking it is only after the 1980s that greater interest begins to be placed on the study of bereavement and its impact on the family (Black, 1981; Bowlby-West, 1983), on how families function during bereavement (Davies, Spinetta, Martinson, McClowry, & KulenKamp, 1986; Lieberman & Black, 1982) and on considering grief as a family process (Gelcer, 1983). Subsequently, a certain number of studies appear on family grief, not only from the perspective of the impact of the loss on the family, but also in an attempt to describe the grief process from a systemic and on occasions a constructivist point of view (Bloch, 1991; Book, 1996; Detmer & Lamberti, 1991; Gilbert, 1996; Goldbetter, 1998, 2003; Kissane & Bloch, 1994, 1996a, 1996b; Lamberti & Detmer, 1993; Moos, 1995; Payas, 2010; Pereira, 1998; Saphiro, 1996; Walsh & McGoldrick, 1991), or from the narrative point of view (Neimeyer, 2000; Neimeyer, Prigerson, & Davies, 2002).

The study of grief from the family perspective does not exclude, rather it complements the individual approach. The observation of grief from a purely individual angle, without taking into account the interactions that take place both within the family and within its nearby network, overlooking the family process that grief instigates and the influence that this process has on the emotional expression and evolution of its members, is impoverishing, biased, and limiting when it comes to proposing an intervention. If this intervention focuses only on the individual—and by the way, on which one? Is the role of the mourner always predefined in the family? Is there only one or are there several mourners?—It will be no surprise if at one time or another symptomatic behaviour appears in other members of the family system, even though the referred individual may be responding positively to treatment.

Definition of Family Grief

Starting from Bowlby's precise definition of grief (1980), we can define family grief as the "family process that is set in motion as a result of the loss of one of its members".

As we have already said, we know that from a systemic point of view, the loss or the threat of the loss of a member is the greatest crisis a system has to deal with (Bowen, 1976). Faced with such a crisis, if the system has sufficient resources, it will react by adapting and changing. If it does not, the system may disappear, as often happens when the only child dies—the parents separate in the aftermath and the family disappears. But this reorganization of the family system needs time; the processes of homeostasis and change must be balanced, and meanwhile, the threat of disappearance hangs over the family system (Pereira, 2002a).

It is therefore necessary to implement a conduct that defends the integrity of the system. The family sets in motion a series of culturally reinforced self-preservation processes designed to maintain the existence of the family and to ensure that it is not dissolved and that it does not cease to serve its members. We can see how different mechanisms for the survival of the system are set in motion:

1. *Reunification of the nuclear family.*

   The nuclear family, that which is closest to the deceased, strengthens its contact, restricts its area of movement, filters contacts with the outside world, and delegates functions on those close to the family or on members of the extended family. In short, it becomes "entrenched" in the house ("the family is not receiving visitors", a phrase that appears frequently in death notices, well illustrates this process of self-protection) seeking to dedicate more time to mutual contact and to reduce external stimuli.
2. *Intensification of contact with the extended family, or with those who are emotionally close to the family (friends, etc.).*

   The extended family draws close to the nuclear family, offering its support and help if needed, as does the closest circle of friends.

   Depending on the life cycle of the nuclear family, this circle is often called on to organize farewell rituals and the removal of the corpse, or they hurry to the family home to take care of the children or the domestic routine. This support allows the most afflicted family members to focus on coming to terms with the loss, and on sharing the pain that it produces, without the need to dedicate resources to dealing with routine tasks, or to having to take care of arrangements that other family members or friends not so affected by the immediacy of the loss can handle.

3. *Less communication with the external environment and reduction of social activities.*

   In "The House of Bernarda Alba" by F. Garcia Lorca, set in rural Spain at the beginning of the twentieth century, the death of the father of the family implies 7 years of mourning. During this time and in addition to having to dress in rigorous black, not only are the young members of the family not allowed to leave the house, they are not even allowed any contact with the outside world. Without going to the extreme of the social demands of bereavement of a few decades ago, it is still common for there to be a certain reduction in exchanges with the external environment, and a decrease in social activities, especially those considered more frivolous (Pereira, 2002a). Family members go out less, and some recreational activities—such as going out dancing, or establishing new relationships—cannot be taken up too soon, usually because they don't feel like it but also because to do so would question the delicate balance of the system at that time, amen as well as generating social disapproval. The myth of the "merry widow (or widower)", that is to say, when the newly widowed person begins to "have fun" or to "go out" too soon, still arouses rejection, or "suspicions" as to the previous relationship. This is a difficult issue, as currently there are no explicit rules on the matter, but it is widely assumed that a subjectively variable "reasonable period" must pass before we consider it appropriate for the widow or widower of our child or sibling, for example, to take another partner.

   In general, almost all the rules that used to govern mourning, that is to say, the social expression of bereavement, have ceased to be explicit, which creates quite a few problems, given that many of them remain implicitly in force which often gives rise to generational conflict as to what is forbidden or appropriate and for how long.

   The Duarte family had lost a son; the oldest of four brothers, he had committed suicide. During therapy, a conflict arose between the mother and her second son because he had been listening to music, something the mother found intolerable. The son said that he understood his mother being upset, but that no one had told him that he couldn't listen to music, and that when he asked how long it would be before he could do so, no one knew how to answer him. (Personal observation)

4. *Socio-cultural support for the continuity of the family.*

   Within the organization of our social system, the family is one of its pillars, if not its main foundation. That system delegates to it the most basic functions of providing food, care, emotional nutrition, education, etc. From a social perspective, there is an obvious interest in ensuring that the family group continues to exist despite losing one of its members, which has to do with the homeostasis of the system. Thus, in addition to the help it receives from its immediate circle and the extended family, societies that have resources to do so, allocate part of them to promote the continuity of the family, although it may have lost one of its key members. Grants, pensions, allowances, exemptions from military service, schools for orphans, widows' and widowers' associations, life insurance, etc. will seek to provide social and economic support to the new family, perhaps now devoid of its main source of income. In short, it is in everyone's interest that the family should continue to look after its surviving members although curiously enough, no specific therapeutic resources are provided to facilitate the often difficult transition inherent in family grief.

5. *Need for a truce in family conflicts: reconciliation.*

   During bereavement, there is an implicit and indeed often explicit requirement to cease hostilities within the family. When the survival of the family group is threatened, the most important thing is that they should all provide each other with mutual support to cope with the adversity they are facing. A truce must be called in the conflicts, no matter how old they may be. It is even a particularly suitable moment for reconciliation, as the close proximity of death relativizes the importance of any grievances and increases values such as mutual support and solidarity within the group. The theme of someone having to die for ranks to be closed is recurrent in literature, theatre, cinema, and politics. The survival of a certain tribal conception of confrontation with death, in which the loss suffered is common and threatens not only the existence of the family but of the whole tribe, underpins this requirement to call a truce in every issue that weakens us when we face danger, and in the use of the dead to that end.

6. *Frequent behaviour involving weakness as a way to claim protection.*

   As a reaction, bereavement involves intense pain and sorrow, the abandonment of everyday tasks, the loss of habitual behaviour patterns, isolation, and a general situation of weakness that generates an external attitude of compassion and protection. The family environment increases the care it provides. External hostility decreases. It is not socially acceptable to "harass" a "helpless" figure, which is how the family nucleus is presented during grief. The terms of outstanding debts can be extended, the neighbours lend a hand, "the pain of the family is respected" and it is not deemed appropriate to bother them with unimportant issues.

   If pain is by and large respected, the pain of bereavement is always respected, and everyone is expected to follow suit. With some exceptions, linked perhaps to family history, no one has any doubts as to the suffering of the close family after a loss. Anyone can empathize, put themselves "in the shoes" of the family, and get closer to what may be their own pain (in fact, one of the ways you can distinguish the affliction of grief from depressive melancholy is precisely the ability to empathize with the sadness of grief, while that of depression tends to generate more rejection). Hence, external care and social support protect the family and facilitate the labour of grief.

The Family Grief Process

As we have said, the objective of this entire series of actions designed to protect the family system is to facilitate the work of family grief, that is to say, the process that is set in motion on the death of one of its members. This process is characterized by a series of actions designed to defend the integrity of the system that we have just described so that the necessary reorganization of how the family works may take place and result in the generation of a "new" system, based on the previous one, but inevitably different, given that the disappearance of a member of a family system implies the need to:

1. *Reorganize the communication systems.*

   Communication systems are organized in each family system according to their own patterns, with each member playing one of the different roles in the transmission of information both within the system and with the external environment. The removal of one of the channels through which this communication flowed implies the need to establish other alternatives that make it possible for there to be an appropriate relationship. Establishing new channels of communication, often without any previous experience, is not easy and will depend on:

   (a) The communication skills and abilities of the family. A family with many open and working channels of communication will always have alternative ways that it can use, ways that will avoid the isolation of its members or of the family from the outside world, which in turn will facilitate the resolution of the family's grief, as the time required for the reorganization of the communication systems will be less.

   The grief process will also be facilitated in this case by the fact that maintaining adequate channels of communication with the external environment will facilitate the access of external assistance and support networks. In the case of families whose prior relationship with their social environment is somewhat limited, such as migrant families, the suppression of channels of communication with the external environment may prove catastrophic for the integrity of the system, especially if the deceased was the only person capable of overcoming language barriers (Pereira, 2002b).

   (b) Regarding the importance of the deceased in the family communication. Closely related to the previous situation, the disappearance of a specific member of the family is going to have a greater or lesser influence on inter-family communication and on its communication with the external environment, depending on the importance of the role played by that member in such communication. The disappearance of a member who plays a passive or peripheral role in the communication networks is not the same as that of someone who plays an active and central role therein and who facilitates communication.

   Regarding the suddenness with which death occurs: a gradual approximation to death makes it possible to establish alternative channels of communication that in turn allow, once the death has taken place, a more rapid reorganization of the communication systems. This is not always the case and on occasions, despite the fact that the illness has been very long drawn out, the difficulty in accepting the reality of the loss means that the leave-taking is not made progressively, and that death arrives without any preparation, which often leads to a complicated bereavement (Pereira, 2002b).

2. *Reorganize the rules governing how the system works.*

   Family patterns of behaviour correspond, for the most part, to patterns of socio-cultural behaviour, although they always include special features that shape the different way each family works. Family rules are established gradually throughout the existence of the family; they demand continuous modifications to adjust to changes within and outside the family. The flexibility of the family to modify its rules in response to these changes, together with the ability to simultaneously maintain a defined family structure, will establish the functionality and viability of the family system (Pereira & Vannotti, 2011).

   The death of a family member is going to modify that structure and how it works, giving rise to changes that will require new rules to be established so that it can adjust to this new reality in which the deceased is absent. This process also takes time, how long or how little will depend on:

   (a) The number of rules that need to be modified: Again, this depends on the place that the deceased occupied within the system, whether he or she was a central or peripheral character.
   (b) The suddenness of his or her death. An "expected death" allows the family rules to gradually adjust to the new situation; an unexpected death requires an immediate change of the rules of operation.
   (c) The family life cycle: depending on whether it involves a stage of the life cycle in which a negotiation of new rules is already taking place, or a period of stability. In the first case, the process of change will be facilitated or hindered, depending on who has died. In general, periods of change in the life cycle will create more difficulties as the family restructures how it works. Usually, the death of a parent at an advanced stage of his or her life cycle does not have the same impact as that of young children or teenagers, although this is not a defined rule, since there is a high number of factors that aggravate or favour the good evolution of grief at a given time (Walsh & McGoldrick, 1988).

3. *Redistribute roles and functions.*

   The roles played by each family member, along with the communication patterns and rules of operation, organize the various functions and structure of the family. Who looks after what, who is responsible for this or for that, who holds the authority and in which areas, etc., are roles that must be redistributed among the different members.

   By no means a simple matter, this distribution often generated conflict. Hence, the redistribution of the roles held by the deceased is a potential source of conflict. Once again, it will depend on whether the dead person played a central or peripheral role. The disappearance of a family member who played a central role in its operation can produce a severe imbalance in the system. Even when the role of the deceased was to "liaise" with the other members, his or her death may lead to the disappearance of the family system, as is often the case, as stated above, following the death of an only child.

The roles played by the deceased can be redistributed among the other members of the family, they can be assumed by one of them (e.g. in the case of the generation of a parentified child), or they can be kept "on hold" pending the addition of a new member to the family who takes over those roles (substitute children or marriages born out of "necessity", e.g. with the sister of the mother who may have already begun taking care of her nephews).

4. *Adjust to a new reality in which the deceased is absent.*

   This adjustment to the new situation will depend, as has already been said, on the flexibility of the family system when it comes to making the necessary changes. Rigidly homeostatic families will face great difficulties when it comes to such adjustment, which in reality is a compendium of the previous three: changes in communication systems, in the rules governing how the system works, and in the redistribution of roles and functions. These changes may sometimes be massive and will test the functionality of the family system, at a time when its members are usually not particularly well disposed to such changes, overwhelmed as they are by the sorrow caused by the death of a loved one.

Stages of Family Grief

Parallels with individual grief may also be drawn when establishing the "family tasks of mourning". Moos (1995), based on Goldberg (1973), makes a comparison with the "individual tasks of mourning" established by Worden (1991)—accepting the reality of the loss, working through the pain caused by sorrow, adjusting to an environment in which the deceased is missing, and finding an enduring connection with the deceased while embarking on a new life. He also talks about five tasks of family mourning: communicating the knowledge of the death, allowing the sorrow of bereavement to surface, relinquishing the presence of the deceased, realigning the roles within the family and outside the family.

Gilbert (1996), based on Walsh and McGoldrick (1991), identifies three essential tasks:

The acknowledgement of the loss and that each member of the family is in mourning, the reorganization of family roles, the reconstruction of the meaning of the family and the family identity, and the reinvestment on the part of the members of the family in a new identity.

Synthesizing both approaches, we now propose the following stages of family mourning:

1. Acceptance of the loss by the family, allowing and encouraging each member of the family to express the sorrow they feel.

In this first stage, rituals are going to play an important role (Imber-Black, 1991). The wake, the funeral, the burial, visits from family and friends, etc. will make the loss public, encourage its acceptance, and create a suitable context for emotional expression (Imber-Black, Roberts, & Whiting, 1998).

The problem arises when grief is centred on only one member of the family, making it difficult for others to express their own grief process and allowing the figure of the "mourner" to appear, as we shall discuss later.

2. Family regrouping and entrenchment to allow the family to reorganize itself: redistribution of internal communication and family roles.

   The process of family reorganization in which it is necessary to redefine the channels of communication and to distribute the family roles is a delicate process that affects the very structure of the family. It must therefore adopt a defensive strategy that allows it to deal with this process with the least wear and tear possible (Pereira, 1998).

   This also implies that it must definitively accept the loss of the loved one, which implies the additional difficulties inherent in the sorrow caused in the members of the family by their passing.

3. Reorganization of the relationship with the external environment. After the internal reorganization, the family must follow the same process vis-à-vis the external environment, opening up new channels of communication, reassigning roles. This stage occurs when the family feels that it has achieved sufficient stability to begin opening itself up to the outside world, casting aside its entrenchment.

   The end of this stage is marked by the acceptance by its members of a new family structure, born of the old one, but organized in a different way. We have created new channels of communication, and other members play the roles that the deceased once played. The games of alliances may have changed, as the surviving members seek new support. This does not mean they forget the deceased, rather they resituate him or her in their emotions, in an appropriate manner. The figure of the deceased will form part of the history of the family, but it must no longer have a direct influence on how it works. Often, the point of inflection is marked by the recovery of "old" forms of behaviour, which imply the opening of the family, which are accepted by all members of the family.

The Mourner

The family mourning process must be accompanied by a process of individual mourning by all its members, in such a way that no one suffers especially or is left behind, converging finally in everyone becoming involved in the new family that must be born of the one that has just died. When the rhythms are out of step, the entire process becomes complicated, often generating a complicated bereavement. One of the most common complications in this rhythm occurs when the mourning process is individualized in a single member of the family, generating a new family role which we designate as "The Mourner".

We define the "mourner" as that member of the family who assumes the exclusive expression of sorrow during the mourning process. Once this role has been assumed by the family system, the other members organize themselves around the mourner, caring, comforting, and supporting him or her. This care includes the assumption of the tasks that the mourner used to carry out, a delicate approach to the expression of sadness and a conscious effort to avoid adding to that sadness. As a result, the other members of the family avoid expressing their own grief, as expressed by a daughter to her mother in the following paragraph:

> *Wrapped up as you were in your own grief, you displayed absolutely no concern for the way I felt, expecting that I sort out the funeral arrangements, answer the door, take the telephone and make the tea for the people who came to comfort you. I have spent a lot of time crying, mostly in the night because I was not allowed to cry during the day.* (Anonymous, 1994, p. 17)

This unique designation of the role of the mourner is sometimes functional, as it allows the other family members to get on with organizing the practical issues of adjustment that the mourning process also requires. But when, as in the case above, it prevents the expression of sorrow and does not allow them to share their sadness, it often leads to dysfunctional grief.

An interesting question from a systemic point of view is how the role of the mourner is allocated. When someone in a stable relationship dies, the mourner is usually the spouse. On the death of a child, it is usually the mother. But this is not always the case. It may be the father. Or a sibling. And after the death of a parent, it may be a child, even though the spouse is still alive. And if the spouse does not survive, if one of the children assumes the role, which one?

J. Bowlby (1980) proposes that normal grief is a reaction of disconnection within a relationship of secure attachment, and that complicated grief would be the result of insecure attachment, which produces "ties" that hinder the separation. This behaviour would persist and would affect other relationships, which may give rise to intense and often chronic grief. Dysfunctional grief may be understood as the evolution of childhood losses that were not adequately worked out and which lead that person to respond to other later losses in a pathological way.

Which would bring us to the question of the risk factors of complicated grief. Thus, childhood losses involving poorly resolved grief, would lead to the development of a personality that is prone to sorrow, which, if complicated by other risk factors such as mental illness or previous unresolved grief, would create a greater chance of that person being the "mourner".

However, these individual factors alone do not explain the assumption of that role: relational risk factors must also come into play, such as the relationship between the deceased and the future exceptionally "close" "mourner", which often involves a relationship of both emotional and financial dependence, an attachment that may be aggravated by anxiety. This might explain how the role is allocated to one or other parent after the death of a child, or to one of the children, after that of a parent.

Another case would be that of the spouse. To understand this role in the case of one of the spouses, the theory of psychosocial transition formulated by Murray-Parkes (1988) is useful. According to this author, of all the significant life events that affect us in an either expected or unexpected way, bereavement is the one that creates most discrepancy between the world we assume exists, based on our experience, and the real world that we face. In this way, the mourning process should be understood as the reconstruction of a new relationship with the deceased, and of new visions of ourselves and our world. The harder this process of reconstructing our "vision of the world" is, the more rules need to be changed, and the more important these are. This will determine the pain caused by the bereavement, its duration, difficulty, and the energy required to overcome it with success. Therefore, if the partnership relationship has been a lasting one, with great mutual dependence, it is very likely that the spouse will assume the role of the mourner—individual factors included. Furthermore, if the loss occurs at an advanced age, when the energy required to make major changes in our relationship with the world around us is scarce, the possibility of complicated grief ensuing is very high.

Perhaps, however, the main risk factor added to any of these situations that involve claiming the role of the mourner is whether the death was caused by the candidate for that role. Even if it has been in a completely unintentional way, the emotional burden that it entails will make it much harder for that person to free himself or herself from the "guilt" produced by what happened, with such fatal consequences.

The appearance of the "mourner" as the only member of the family who expresses sorrow can be an adaptive role, and it may not therefore be necessarily dysfunctional. But in any case it is a risk factor, one that if it continues for too long can restrict and make it harder for other members of the family system to work out their grief, and who must adopt roles of containment and support of the person who assumes the expression of the family's sadness and pain.

Functional and Dysfunctional Family Grief

We speak of functional family grief when the members of the family share the common purpose of working out their pain in such a way as to generate a new and satisfactory relationship with the deceased—without that implying that he or she is forgotten—enabling them to get the family functioning again without the absent member, without the family falling apart or any particular member of the family suffering during this adaptive process. This period of reorganization will flow more smoothly if it is based on all the family members actively supporting each other: if it functions in an open way that facilitates communication, the frank expression of feelings, tolerating any manner of family expressions, and allowing for different degrees of sorrow. If, in addition, the redistribution of the roles and functions is done in an operational manner, without generating conflicts or power struggles, the probability of a functional evolution will increase significantly.

We talk about dysfunctional family grief when, for some reason or other, the family is not able to make the transition from the old to the new family, either because it does not accept the loss and is therefore unable to change its communication model or redistribute the functions and roles of the family system, or because this transition is done at the cost of disorders appearing in one or more members of the family.

In the first case, the family equivalent of "frozen" individual mourning is produced, with effects that can last a long time. Bowen (1976) spoke of the delayed effects of unresolved family mourning as a network of underground shocks that appear sometime after the death of an important member of the family, producing family crises that can be serious.

This "freezing" that prevents the adjustment changes needed to adapt to the new reality in which the deceased is absent occurs more frequently in rigid families that are unable to negotiate the redistribution of roles and functions or to establish new relationships. This homeostatic rigidity often depends on strict compliance with mandates or wishes that the deceased may have expressed, or on a rigid dependency on religious rituals or cultural traditions that have not evolved to adapt to social changes.

A characteristic of this dysfunctional family grief is an evasive attitude, hardly ever talking about the deceased or expressing their feelings, and concealing their sorrow. To prevent having to express emotions, intimate gatherings are evaded and conflict avoided. Family disruption during bereavement is more likely if the deceased was a core member of the family system, if he or she had a stabilizing role. If this loss occurs suddenly or unexpectedly, at a complicated time in the family life cycle, and in a system with low cohesion, adaptive difficulties, and with scarce contact with and support from the social network, the chances that complicated mourning will develop are very high.

Sometimes the typical reactions of individual pathological grief become widespread in the family: the idealization of the deceased even when the previous relationships had been bad, blaming the environment or a disproportionate sense of guilt, lack of emotional response and mummification of the nearby environment of the deceased (his or her room, photographs, clothes, etc.).

A situation that often generates complications, without being dysfunctional in itself, is caused by the different rhythms of grief in the parental couple in the event, for example, of the loss of a child. In general, fathers and mothers experience bereavement with different rhythms and in different ways, using different means of combating the affliction. Fathers tend to be more angry and aggressive, controlling how they express their sorrow somewhat more and coping with it in a more cognitive way. Mothers, on the contrary, tend to express more anxiety and sadness and to appear as more distressed and inhibited, blaming themselves more and feeling more guilty. She assumes the role of the "mourner" more frequently than the father, while the role he has to assume is that of supporting his wife. From the outside, the impression is that the father goes through a less emotionally intense bereavement, which is often not "understood" by their spouses, who find it difficult to understand why their husbands do not seem as distressed as they are.

Another source of problems in the reaction of the married couple faced with such loss has to do with the different ways they handle sexuality. Fathers usually want to resume sexual relations "too quickly", from the point of view their wives who are not yet prepared for such a step.

Nor can we forget how grief can be "used" as a way to avoid certain conflicts which are "put on the back burner" given that their sorrow does not allow them or justifies their not attempting to resolve such conflicts if they imply an increase in tension and sadness. Marital conflicts that are postponed indefinitely by the immediacy of a sorrow that has not yet been resolved can be covered up.

Bereavement may generate a very complex crisis in the family system, which affects all levels of organization, and can be, as we have already said, the most difficult crisis the system has to confront. It is not enough to reorganize the family system, rather each one of its members must modify their version of the world and adapt to a new reality from which the deceased is absent. And this process of adjustment of the family system and its members, in which the support of the social and family network is an essential factor, must be done simultaneously to avoid the appearance of problems that have been deferred over time.

Family Intervention in Grief

Family intervention during bereavement must distinguish, in the first place, if we are dealing with grief of a normal nature, in which case it will help prevent the grief from becoming complicated, or if we can already diagnose pathological grief. To determine which will be most appropriate, we must start by assessing how the family works and how it is adjusting to its loss. According to Bowen (1976), we must first know how the family is configured, the role of the deceased in the system and the latter's ability to undergo adaptive changes, which together with whatever social and family support it can obtain, will guide us as to how likely it is that the family's bereavement will be functional or if it might become complicated.

Responding to the following questions will give us a good idea of how the organizational process that the mourning family requires is progressing:

- What changes have the illness and death of the deceased produced in the family system?
- What member of the family has, or what members of the family have, assumed the functions of the deceased?
- How are the alliances and supports being distributed and how have they been reorganized in the new system?
- Do they talk about the deceased? Do they allow and share the expression of both positive and negative emotions?
- Have the needs of the members of the family changed? Has their behaviour changed notably? In what way?

- If there are differences of opinion, especially as to how to handle the death and memory of the deceased, how are these being managed?

If the changes that have taken place are relevant and appropriate to the role played by the deceased, if they have distributed his or her roles after due negotiation and without overburdening anyone, if the new alliances and supports do not sideline any family member and are not structurally destabilizing, if the family speak of the deceased with humour appropriate to the situation, putting the emphasis on their positive memories but without fear of speaking about negative aspects, if no sudden changes in behaviour have been recorded, and any possible differences of opinion are negotiated in such a way that allows everyone to participate insofar as the memory of the deceased is concerned, in all probability we are dealing with a functional family.

In that case, the purpose of the intervention, if it occurs, will be to convey messages of support and participation, focusing on the most appropriate rituals for the removal of the deceased, facilitating the expression of emotions, allowing different rhythms during the bereavement, reassuring them as to the inevitability of changes, confirming how important it is to meet and strengthen family relationships at that time and to take advantage of the offers of support from the external environment, placing the emphasis on the need for mutual support and the importance of making sure every member of the family can participate and express the inevitable sadness caused by the loss (Pereira, 2010).

Family Intervention in Complicated Grief

We talk about complicated family grief when the family mourning process that we have described is blocked and lasts for more than 13 to 24 months,[1] or when there is a generalized reaction of non-acceptance of the loss, or when there is an absence of an appropriate emotional reaction to that loss, or when the functional isolation of the first moments is prolonged excessively over time. In any of these cases, a diagnosis of complicated or pathological grief can be made, which requires psychotherapeutic intervention.

We should defend family intervention in the first instance, given how important it is to check if the mourning process is affecting all members of the family equally, or if any of them has been designated as the "mourner", preventing others from reacting emotionally to the loss. Or to assess whether the blockage of the process is affecting one member of the family in particular, giving rise to the appearance of some form of prolonged symptoms, or sudden changes in behaviour, or if some kind of blame is being generated because they do not tolerate different rhythms of mourn-

[1] The extent of the period indicated above is due to socio-cultural influences that have a significant impact on what is considered a "normal" duration of a mourning process. Up to 12 months is considered normal in any culture; over and above 24 months seems to us a time from which the mourning process may be considered "complicated".

ing, or emotional expressions that stray from the family "rule" of not expressing emotions that are deemed "negative".

It is also important to be aware of those cases in which a family presents ambivalent grief, in which the initial feelings after the loss are of relief or satisfaction, without a shadow of sadness, after the death of a family member who has abused one or more of its members. After some time, this total absence of sorrow usually leads to a more intense mourning process than is normal, among other things because it entirely lacks the support of social and family networks, which are so important if mourning is to progress in a positive manner.

After an initial proposal for family intervention, we can combine joint sessions with work aimed at subsystems or with individual sessions, in order to ensure not only that the family system begins to reorganize itself in order to appropriately resituate the deceased in the family history and to create a new family with new roles, rules and, where necessary, channels of communication, but also that all members of the family change their vision of the world and adapt to a new one in which the deceased is absent.

The purpose of psychotherapeutic intervention will be to set up or strengthen the "tasks" of mourning, whether individual (Worden, 1991) or family (Pereira, 2010): dealing with the evidence of the loss, encouraging the family members to talk about the deceased, that they do so in the past tense, highlighting the positive aspects of the relationship but also allowing negative ones to emerge. The emotional expression of pain should be encouraged, without allowing the sessions to become a "plaintive choir" that hinders them. The therapist must empathize with the emotions of the members of the family, but without losing control of his or her own emotions, which in certain cases of bereavement, may well put their training to the test.

Therapy should emphasize the need to move through the mourning process, allowing sorrow to manifest itself even though it may prove painful, always reinforcing the importance of sharing that sorrow, both within the family and with the social network. The expression of emotions, especially in men, must be redefined as something positive, helping to "translate" feelings of anger and rage as manifestations of sadness.

In some cases, conflicts within the family circle or the extended family may have to be confronted, conflicts related to the management of the illness, or to the side effects of the loss: non-equitable wills, comparative grievances, blame, etc. This task is one of the most complicated as sorrow often serves as a way to justify not changing one's own attitudes in relational conflicts, and vice versa. When these conflicts arise, we must be aware that the psychotherapy of mourning will continue until a solution is found for these conflicts (which sometimes cover up old grievances) or at least until they no longer interfere in the mourning process.

And one should never lose sight of the possible use of prolonged mourning as a mechanism to maintain the family homeostasis to prevent or hinder a family member from leaving the system or the entry of a new one, paying special attention to the stage in the life cycle at which the family finds itself.

The use of rituals will be of great utility throughout this entire process, as well as methods to "bring" the deceased to the therapy room: "the empty chair", dramatizations, the use of symbolic objects closely related to the deceased, looking through photo albums. It will be necessary to explore the history of loss and death in the family, as well as the family myths underlying these, not to mention any unresolved conflicts that may have been activated.

The facilitation of the process will involve clarifying the roles that the deceased played and their negotiated redistribution, ensuring that no one is excluded, thereby preventing dysfunctional parentification, and also the reorganization of the family communication, creating direct channels if these used to pass through the deceased.

References

Anonymous. (1994). Dear Mum. *Bereavement Care, 13*(2), 16–18.

Ariés, P. (1977). *El hombre ante la muerte en el mundo occidental*. Madrid: Taurus.

Black, D. (1981). Mourning and the family. In S. Walrond-Skinner (Ed.), *Developments in family therapy*. London: Routledge.

Bloch, S. (1991). A system approach to loss. *Australian & New Zealand Journal of Psychiatry, 25*(4), 471–480.

Book, P. (1996). How does the family narrative influence the individual's ability to communicate about death? *Omega, 34*(4), 323–341. https://doi.org/10.2190/3J4E-2X29-YEVE-JH14

Bowen, M. (1976). Family reactions to death. In P. Guerin (Ed.), *Family therapy. Theory and practice*. Lakeworth, FL: Gardner Press.

Bowlby, J. (1980). *Attachment and loss, Vol. 3: Loss. Sadness and depression*. London: Tavistock.

Bowlby-West, L. (1983). The impact of death on the family system. *Journal of Family Therapy, 5*(3), 279–294. https://doi.org/10.1046/j..1983.00623.x

Clayton, P., Desmarais, L., & Winokur, G. (1968). A study of normal bereavement. *American Journal of Psychiatry, 125*, 168–178. https://doi.org/10.1176/ajp.125.2.168

Davies, B., Spinetta, J., Martinson, I., McClowry, S., & KulenKamp, E. (1986). Manifestations of levels of functioning in grieving families. *Journal of Family Issues, 7*, 297–313. https://doi.org/10.1177/019251386007003005

Detmer, C., & Lamberti, J. (1991). Family grief. *Death Studies, 15*, 363–374.

Freud, S. (1915). Duelo y Melancolía. En S. Freud, *Obras Completas, Tomo I*. Madrid: Biblioteca Nueva, 1961.

Gelcer, E. (1983). Mourning is a family affair. *Family Process, 22*, 501–516. https://doi.org/10.1111/j.1545-5300.1983.00501.x

Gilbert, K. (1996). We've had the same loss, why don't we have the same grief? Loss and differential grief in families. *Death Studies, 20*, 269–283. https://doi.org/10.1080/07481189608252781

Goldberg, S. (1973). Family tasks and reactions in the crisis of death. *Social Casework, 54*, 219–228.

Goldbetter, E. (1998). *Dueil et fantômes. Cahiers critiques de thérapie familiale et de pratiques de réseaux* (Vol. 20, pp. 51–87).

Goldbetter, E. (2003). *El duelo imposible*. Barcelona: Herder.

Imber-Black, E. (1991). Rituals and the healing process. In F. Walsh & M. McGoldrick (Eds.), *Living beyond loss. Death in the family* (pp. 207–223). New York: Norton.

Imber-Black, E., Roberts, J., & Whiting, R. (1998). *Rituals in families and family therapy*. New York: Norton.

Jensen, G., & Wallace, J. (1967). Family mourning process. *Family Process, 6*, 56–66. https://doi.org/10.1111/j.1545-5300.1967.00056.x

Kissane, D., & Bloch, S. (1994). Family grief. *British Journal of Psychiatry, 164*, 728–740.

Kissane, D., & Bloch, S. (1996a). The Melbourne family grief study, I: Perceptions of family functioning in bereavement. *The American Journal of Psychiatry, 153*(5), 650–658. https://doi.org/10.1176/ajp.153.5.650
Kissane, D., & Bloch, S. (1996b). The Melbourne family grief study, II: Psychosocial morbidity and grief in bereaved families. *American Journal of Psychiatry, 153*(5), 659–666. https://doi.org/10.1176/ajp.153.5.659
Klein, M. (1940). Mourning and its relation to manic-depressive states. *The International Journal of Psychoanalysis, 21*, 125–153.
Lamberti, J., & Detmer, C. (1993). Model of family grief assessment and treatment. *Death Studies, 17*, 55–67. https://doi.org/10.1080/07481189308252604
Lieberman, S., & Black, D. (1982). Loss, mourning and grief. In A. Bentovim, G. Barnes, & A. Cooklin (Eds.), *Family therapy complementary frameworks of theory and practice* (pp. 373–387). London: Grune & Stratton.
Lindemann, E. (1944). Symptomatology and management of acute grief. *American Journal of Psychiatry, 101*, 141–148. https://doi.org/10.1176/ajp.101.2.141
Moos, N. (1995). An integrative model of grief. *Death Studies, 19*, 337–364. https://doi.org/10.1080/07481189508252737
Neimeyer, R. (2000). *Aprender de la pérdida*. Barcelona: Paidós, 2002.
Neimeyer, R., Prigerson, H., & Davies, B. (2002). Duelo y Significado. *Revista de Psicoterapia, 49*, 5–24.
Parkes, C. M. (1972). *Bereavement. Studies of grief in adult life*. London: Tavistock.
Parkes, C. M. (1988). Bereavement as a psychosocial transition: Processes of adaptation to change. *Journal of Social Issues, 44*(3), 53–65. https://doi.org/10.1111/j.1540-4560.1988.tb02076.x
Parkes, C. M., & Weiss, R. (1985). *Recovery from bereavement*. New York: Basic Books.
Paul, N., & Grosser, G. (1965). Operational mourning and its role in conjoint family therapy. *Community Mental Health Journal, 1*, 339–345.
Payas, A. (2010). *Las tareas del duelo*. Barcelona: Paidós.
Pereira. (1998). *Le deuil: de l'optique individuelle a l'approche familiale. Cahiers critiques de thérapie familiale et de pratiques de réseaux* (Vol. 20, pp. 31–49).
Pereira, R. (2002a). Hacia un modelo familiar de duelo. *Mosaico, rev. de la Featf, 23*, 9–14.
Pereira, R. (2002b). Duelo familiar. *Sistemas Familiares, 18*(1–2), 48–61.
Pereira, R. (2010). Evaluación y Diagnóstico del Duelo normal y patológico. *Formación Médica Continuada, 17*(10), 656–663. https://doi.org/10.1016/S1134-2072(10)70267-X
Pereira, R., & Vannotti, M. (2011). Caso clínico: Un caso de duelo familiar. *Rev Formación Médica Continuada, 4*, 200–204.
Pollock, G. H. (1961). Mourning and adaptation. *International Journal of Psychiatry, 42*, 341–361.
Raphael, B. (1984). *The anatomy of bereavement*. London: Hutchinson.
Saphiro, E. (1996). Family bereavement and cultural diversity: A social development perspective. *Family Process, 35*(3), 313–332. https://doi.org/10.1111/j.1545-5300.1996.00313.x
Walsh, F., & McGoldrick, M. (1988). La pérdida y el ciclo vital de la familia. Cap. 13 del libro de C. In *Falicov (comp.): "Transiciones de la Familia"* (pp. 429–464). B. Aires, 1991.
Walsh, F., & McGoldrick, M. (1991). Loss and the family: A systemic perspective. In F. Walsh & M. McGoldrick (Eds.), *Living beyond loss: Death in the family* (pp. 1–29). New York: Norton.
Worden, J. (1991). *Grief counselling and grief therapy*. London: Routledge.

[illegible]

Correction to: Family Therapy with Involuntary Clients. The Therapeutic Alliance as a Major Key to Therapy Success

Ana Paula Relvas and Luciana Sotero

Correction to:
Chapter 13 in: R. Pereira, J. L. Linares (eds.), *Clinical Interventions in Systemic Couple and Family Therapy*, European Family Therapy Association Series, https://doi.org/10.1007/978-3-319-78521-9_13

In chapter 13, the affiliation of the co-author **Luciana Sotero**, along with Ana Paula Relvas was incompletely published in the original version of the book. It only mentioned the Faculty of Psychology and Education Sciences. Both of them are also researchers at the Centre for Social Studies of the Coimbra University (CES).

This has been updated in this version of the book.

The updated online version of this chapter can be found at
https://doi.org/10.1007/978-3-319-78521-9_13

R. Pereira, J. L. Linares (eds.), *Clinical Interventions in Systemic Couple and Family Therapy*, European Family Therapy Association Series,
https://doi.org/10.1007/978-3-319-78521-9_16

Index

R. Pereira, J. L. Linares (eds.), *Clinical Interventions in Systemic Couple and Family Therapy*, European Family Therapy Association Series,
https://doi.org/10.1007/978-3-319-78521-9

MIX
Papier aus verantwortungsvollen Quellen
Paper from responsible sources
FSC® C105338

If you have any concerns about our products,
you can contact us on
ProductSafety@springernature.com

In case Publisher is established outside the EU,
the EU authorized representative is:
Springer Nature Customer Service Center GmbH
Europaplatz 3, 69115 Heidelberg, Germany

Printed by Libri Plureos GmbH
in Hamburg, Germany